A CUTTER LAYS THE HOODIE PATTERN MARKER OF FLEECE AND CUTS OUT PIECES, THEN BUNDL AND SENDS THEM TO WESTBROOK, MAINE.

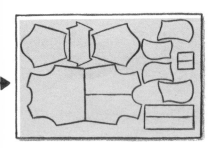

IT TAKES THIRTY-ONE PEOPLE ABOUT FORTY-FIVE MINUTES TO TURN THE PIECES INTO A GARMENT.

FOUR WORKERS PREPARE THE CUFFS AND WAISTBANDS, MADE OF RIB-KNIT, WHILE A SECOND TEAM OF FIVE CLAMPS GROMMETS ONTO DRAWSTRING HOLES AND SEWS TOGETHER THE HOOD PANELS.

GROMMETS ARE MADE IN MASSACHUSETTS.

DRAWSTRING IS MADE IN VIRGINIA.

FIVE WORKERS SET THE FRONT POCKETS AND TOPSTITCH THE HOOD SEAMS FOR A FINISHED LOOK.

A MACHINE OPERATOR ADDS SCREEN PRINTING OR EMBROIDERING.

THE SHIPPING TEAM TAGS, POLY-BAGS, AND BOXES HOODIES.

GARMENTS ARE SHIPPED TO CUSTOMERS AROUND THE COUNTRY.

ALSO BY RACHEL SLADE

Into the Raging Sea

MAKING IT IN AMERICA

RACHEL SLADE

MAKING IT IN AMERICA

THE ALMOST IMPOSSIBLE QUEST TO MANUFACTURE IN THE U.S.A. (AND HOW IT GOT THAT WAY)

Pantheon Books

New York

All rights reserved. Published in the United States by Pantheon Books,
a division of Penguin Random House LLC, New York, and distributed
in Canada by Penguin Random House Canada Limited, Toronto.

Pantheon Books and colophon are registered trademarks
of Penguin Random House LLC.

Library of Congress Cataloging-in-Publication Data
Name: Slade, Rachel, author.
Title: Making it in America : the almost impossible quest to manufacture
in the U.S.A. (and how it got that way) / Rachel Slade.
Description: New York : Pantheon Books, 2024.
Includes bibliographical references and index.
Identifiers: LCCN 2023009052 (print) | LCCN 2023009053 (ebook) |
ISBN 9780593316887 (hardcover) | ISBN 9780593316894 (ebook)
Subjects: LCSH: Textile industry—United States—History.
Clothing trade—United States—History. Free trade—
History. Labor unions—United States—History.
Classification: LCC HD9855 .S53 2023 (print) |
LCC HD9855 (ebook) | DDC 338.4767700973—dc23/eng/20230316
LC record available at https://lccn.loc.gov/2023009052
LC ebook record available at https://lccn.loc.gov/2023009053

www.pantheonbooks.com

Jacket design and photograph by Tyler Comrie

Endpapers infographic by Max Temescu

Printed in the United States of America

1st Printing

To all the people in the world who earn
a living by making things.

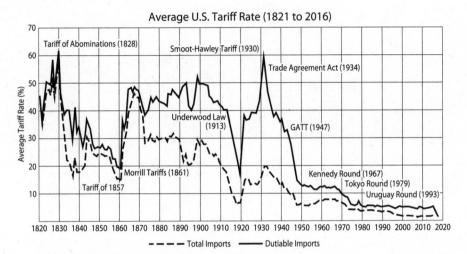

Average U.S. Tariff Rate (1821 to 2016)

Tariff of Abominations (1828)
Smoot-Hawley Tariff (1930)
Trade Agreement Act (1934)
Underwood Law (1913)
GATT (1947)
Morrill Tariffs (1861)
Tariff of 1857
Kennedy Round (1967)
Tokyo Round (1979)
Uruguay Round (1993)

Average Tariff Rate (%)

- - - - Total Imports   ———— Dutiable Imports

Sources: U.S. Department of Commerce, Bureau of the Census, Historical Statistics of the United States,
U.S. International Trade Commission, dataweb.usitc.gov

To be independant [*sic*] for the comforts of life, we must fabricate them ourselves. . . . He therefore who is now against domestic manufacture must be for reducing us either to dependance [*sic*] on that foreign nation, or to be clothed in skins. . . . Experience has taught me that manufactures are now as necessary to our independance [*sic*] as to our comfort.

—Thomas Jefferson, during the War of 1812

CONTENTS

PREAMBLE

The Traffic Jam That Never Ends

No one had ever seen anything like it—an infestation of cargo ships—at least seventy of them—clogging up miles and miles of ocean off the California coast. The armada of container ships south of L.A. offered the clearest picture yet of how extensively Americans had exported their economy. Each ship was an enormous floating warehouse packed with more than 7,000 shipping containers. Inside those containers was all the stuff of modern life, including electronics, plastics, furniture, and clothing, the kinds of things people used every single day. More than 90 percent of the cargo had come from East Asia—China, Vietnam, South Korea, and Taiwan—and all of it was stuck, frozen in time, trade interrupted, because Americans couldn't unload those ships fast enough.

The container ships had been idling at anchor for days, sometimes weeks, belching diesel fumes into the salty air, as far as the eye could see, waiting for a berth at one of America's top two busiest ports—Long Beach and L.A.—where 140 gantry cranes worked night and day unloading and loading containers. By the fall of 2021, people familiar with the ports thought they'd seen it all. Thanks to the pandemic, major backups were old news. Even the *New York Times* and *Wall Street Journal* got tired of covering it. But somehow, the traffic jam was more impressive than ever. Demand for imported goods hadn't even peaked yet. In the U.S., 4,000 orders were coming through Amazon every minute, and nearly all those orders were for goods manufactured abroad.

Jammed into containers and shipped across the Pacific, all that stuff was baking in the heat of another California day.

It's impossible to wrap your head around how much stuff goes through these two ports alone, but I'll throw a few more numbers at you. Each year, the ports handle a combined $370 billion worth of cargo. They load and unload 156.8 million metric tons, or 346,000,000,000 pounds of stuff. That's roughly equivalent to the weight of the earth's moon . . . doubled. And that represents only one third of the goods coming into the United States.

In the fall of 2021, the global supply chain was cracking under our insatiable need for things.

The port was experiencing "unparalleled import surge, driven by unprecedented demands by American consumers," said Gene Seroka, the executive director of the Port of Los Angeles.

There weren't enough berths to handle the number of vessels arriving. There weren't enough cranes to unload the vessels. Crane operators, who make up to $300,000 a year, there weren't enough of them either. There weren't enough longshoremen to drive the shipping containers to the vast parking lots surrounding the ports for short-term storage, and there weren't enough warehouse workers to steer all that stuff to the proper tractor trailer before it hit the interstate. There weren't enough truckers to pick up the cargo once it was loaded into trailers, and on the other end of the interstate, wherever those trucks were heading, there weren't enough warehouses and warehouse workers to distribute the goods fast enough.

"We basically took a year's worth of product and jammed it into six months of entry," Matt Priest, president and CEO of the Footwear Distributors & Retailers of America (FDRA), told *Sourcing Journal.* "We've just been jamming it through the ports and that's going to create a lot of challenges, especially when you couple that with the fact that the longshoremen and others have been impacted by Covid like everyone else. It's the perfect storm."

This is what we've become: a nation of shoppers, clickers, and waiters. We fancy something, we hunt for it, we get giddy at the magical words "free shipping" (nothing is ever free), and then we wait, wait, wait for those packages to arrive. Our shoes and dehumidifiers and computers and lifesaving medications are manufactured far away, and often have to travel 10,000 miles to get to our doorsteps. Who has time to think about that? We unbox and unpack so much that watching unboxing and unpacking is a popular genre on YouTube. Our trash bins overflow with cardboard boxes and plastic wrappers, inflatable packing strips, plastic tags, and instruction leaflets written in a dozen languages—some of which gets shipped back to Asia to be turned back into pulp.

The most destructive myth about it all is that Americans have no choice in the matter.

But we do.

MAKING IT IN
AMERICA

INTRODUCTION: THE HIGH COST OF CHEAP STUFF

When we consider the role of manufacturing in our lives, there's no better place to start than with textiles, which are both ubiquitous and essential to human survival. In the intervening years between our swaddling and shrouding, we wrap ourselves in an astounding array of decorative and protective layers.

Worldwide, the textile industry is worth about $3,000,000,000,000. That figure includes the production, refinement, and sale of synthetic and natural fibers used in thousands of industries that employ more than 60 million people.

For most of history, textile and clothing production was as central to society as finding food and shelter.

Let's take a moment to thank our ancestors for their ingenuity; it took tremendous imagination and skill to transform plants, animal fibers, and insect threads into fabric. It also took tremendous commitment: preindustrialization, producing clothes could require the combined energy devoted to food cultivation and shelter-building. That's a lot of work, which may be why "clothe thyself" was one of the Judeo-Christian god's first commandments when jettisoning Adam and Eve into the world, and we've been cranking out garments ever since.

Many of the fabrics we wear today have been continuously produced for more than five millennia, though the precise dates of their
invention are impossible to know due to the inherent vulnerability
of natural fibers. Woven cotton fabrics crafted more than 6,000 years
ago have been found in Peru, Africa, and India. Linen was extrava-
gantly difficult to make before industrialization; it could take a village a full year to transform the flax plant into ready-to-weave linen
threads. When you're in London, you can marvel at the oldest extant
woven garment in the world—a V-neck floor-length fine linen dress
with smartly pleated sleeves and bodice, made in Egypt, carbon-
dated to around 3400 BCE. The oldest woolen garment is a pair of
trousers found in a herdsman's grave buried 3,000 years ago in what
is now western China. And silk threads, made from the hardened spit
of the lowly silkworm, was an established Chinese industry by the
fourteenth century BCE.

Perhaps because production of clothing was offshored decades
ago, most Americans don't spend much time thinking about what
it takes to make the things we wear. When I first proposed writing a
book about domestic apparel manufacturing, everyone in my orbit
had something to say, and most of it was discouraging. One friend
who teaches at Harvard Business School dismissed the entire project.
"Why should Americans care about manufacturing?" he asked. We're
a service economy now, he declared, as if there was something unsa-
vory about making things.

With all due respect to our nation's business schools, there seems
to be a disturbing lack of knowledge about how the American economy works. In the fourth quarter of 2022, domestic manufacturing
contributed $2.9 trillion to the U.S. economy and employed nearly
13 million workers who earned an average salary of nearly $96,000.
Further, the National Association of Manufacturers calculated that
every dollar spent in this sector injects $2.60 into the overall economy,
and for every 1 manufacturing worker, 4.4 are added into the labor
force. Those are impressive numbers. In fact, in spite of the offshoring

trend hastened by free trade agreements, domestically made exports have doubled over the past two decades, much of it going to Europe.

Maybe the real thing holding us back from talking about manufacturing is that it's not as sexy as the billion dollar tech companies that thrive off of selling others' content, labor, and products. Jimmy Fallon gets more viewers talking about *Bored Ape* NFTs with Paris Hilton than interviewing a woman making quality underwear in Burlington, Vermont. American manufacturers tend to be small companies. The U.S. Census Bureau reports that a vast majority of the nation's 250,000 manufacturers have fewer than fifty employees. They're everywhere, except top of mind.

There are a thousand political and economic reasons why Americans need to reclaim manufacturing, but first, consider that Americans owe their very independence from England to the homegrown industry.

The English colonists who made their home in bitter-cold New England depended on regular shipments from the motherland to clothe themselves. Digging through the archives at the Boston Athenaeum, I found the manifest of a supply ship sent from England in 1635 to outfit the colonists of the Portsmouth Plantation (New Hampshire). The ship carried dozens of imported cassocks, breeches, shirts, hats, stockings, coats, along with twelve bolts of canvas and 375 yards of sailcloth—all made in England. Shivering colonists must have been overjoyed to get their hands on these goods.

But imported clothing was expensive, and in the colonies hard currency was scarce. Because people needed clothing, they turned to home production. Lucy Crawford, a nineteenth-century memoirist from New Hampshire, noted that the men in her family originally wore moose skins, "dressed as the Indians had taught them," she wrote, "until the country began to be opened a little, and then they got sheep."

With a flock of sheep, colonists could gather wool, spin their own yarn, and weave their own fabrics, but clothing production in New

England was slow going. "I have heard Grandmother say that she used frequently to work a whole week, both night and day, without undressing herself, while carding and spinning," Lucy wrote. This slowness was by design: English weavers, continually threatened by the specter of self-sufficient colonists, were assured by the British Parliament in the eighteenth century that only flimsy, cheaply made carding tools were being exported to America.

After carding the wool and spinning it into yarn, Crawford's grandmother used a handloom to weave the wool, then dyed the fabric with tree bark and cut and sewed it into garments. "In this cheap, humble, but happy way, these people lived for many years," Crawford wrote.

But American homespun was crude and rough. Urban sophisticates wouldn't deign to wear it. Those folks who suffered scratchy shirts and bulky skirts could feel either shame for being poor or virtue for being self-sufficient and thrifty. Crawford imagined her ancestors in the latter camp. She wrote, "The purity of our forefathers taught simplicity of dress . . . they then had no ruffles, no ribbons . . . but all was neat and tidy."

While Crawford's grandmother was carding wool day and night, the British were figuring out how to industrialize their own textile production. Englishman John Kay invented the flying shuttle in 1733, enabling weavers to work faster. In 1770, James Hargreaves received a patent for the spinning jenny—a multiple-spindle machine that semiautomated the task of hand-spinning wool into yarn, greatly increasing the speed at which material was produced.

Five years later, Richard Arkwright patented the spinning frame, which spun yarn even faster. Once he mastered the machine works, Arkwright built a huge, multistory water-powered carding and spinning factory in Cromford, Derbyshire, and became a very wealthy man. Arkwright's impact on the textile industry didn't stop there. As one of the first industrialists, Arkwright was the grandfather of the modern factory. He built an entire town to accommodate the men, women, and children who worked dreary thirteen-hour shifts at his factories. For the first time in history, humans were working in the service of machines, and Arkwright constantly sought ways to increase their efficiency.

The British fiercely guarded the secrets of their mechanized mills while flooding American ports with inexpensive textiles. Cheaper imports, in turn, disrupted colonists' self-sufficiency, destabilizing the barter economy and domestic production on which so many of them depended. "The enemy of contentment began to introduce articles of merchandise, which soon created pride," Crawford wrote with bitterness. "As soon as one came in possession of a newly imported dress, it stimulated others to follow the fashion. In this way has our country since been infested with this foolish pride of dress, making gay the outside; while some, it is feared, have neglected the most important part, the soul."

Addicted to imports, early Americans were slow to develop domestic manufacturing. When they finally broke with England, their industry was so undeveloped that even the uniforms the American soldiers wore were made of British wool cloth, imported on Dutch and French ships.

How to stimulate manufacturing became a central question of George Washington's administration. In fact, the first piece of major legislation passed by Congress was the Tariff of 1789, which imposed fees on imported goods—in part to finance the federal government, but also to slow the flood of imports into the country.

But tariffs alone wouldn't solve the new country's financial problems. In his first address to Congress in 1790, Washington declared that the United States' survival depended on building robust domestic production. He warned that when people don't make things for themselves, they lose control—of their livelihoods, their politics, and their economy. He then asked Congress to "promote such manufactories as tend to render them independent of others for essential . . . supplies." And he put thirty-five-year-old Alexander Hamilton in charge of figuring out how the new government could support nascent American industry.

Economic independence, freedom, solidarity—these were the foundational principles of the United States.

Alexander Hamilton was keenly aware of the vulnerability of America's young industries to imports. The threat of ever-cheaper goods from abroad increased every day. Around the time Hamilton was researching his "Report on Manufactures" for Congress, Edmund Cartwright was hooking up the brand-new steam engine to a loom in Doncaster, England, exponentially increasing the speed of production while dooming what was left of the nation's handweaving industry.

After a year spent thinking about how to stimulate domestic production, Hamilton convinced the first Congress that the price of American economic and political independence would be a combination of tariffs (to stem the flow of imports) and subsidies (to reduce investors' financial risk). Entrepreneurs also needed easy access to capital, so Hamilton set up a national bank charged with granting low-interest loans to the country's first industrialists.

Finally, Hamilton lobbied Congress to sever dependency on foreign shippers. When you control your supply chain and logistics, he argued, you control your economic destiny. Only American-made ships owned by Americans and sailed by an American-majority crew could move goods from American port to American port. (An updated version of this law, commonly called the Jones Act, is still on the books today.) It's a tactic China would copy two hundred years later.

The United States wouldn't have survived the nineteenth century if it weren't for the tariffs and shipping laws that Hamilton proposed. Together, they spawned New England's textile industry, which fueled the early American economy while creating opportunities for America's best and brightest, such as Eli Whitney.

After the Massachusetts native graduated from Yale in 1792, Whitney was too short on funds to pursue a law degree, so he traveled to Georgia, where he witnessed the brutal reality of plantation life. It was there that he invented the cotton gin—a simple mechanism that quickly removed the seeds from cotton, the most time-consuming step of cotton production. Whitney hoped that his gin would ease the work of enslaved laborers in the South, but it had the opposite effect. As the price of cotton dropped due to ease of processing, demand increased for both cotton and workers to grow and harvest the crop.

Seven years later, Bostonian Francis Cabot Lowell would commit one of the most egregious acts of international corporate espionage, thereby jump-starting the American industrial revolution. Lowell was already a wealthy merchant in 1810 when he traveled to England posing as an American bumpkin, which aligned nicely with British views of the former colonists. Feigning ignorance, Lowell talked his way into textile factories, where he used his photographic memory to record the inner workings of power looms. As soon as he got back to Boston, he drew up what he remembered of the machinery. He didn't quite get the whole story, but aided by English, Welsh, and Scottish mechanics, Lowell and several other investors successfully built America's first fully integrated cotton mill in Waltham, Massachusetts, in 1814, powered by the Charles River.

Swept up in the Second Great Awakening, the Transcendentalist movement, and lingering revolutionary fervor, Lowell was America's first utopian industrialist. He shared Thomas Jefferson's vision of the American manufacturing town as a safe place where decent people (mostly New England farm girls) could earn cash, worship, read classic texts, and attend lectures from learned and spiritual men. When Lowell's textile mills were up and running, they drew much admiration from philosophers, writers, and legislators, domestic and foreign alike, including Charles Dickens, who admired the stamina and morality of the girls and women living and working there.

Soon, mill towns popped up all over New England, many founded on utopian principles.

It wouldn't last. As the nineteenth century progressed, Europe and Russia became increasingly unstable, and immigrants began arriving in the States in great numbers—first the Irish in 1846, then the

Italians, Quebecois, Eastern Europeans, Chinese, and eventually South Americans. They came with new religions, languages, and traditions. New England's wealthy, second- and third-generation factory owners began to see less of themselves in their workforce and consequently took less responsibility for their employees' welfare.

By the 1850s, New England's factories looked much like the dire English factories Lowell had tried to avoid. Men and women were poor and powerless, children as young as five years old were working long days in the dangerous mills, labor organizers were castigated, and strikes were sometimes broken by violence.

The immigrants may have been desperately poor, but they also brought novel ideas about the role of government, labor, and workers' rights to the United States. In the stifling, deafening textile mills where tens of thousands of workers enriched the few at the expense of the many, factory workers occasionally united to demand better pay, more humane shifts, and safer conditions in a world where unions, the forty-hour workweek, and the weekend were still unknown.

Collective bargaining, as well as ideas about workers' rights, spread from New England textile factories to West Virginian coal mines to Pennsylvania steel mills. It took more than a century of organizing—and bloodshed—for worker protections to be enshrined by American law. But once they were, the movement gained incredible momentum.

By the 1960s, roughly one third of the American workforce was unionized, and Americans made nearly everything they wore.

And then . . . the unions destroyed American manufacturing, right?

When I was growing up in the 1980s, the United States was recovering from a tumultuous decade marked by the war in Vietnam, the OPEC oil embargo, and runaway inflation. Europe and Asia had recovered from the devastation of World War II and were beginning to produce things for themselves. American exports dropped.

Nostalgia for an imagined past glory swept across the nation, and plenty of Americans began to buy the antiunion narrative being pushed by big business.

Ronald Reagan rebranded the U.S. based on a distorted vision of mid-century America: fightin' mad eagles, flags-a-flying, roaring anthems. Freedom was the zeitgeist—an angry, aggressive freedom, the kind that might use a flagpole as a spear.

One major difference between 1950s and 1980s populist conservatism was the demonization of unions, wrapped in the new mystical language of free trade.

Conservatives had always alleged that labor laws were hostile to business. Since the New Deal, they'd been hard at work unraveling worker protections (as well as banking regulations, shipping laws, and protectionist tariffs) via constitutional challenges. In the 1980s, those ideas took flight.

Free trade wasn't a new idea, but it got considerable traction on both sides of the aisle. In his brilliant book *Evil Geniuses: The Unmaking of America,* Kurt Andersen details how free market theory—a radical, reactionary hypothesis developed by then-fringe economists Milton and Rose Friedman in the 1960s—crept into intellectual circles, then oozed into the Beltway, and finally exploded into the mainstream, captivating Democrats and Republicans alike.

The Friedmans preached the idea that the market had a magical natural order. If left on its own, free of the corrupting influences of tariffs, labor regulations, and checks of any kind, the market would not only self-correct, but ultimately benefit all of humanity.

Their theories took on Darwinian tones but were about as scientific as palm-reading.

In human society, there never was a free market, nor would there ever be. Someone is always putting a thumb on the scale. Actually, there are a million thumbs everywhere. But socialism and communism and trade unions were convenient scapegoats, said to be choking the life out of a stunning, yet fragile, natural order.

The Friedmans' theory was based on a misreading of a then-little-known phrase in Adam Smith's *Wealth of Nations,* published the year the American colonists revolted against Mother England. The

Friedmans repackaged Smith's so-called invisible hand, a divine force that led humans to act selfishly, which paradoxically would lead them down the most beneficial path.

In fact, Smith mentions the invisible hand only three times. Most importantly, he uses it only to refer to domestic industries, *not* international trade. Smith argued that when entrepreneurs are bound to place, they keep their money in their community. Local banks, for example, have a natural incentive to lend locally, spurring investment in the people and businesses that in turn drive the bank's revenue. That marks the extent of the invisible hand in Smith's world.

International trade, in contrast, often involves exploitation of an imbalance in resources, political power, or wealth between nations. That's why Smith absolutely believed that international commerce should be carefully regulated. Otherwise, he argued, multinational corporations would mercilessly exploit weaknesses and become destructive.

Smith had seen the devastation wrought by free trade in real life. While he was writing his treatise, the British East India Company (EIC) was choking the life out of India, once the world's fourth-largest manufacturing economy. Chartered by the English crown in 1600, the EIC was founded to launch a British spice trade, but when the Dutch locked up Indonesia, the EIC looked to India. The Indian subcontinent was enjoying a period of relative peace that allowed manufacturing and trade to flourish. A robust supply chain of fantastic raw materials stretched all the way from Persia to China to the tip of India, enabling an eye-popping variety of textile-making traditions.

The EIC traders loaded up their ships with luxurious dyed silks, opulent brocades, and bright calicos, chintz, paisley, palampore, bandanna, plus fine muslins, khaddars, and ikats and sailed back to England. One can imagine what it was like when a seventeenth-century Londoner—clad since birth in earth-colored woolens and linens—first laid eyes on the vibrant, lushly patterned textiles fashioned by Islamic, Hindi, and Buddhist craftspeople in the exotic East.

Cottons and silks were soft to the touch, cool in summer, and eagerly took on dyes of every imaginable hue. Under the gray skies of London, how could anyone resist?

But Indian fabrics threatened England's domestic wool industry, so Mother England enacted high tariffs, patents, royal charters, and outright bans to protect her textile manufacturers. These were the regulations that Smith was thinking about when he published *The Wealth of Nations* on the eve of the American Revolution in 1776.

Here's where things get spooky for twenty-first-century readers: to keep prices down and maximize profits, EIC operatives began to stoke rebel factions against the Indian ruling class. Eventually, the British corporation employed its own private army of highly paid native Indians to use terrorist tactics to break up the remains of India's empire. Which sounds much like the CIA's work in South America, the Middle East, and Asia during the Cold War.

Between 1750 and 1800, destabilization led to widespread de-industrialization in India. Travel and trade became dangerous, which prevented exchange of goods, people, and ideas. To protect populations, resources were redirected from manufacturing and growing crops to outfitting militias. Food became scarce. India stopped producing goods for trade, let alone for domestic use.

When the Indian trade collapsed, the East India Company looked elsewhere for opportunities and began importing Bengal-grown opium to China to trade for tea. Soon, Chinese cities and towns were flooded with the narcotic; addiction was endemic. When the Chinese emperor tried to ban the opium trade, the British government—now inseparable from the EIC—sent ships and guns. British naval forces crushed the emperor's armada in 1838.

British conquerors forced the Chinese emperor to sign a series of "free trade" treaties that gave the EIC carte blanche to pillage. Twenty years later, the opium trade and human trafficking were so lucrative that European allies—including the United Kingdom, France, and the Russian Empire—again invoked the free trade trope (backed by bombs and bullets) to force China to fully legalize opium, expand the export of "coolies" (Chinese laborers), and grant British merchants and opium traffickers access to all of China while removing any duties on foreign imports.

Free trade indeed. Adam Smith would have scoffed at the Friedmans' oversimplification of his precepts, especially the childlike belief that unchecked globalization—multinational corporations financed by free-floating capital—would lead to a harmonious future. Smith wrote, "I have never known much good done by those who affected to trade for the public good."

In the U.S. in the 1980s, free market jargon made mediocre thinkers sound smart. It had an aura of magic and mystery, plus it was illogical, like a religion. When an ideological construct can't be explained because it's based on specious arguments, advocates lean heavily on the language of faith.* Then the herd mentality kicks in. Afraid of missing out on the next big thing, people sign up, attributing their lack of understanding to their outsider status rather than a shortage of reason.

Some American policymakers argued that the free market would be good for business *and* good for workers. Others thought workers might lose their jobs, but in the new economy, they'd simply find new jobs. At the very least, America's consumers would love the low, low prices of foreign-made goods—cheaper to produce, cheaper to buy.

The free market also promised to boost the middle class, now heavily invested in the stock market through their brand-new 401(k)s, because cheaper production would leave more room for profit. And a more economically robust Mexico would create a new market for American exports.

Besides, free market had the word *free* right there in its name, and if you weren't for freedom, you were against it.

---

* Consider all the hype around cryptocurrencies. Apparently smart people breathlessly tossed around inscrutable jargon, enticing investors who didn't want to miss out on something big. With the collapse of the cryptocurrency exchange FTX in November 2022, the skeptics were vindicated: it was all just a massive Ponzi scheme, after all.

—

When I got to college, George H. W. Bush was hammering free trade theory into law. He was the perfect guy for the job. As America's first industro-intelligence president, he'd built his career on forging an unholy union of big business and the intelligence community to bend foreign governments to the corporate will.

During Bush's brief time as the head of the CIA in 1976, for example, the agency was mucking about with Operation Condor, a cartel of seven military dictatorships in South America. The CIA's charge was to keep South America wide open to big business and hostile to socialists and Marxists who might want to nationalize resources. The cartel's main weapon was terror. An estimated 80,000 people—trade unionists, socialists, political activists, and students—were murdered during Operation Condor, and at least 400,000 more people were imprisoned.

Bush unlocked the agency's potential to bend smaller nations to capitalism's will. Four years later, he became vice president under Ronald Reagan. It's not difficult to see his fingerprints in the secret sale of arms to Iran to fund the anti-Marxist, paramilitary Contras in Nicaragua.

Bush's first attempt at freeing the market would be an agreement among the United States, Mexico, and Canada. Bush was so confident that Congress would support his treaty that he demanded more than permission to negotiate. He insisted that all of America's elected lawmakers allow his agents to negotiate with Mexico and Canada behind closed doors. Once his appointees agreed on terms, Congress had to either accept the North American Free Trade Agreement (NAFTA) in its entirety or kill the whole deal.

Bush's gamble paid off. Few legislators wanted to be "freedom killers," and a Democrat-majority Senate passed the treaty under Bill Clinton in 1993, 61 to 38.

Cooked up during the mergers and acquisition fervor, steeped in antiregulation and free market dogma, NAFTA was much more than just a trade pact among three nations. NAFTA eliminated tariffs for goods mostly sourced within the three countries. Another alarming new feature baked into NAFTA: the agreement gave foreign investors the right to sue a nation for implementing environmental, labor, and health regulations that the investors believed undermined their profits. As such, it was a grand free trade experiment that created a radically new model, one that privileged corporate power over government sovereignty and organized labor. By accepting the terms, signatory governments agreed to waive domestic procurement preferences (in other words, *adios* "Buy American"); limit their regulation of services ranging from trucking to banking; honor pharmaceutical patents; and limit regulation of food, product, and workers' rights.

Since America's founding, taxes and tariffs had protected domestic goods from foreign competition, but these required extensive negotiation. NAFTA bypassed that process. In its place, NAFTA established new privileges and protections for business, testing world leaders' stomach for the coming corporatocracy.

Shortly after NAFTA passed, the United States and dozens of other countries established the World Trade Organization (WTO), the sole international organization dedicated to setting and enforcing the rules of global trade. The WTO was the successor to a post–World War II organization, known at GATT, but charged with a broader mission that included agriculture. Birthed during the height of free trade zeal, the WTO's main mission remains to lower trade barriers among all nations to stimulate global growth.

Volumes have been written about the impacts of this organization since its inception. Great thinkers have interrogated whether the WTO's complex tangle of rules fostering ever-freer trade privilege multinational corporations, wealthy nations, and large-scale industry at the expense of Indigenous groups, labor protections, and the environment. Back in 1999, the answer for an estimated 40,000 protestors was decidedly yes. When the WTO convened in Seattle in late fall of that year, a loose coalition of anti-globalization groups showed up to demonstrate against what some called the "World Take Over."

When evaluating the WTO now, there's a tremendous amount to tease out, but here's where I fall on the question: the unconsidered pursuit of constant growth will only hasten environmental decline. Recently, more thoughtful economists have begun to question our slavish commitment to gross domestic product as a full measure of a nation's health.* Some economists are now arguing for alternative metrics that tell a much richer story about how a nation's economics intertwine with the welfare of its citizenry and environment.

What economists are realizing is that growth alone, without societal and environmental safeguards, often makes everyone unhappier. Multiple studies have shown that as the rich get richer, they find

* This isn't a new concept. Two days after Robert Kennedy announced his presidential candidacy in 1968, he gave a speech at the University of Kansas which included this remarkable passage: "Even if we act to erase material poverty, there is another greater task. It is to confront the poverty of satisfaction, purpose, and dignity, that afflicts us all. Too much and for too long, we seemed to have surrendered personal excellence and community values in the mere accumulation of material things. Our Gross National Product, now, is over $800 billion a year, but that Gross National Product, if we judge the United States of America by that, that Gross National Product counts air pollution and cigarette advertising, and ambulances to clear our highways of carnage. It counts special locks for our doors and the jails for the people who break them. It counts the destruction of the redwood and the loss of our natural wonder in chaotic sprawl. It counts napalm and counts nuclear warheads and armored cars for the police to fight the riots in our cities. It counts Whitman's rifle and Speck's knife, and the television programs which glorify violence in order to sell toys to our children. Yet the Gross National Product does not allow for the health of our children, the quality of their education, or the joy of their play. It does not include the beauty of our poetry or the strength of our marriages, the intelligence of our public debate or the integrity of our public officials. It measures neither our wit nor our courage, neither our wisdom nor our learning, neither our compassion nor our devotion to our country, it measures everything, in short, except that which makes life worthwhile. And it can tell us everything about America except why we are proud that we are Americans."

themselves stuck in a numbers race with those who have even more. Those citizens who don't directly benefit from growth "feel excluded and frustrated by not being able to keep up" with those around them, notes British sociologist David Bartram, and their happiness sinks.

Of course, globalization has had real material effects on people's livelihoods. In January 1997, Public Citizen's Global Trade Watch found that in three years, NAFTA had already cost the United States a net loss of close to 400,000 jobs. Some estimate that up to a third of those job losses were due to increased automation of production methods. But the worst-hit industry in those early years of NAFTA? That would be apparel, which is extremely difficult to automate and thus remains labor-intensive. American clothing companies shifted the most mobile (and worker-centric) part of their industry—stitching—to Mexico. Textile-producing looms followed.

As a result, the first victims of this iteration of free trade in the U.S. were the highly trained women, mostly people of color living in rural communities, who once made America's shirts, pants, jeans, underwear, and sweatshirts.

Few people spoke up for America's needleworkers and textile workers when NAFTA passed, but maybe they should have. Once apparel companies proved that offshoring worked, nearly every industry in America began offshoring—sending the "work" part of its operations to Canada or Mexico.

When China earned most-favored-nation status from the WTO in 2001, many of those same companies, along with the remaining domestic holdouts, shifted their manufacturing to Asia.

Communications technology, shipping containerization, and the internet expedited the process.

Since NAFTA's implementation, more than 60,000 American manufacturers permanently shut their doors. Five million American manufacturing jobs vanished between 1994 and 2013. In textiles alone, more than a million manufacturing jobs evaporated between 1990 and 2019.

Americans who had worked good-paying manufacturing jobs were forced to take new low-paying, low-skill service sector jobs. From 2001 to 2003, the average manufacturing worker's income plummeted from $40,154 to $32,123 when that person was re-employed in the service industry, a 20 percent drop in earnings. In general, U.S. workers without college degrees (more than 65 percent of the workforce) lost about 12.2 percent of their wages under NAFTA-style trade, even after adjusting for the benefits of cheaper goods. That means any worker, not just in manufacturing, who earned $27,000 before NAFTA is now earning the equivalent of $23,700. With recent inflation, that spending power is further diminished.

Income inequality also went through the roof. Since NAFTA's implementation, the richest 10 percent of Americans have taken 18 percent more of the pie, while the top 1 percent's share has increased by nearly 40 percent.

After thirty years of free trade policy, the American economy has drifted from producer-exporter to buyer-importer and American consumers now find themselves in a dire situation. They are dependent on other nations to provide the bulk of their basic needs—medicines, technology, vehicles, energy, furniture, and, of course, clothing. This dependency was felt very acutely when Covid shut down trade between the States and China and imports were abruptly cut off.

In January 2020, NAFTA was so roundly despised, its destructive nature laid bare after years of economic trauma, that a bitterly divided Congress overwhelmingly ditched it for Trump's new United States-Mexico-Canada Agreement (USMCA), which was essentially NAFTA, but with a few tweaks.

So maybe free trade played a much bigger role in destroying domestic manufacturing than the unions.

—

I grew up in a postindustrial landscape surrounded by the evidence of our dwindling manufacturing economy. I could see the scars of offshoring everywhere. Traveling by train back and forth from New York to Philadelphia, I saw the wasteland that mill closures left in their wake, especially in North Philadelphia, where the ruins of huge brick factory buildings where people once made Stetson hats, Baldwin locomotives, and Schomaker pianos cast deep shadows across once-vibrant neighborhoods.

Acres and acres of vacant row houses stared blankly at empty streets.

When the train crossed the Delaware River into New Jersey, I puzzled over the bridge emblazoned with the words "Trenton Makes, the World Takes." Because by the time I'd found myself on that train, it seemed the world had already taken all that it could.

I asked myself how anyone could do this to their own city, their own countrymen.

Whenever we buy stuff made abroad, we leave a lot of questions unanswered. Was someone exploited to make that thing? Did they earn a living wage? Did they have the freedom to leave the factory when they needed to? Did they have access to protections in the factory, like masks or helmets? Did they have a safe place to report sexual harassment? Did they get regular breaks? Were they expected to work reasonable hours? What happened when they got sick or their children fell ill? Was the factory building even safe?

In 2017, Americans spent $380 billion on apparel and footwear, nearly all of it made somewhere else. Buying a sweatshirt manufactured abroad means you won't ever know the true price that humans, animals, and the environment paid to get it to market for $28. You can be sure, however, that the money didn't go into workers' pockets in other countries. Most of it went into marketing and profit.

One sweatshirt, cheaply made abroad, gives middlemen and brands a dozen opportunities for profit. A few years ago, the Swiss-based watchdog group Public Eye broke down the cost of a $28 Zara hoodie. (See pie chart below.) Nearly 70 percent of the retail price went to tax, profit, and Zara's operational costs (including marketing, rent, and staff). Just over 7 percent of that price went to the women and men in Turkey who cut and sewed the garment.

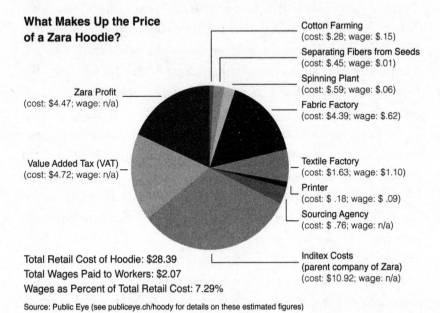

What Makes Up the Price of a Zara Hoodie?

Cotton Farming (cost: $.28; wage: $.15)

Separating Fibers from Seeds (cost: $.45; wage: $.01)

Spinning Plant (cost: $.59; wage: $.06)

Fabric Factory (cost: $4.39; wage: $.62)

Zara Profit (cost: $4.47; wage: n/a)

Textile Factory (cost: $1.63; wage: $1.10)

Value Added Tax (VAT) (cost: $4.72; wage: n/a)

Printer (cost: $.18; wage: $.09)

Sourcing Agency (cost: $.76; wage: n/a)

Total Retail Cost of Hoodie: $28.39
Total Wages Paid to Workers: $2.07
Wages as Percent of Total Retail Cost: 7.29%

Inditex Costs (parent company of Zara) (cost: $10.92; wage: n/a)

Source: Public Eye (see publiceye.ch/hoody for details on these estimated figures)

Public Eye concluded that Zara's demand for a low price point and a 16 percent profit reverberates across the global supply chain, impoverishing the people harvesting the cotton, transforming raw materials into fabric, and cutting and sewing the hoodie. So what does Zara actually pay workers per hoodie? Just over $2. (For reference, an American cut-and-sew team of stitchers paid an average of $20 per hour can produce a zip-up hoodie for around $4.) Given the cost of living in Turkey, were the workers manufacturing the Zara hoodie paid fairly? When Public Eye calculated the living wage in regions where the garment was made, the answer was a hard no. From the cotton fields to the textile factories to the shops, if workers had been properly compensated for their labor, that Zara hoodie would retail for an additional $3.60.

Buying foreign-made goods allows us to ignore the environmental impact of our choices as well. Textile manufacturing is the second-most-polluting industry in the world. While American factories are highly regulated, developing countries lack the political will, resources, or international permission to monitor everything that goes on. (The WTO, for example, is forever on the watch for environmental or labor laws that could be said to impede free trade.) Fabric dyes, which can be quite toxic, might be dumped into the closest river, turning a region's water supply lethal. It's precisely that lack of regulation in developing countries which contributes to making some foreign goods so cheap to produce.

There's also the question of quality. When compared with garments manufactured just a couple of decades ago, it's difficult to express how poorly our modern clothes are made, even those sold by higher-end brands. Well-made clothes are exponentially more expensive than they once were, and more difficult to find. We might think we spent a lot for that wool skirt or silk tie, but only the wealthiest among us can afford to clothe themselves with dignity.

Because our clothes are cheaply made, Americans discard more than a billion and a half pounds of used clothing a year, exporting much of it to sub-Saharan Africa. At the Kantamanto Market in Accra, Ghana, 30,000 vendors pick through more than a billion pounds of secondhand T-shirts, jeans, and jackets exported from the U.S. each year. Some of the garments will be sold as-is, but many will be locally tailored (few people wear size XL in Ghana, for example), dyed, and otherwise fashioned to appeal to the regional consumer.

Finding clothes to resell in Kantamanto isn't as easy as it used to be. When bundles of used clothing first began showing up in the early 1970s, locals called them *obroni we wu,* meaning "the white person has died," death being the only logical reason why, to a Ghanaian, anyone would give away their personal garments. These days, much of the used clothing sent to Africa from those ubiquitous donation bins in parking lots is literally garbage. The quality of the garments we wear and discard has dropped so low that 40 percent of shipments to Ghana end up in landfill, or worse, on the country's beaches. Tons of unwanted cast-offs dam up rivers, contaminating water supplies with petroleum-based yarns and chemical dyes. And sometimes the piles of cheap T-shirts and sneakers inexplicably combust. Kantamanto was leveled by such a conflagration in 2014. European and American cast-offs have created an environmental catastrophe halfway across the globe.

The imported sweatshirt also embodies political problems. Many watchdogs would argue that unfettered capital causes democratic erosion. More than two thirds of the world's population is now living under authoritarian rule, reports the International Institute for Democracy and Electoral Assistance (IDEA). The "number of countries undergoing 'democratic backsliding' (a more severe and deliberate kind of democratic erosion) has never been as high as in the last decade," IDEA reported in 2021, with more than a quarter of the world's population living in democratically backsliding countries.

The reason for backsliding may be free-range capital, which has no ethical or social agenda.

It has no inherent concern for any one nation's political fate. Foreign buyers just want manufacturers who can deliver. Factory owners scramble to get contracts. It's a purely transactional relationship.

Contract buyers for big brands hunting for cheap producers prefer to operate within clear political structures that are easy to control and navigate. They're looking for predictability and a compliant workforce.

Democracy can be messy and slow.

When a developing country lowers barriers to trade and capital flows in, the local people in power tend to use their influence to secure their positions by selling access to foreign contracts, shunting work to their most ardent supporters. Income inequality rises as a result and political power becomes more concentrated.

Once factories are up and running, people with little education (usually young women) relocate to manufacturing centers (often unequipped for the influx of workers), where they work long hours for chronically low wages without employment protections. As soon as the workers begin training, the clock is ticking. In the world of borderless capital, workers will always be vulnerable to competition from an even cheaper source of labor waiting to be cultivated in some other part of the globe.

Contractors dictate prices, then put on the squeeze. Factory owners scramble to make more for less, operating under the assumption that if they can't match the prices the contractors demand, the money will dry up. They operate on ever-slimming margins, and impoverished garment workers take the hit.

Courting global capital operating under the free trade paradigm doesn't offer a nation a path toward a diverse and robust economy. While multinational brands strive to monopolize their own markets, they foment fierce competition among small, local manufacturers to keep production prices down.

When capital pulls out of a country in pursuit of cheaper labor, which it inevitably does, the effects can be devastating. Developing countries that build their economies around a single industry—say, Bangladesh and textile manufacturing—lack the economic resiliency to care for abandoned workers. As a result, they find themselves at the mercy of aid organizations.

That's a phenomenon we witnessed in real time when Covid-19 hit in 2020.

When Americans and Europeans stopped buying clothes during the pandemic, major brands canceled orders with their small manufacturers around the world. The Worker Rights Consortium (WRC), a D.C.-based organization that investigates global factory conditions, estimates that between April and June 2020, clothing orders worth $16 billion were canceled by brands such as Adidas, The Children's Place, Express, Gap, H&M, JCPenney, Nike, PVH Corp (which owns numerous brands, including Tommy Hilfiger and Calvin Klein), Gildan (owner of American Apparel), and Walmart.

Throughout the pandemic, WRC reports, these mega-buyers demanded steep discounts from producers, "greatly exacerbating a state of emergency that has already resulted in widespread factory closures and the loss of *millions* of jobs." Many of these brands remained profitable, with some reporting record sales.

The result was stress, and in some cases, starvation. WRC investigators interviewed one Indonesian worker who said she sewed clothes for Nike, the biggest clothing brand in the U.S. ($37.4 billion annual revenue in 2020) but was "curtailing her food intake because she was drowning in debt and wary of taking on more."

Things didn't get better. In April 2021, Elizabeth Paton wrote a *New York Times* story describing the continuing effects of capital's retreat in the global garment industry. The people in Paton's story were making clothes and shoes for companies like Nike, Walmart, and Benetton, but in the last twelve months, she writes, "those jobs have disappeared, as major brands in the United States and Europe canceled or refused to pay for orders in the wake of the pandemic and suppliers resorted to mass layoffs or closures."

Paton detailed stories of despair. She described Ashraf Ali, a thirty-five-year-old father and garment worker in Bangladesh, who was "desperate to feed his family." In Cambodia, garment worker Sokunthea Yi told Paton that "she spends sleepless nights worrying about how she will pay off loans she took out to build her house." Dina Arviah in Indonesia told Paton "she was hopeless about her future as there were no longer any jobs in her district."

"The high levels of hunger reported by workers in our survey are alarming, especially since so many of these workers are still in employment," Genevieve LeBaron, coauthor of the WRC study, said in a statement. "Hunger and food insecurity appears already to be widespread and is growing across the supply chain."

International labor organizations and watchdog groups have been hard at work trying to get workers back pay, and fortunately, they've had some success.

Now think about how these phenomena are playing out at the Mexican-American border.

Following the ratification of NAFTA, agricultural work in Mexico was consolidated, local economies were gutted, jobs disappeared and wages sank, forcing rural Mexicans to leave their villages and join the 11 million undocumented workers competing for low-wage jobs in the United States, a labor pool compounded by the influx of Americans who had also lost their manufacturing jobs to Mexico and beyond. The World Bank, a major cheerleader of trade liberalization, estimates that the number of people struggling to earn enough to eat doubled in the first four years of NAFTA alone.

Incidentally, the Pentagon warned in 2009 that Mexico now "bear[s] consideration for a rapid and sudden collapse."

Yet the U.S. government continues to encourage offshoring.

I shouldn't have been surprised when the U.S. Agency for International Development (USAID) sent out a press release in 2021 recommending that American companies consider shifting their manufacturing to Africa. USAID was founded in 1961 during the Cold War to promote U.S.-friendly development throughout the world and expand markets via economic and intellectual assistance. For decades, countless NGOs (nongovernmental organizations) funded by the American government had been priming the continent to become a reliable source of inexpensive labor. I'd seen the same phenomenon when I visited Vietnam in 2012—traveling the countryside by bus and motorcycle, I passed dozens of sewing training schools filled with students recruited from villages. A decade after my visit, it seems like all the running sneakers, puffer jackets, and snow pants sold in America were made in Vietnam.*

Indeed, in 2021, nearly all big American apparel brands now come with an asterisk. Nike makes nothing here. New Balance makes a few things domestically, thanks to government contracts. Pendleton

---

* And the wheel keeps turning: in December 2022, as I was finishing a draft of this book, Agence France-Presse reported that more than 1,200 companies— "mostly foreign businesses in the garment, footwear and furniture sectors"— have laid off people, as orders from the U.S. and Europe have plummeted up to 50 percent since last year due to inflation and the war in Ukraine. The Vietnam General Confederation of Labour reported that more than 470,000 workers have had their hours slashed in the last four months of the year, while about 40,000 people have lost their jobs—30,000 of them women aged thirty-five or older. One worker told Agence France-Presse, "We have no one to help us. I will have to get us through this on my own."

may make fabric in the U.S., but the company sends much of it abroad to be cut and sewn. L.L. Bean, with its iconic Maine hunt-and-canoe culture, is essentially an importer of Asian-made goods, with the notable exception of *some* Bean Boots, canvas boat bags, and, curiously, dog beds.*

Or consider Carhartt, "an American apparel company," around since 1889, whose website features laborers (men *and* women) tugging, pulling, pushing, or leaning on heavy equipment—always in the great outdoors. Carhartt's website would make a nice pairing with a Chevy Silverado 2500 HD. In fact, the Carhartt edition of that pickup launched with the brilliant tagline, "The uniform of hard work now comes in a truck." It boasts a towing capacity of 36,000 pounds.

Carhartt's rugged-looking models wear leather work gloves, thick knit hats, and heavy canvas duck coveralls sporting the Carhartt logo. I wonder how its wearers would feel knowing that most of that gear is made abroad, as reported in *Esquire* in 2017: "Despite its appeal to right-leaning values," wrote journalist Tonya Riley, "the reality of the brand's operations are a conservative nightmare: Since 1997 it's been predominantly produced in Mexico."

What once seemed impossible now feels inevitable. Americans don't make things. It's too messy. It's too expensive. It's too complicated.

Americans are good at justifying things that turn out to be bad for them. We have a bad habit of thinking that the twists and turns of history are inevitable or irreversible. That the internal combustion engine was destined to rule the world. Or that Reconstruction was doomed to fail. Or that offshoring manufacturing and the growth of the service economy was as natural as evolution.

* The balance of L.L. Bean's snow pants, fly rods, and fleece vests are labeled "imported," and you can find an eleven-page list of the more than two hundred facilities Bean worked with in 2021, including plants in Bangladesh, India, Vietnam, Dominican Republic, and Sri Lanka.

Thinking about all the critical items we import every day, and how much we depend on shipping to move all those goods across the ocean, I began looking for someone who was trying to correct course. Someone actually attempting to manufacture things in the U.S.

What I sought was a unicorn: a person as committed to manufacturing—completely and totally—in America as they were to running their company ethically.

That quest became my obsession. Lots of companies swear up and down they'll never offshore, but even when they peddle the Made in USA ethos as a key part of their brand, they often end up sending work abroad just the same.

When companies do offshore, they don't post a big banner across their website. And they might continue making a few things domestically or do a little finishing work here in the States just to maintain the illusion. There's a lot of bait-and-switch going on. I nearly gave up. Then, in the summer of 2020, I finally found the real deal. While working on a story for *Down East* magazine, I met Ben and Whitney Waxman, founders of the Maine-based, union-made apparel company American Roots. The Waxmans' factory manufactured 100 percent American-sourced cotton hoodies.

As soon as I got Ben on the phone, I had to pinch myself. He seemed like the real deal. He was unwavering about his commitment to rebuilding manufacturing and organized labor in America. He truly believed that reviving both would stitch together communities and reshape our fractured political narrative. When Ben and Whitney started American Roots, they were young and childless, two fiercely independent millennials hunting for something that would give their lives more purpose. They opened their factory, invited in the union, and gave their employees everything they could afford, including health insurance, paid sick leave, and vacation time.

Their mission statement went something like this: "For people who actually give a shit about how and where their clothes are made—and want others to know it—American Roots is the only maker of socially responsible and ethically made clothing for hands-on life.

With American Roots, you can wear your values with confidence knowing your clothes are completely sourced from and made in America by American union labor."

Ben and Whitney trusted that profit would happen along the way, that good things happen to good people. Since their founding in 2015, they pulled some seventy Portland families out of poverty.

Manufacturing hoodies in the U.S. seemed like the perfect marriage of product and consumer. Americans love their sweatshirts; in 2020, they spent $5.5 billion on them, which makes the U.S. the world's top sweatshirt importer—comprising a quarter of the global market. Nearly half of those sweatshirts are made in China, Bangladesh, and Vietnam. Maybe it was time to make some here.

Ben and Whitney had committed their lives to doing the impossible. To prove the naysayers wrong. To show how ethical manufacturing of even the most basic goods could return to our shores.

By following Ben and Whitney's journey, I hoped to understand the stories that shaped their vision and the history that informed their quest. And finally, I hoped to see how manufacturing could be revived. Because actually, I'm convinced that Americans don't have a choice.

The stakes are sky-high. If Americans want to control their fate, if they truly want to innovate, if they want to forge an ethical future, if they really care about the environment and each other, then they need to start making things for themselves.

MAINE ROOTS

On April 28, 2012, Dory Waxman sat very still at the kitchen table listening to the family van as it climbed the steep driveway and stopped at the barn door. She heard the engine shut off with a resentful knock. At her ankles, the dog whimpered, then sat back on his heels, swishing his tail back and forth across the floor.

Dory took off her reading glasses and tossed them onto the mounting hill of bills, invoices, letters from the city council, school board minutes on the table.

"Well," she announced to the empty room, "Ben's back."

She ground her palms into the table, pushing herself up, wisps of hair slipping free from her loose bun. Wiping her hands on her apron, she maneuvered around the dog, now ecstatic, and swung the storm door into the cool afternoon air while reflexively grabbing the animal's collar to keep him from leaping into the wet grass.

The storm door's spring had stretched out forever ago; the door gaped wide and stayed there. The heat of the kitchen rolled out.

Dory studied two of the people she loved most in the world— her husband, Dan, and her oldest son, Ben. Over the past decade, he'd evolved from a skinny redhead in cargo shorts to a sturdy, commanding union man. Dory always wondered what side of the family the red hair came from.

Ben looked up from unloading the van and waved. "Hi, Ma."

After four months of rehab, Ben looked fit, trim, and tan, healthier than she'd seen him in years. That was the moment she realized he'd been hiding his addiction for a long time.

Ben trudged up the rotting front steps, which sagged under his weight. "One day, someone's gonna fuckin' kill themselves on these," he told her for the thousandth time.

The running joke melted any tension between them. After leaving Maine a decade ago, Ben was home again.

"Well, come in, come in," Dory said as the dog wriggled at the end of her arm like a fish on a hook.

Ben leaned over the mutt to give Dory a perfunctory peck, wiping his sneakers on the mat. In the kitchen, Dory stood next to Dan in solidarity and gave Ben her best *I'm not worried* impression. "I'm good," Ben said impatiently. Dan reached for Ben's duffel, but Ben grabbed it and hefted it over his shoulder, then headed upstairs to his boyhood room.

Dory stood listening for the familiar creak of floorboards above them. It was the sound of her boys in her house, under her roof, in her care. But no, this wasn't right. There was addiction in Dory's family, and in Dan's, too. No matter how far you run away from it, it still finds you. Would their oldest find his way out?

She called up to Ben in her resonant alto, "Fresh linens on your bed, Ben. And the shower's working again. Towels are up there, too."

Dan and Dory Waxman knew that life was a journey full of false starts and dead ends. The trick was to keep going. They'd met in Boston in the mid-1970s—two free spirits, bound together by their sense of justice. Dan had a mass of black curls and a handsome cleft chin. Dory was a blond-haired, blue-eyed, farm girl from central Massachusetts. Dan dreamed of becoming a professional musician and dropped out of the University of Delaware to immerse himself in Boston's folk rock and jazz scene. Dory was energetic and independent, eager for adventure. She didn't bother with college. Her father had worked in a factory; her mother had been a nurse. She'd moved to Boston to build a life for herself.

Dory was one of those New Englanders whose roots go "all the way back to the *Mayflower*," she'd say, which was local shorthand for "We've been here a while." Her grandfather, a Harvard man, won Olympic gold in the high jump. Her grandmother came from Wales. Some close family members struggled with alcoholism and mental illness.

She viewed her heritage with a mix of pride and sadness.

Dan's family embodied the Eastern European Jewish immigrant experience. His father's mother had escaped the pogroms in Odessa, Russia, to raise five children in Wilmington, Delaware. She never learned to read or write. Dan's grandfather had been a professional boxer who fought in the early twentieth century under a pseudonym to hide his Jewish roots. Later, he became an officer in the U.S. Army. Dan's maternal grandfather founded a dry-cleaning business in Wilmington in the 1930s, which exists to this day. Dan's father enlisted in the Army Air Force during World War II and fought in the Battle of the Bulge, then took over his in-laws' dry-cleaning business. He loved telling people that Delaware's young senator, Joe Biden, was a regular customer.

Although Dan and Dory eschewed conventional life, the cult of hard work was in their DNA. They moved to Midcoast Maine so that Dan could study jazz at the University of Maine, Augusta. Earthy and gregarious, Dory hustled to support them both. She gardened, waited tables, and worked as a line cook. It didn't take long before everyone in town knew her. Like Dory, Dan began building a mile-long CV of odd jobs—dishwasher, busboy, cashier, short-order cook, house painter, a farmhand for haying, a counselor at a tiny residential high school for troubled teens. In the winters, they'd house-sit for wealthy absentee owners in large, drafty "summer cottages" along the coast, waiting out the cold under piles of quilts while keeping out the raccoons and making sure the pipes didn't freeze.

In 1978, Dory was pregnant with Ben. She carried him so long that he became known around town as "the egg that wouldn't hatch." When he finally came out on June 15, 1979, the local newspaper ran a front-page story about him.

That year, Dan and Dory bought a 1965 beige and red VW bus with an engine that would start only when rolling downhill, with one foot working the clutch, another pumping the gas, and one hand gripping the emergency brake. If they couldn't find a hill to park it on, they'd have to crawl underneath and cross the solenoid. Ben's brother, Adam, arrived a year later.

Throughout the Reagan years, when much of America was embracing Ralph Lauren and free trade, Dory and Dan held tightly to their progressive beliefs. Maine was a refuge for idealists like them. Utopian fervor was a northern Yankee tradition. It spanned across the centuries and across the political spectrum—from celibate Shakers to right-wing libertarians and doomsday preppers. Countless descendants of the self-righteous Protestants who'd fled England in the seventeenth century still lived in the Maine woods, alongside back-to-the-land types, artists, and writers. Maine was big enough (and rural enough and cheap enough) that someone could even slip off the grid, like Christopher Thomas Knight, the so-called North Pond Hermit, who survived alone in the woods for twenty-seven years until he was arrested in 2013 for multiple burglaries.

In 1983, Dan began selling ads for *Farmstead Magazine,* a homespun-looking stapled affair founded a few years earlier. The magazine was geared toward the new crop of back-to-the-landers arriving in Maine. The cover of the first issue, published in 1974, featured a woodcut of a farmer riding a plow drawn by two muscular horses, their heads bending elegantly toward each other, forming the shape of a heart. Stories included a Maine planting calendar; a feature called "You Can Raise Turkeys"; something about E. B. White; and "Helen Nearing's Rosehip Recipes."

Helen and Scott Nearing had fled the cacophony of their native New York City to rural Vermont forty years earlier, and resettled on a saltwater farm in Midcoast Maine in the 1950s when the skiing craze made Vermont too popular for their taste. Throughout their long lives (Scott died at one hundred; Helen lived to age ninety-one), the Nearings published dozens of books about the farming life, guiding others in the art and craft of rural self-sufficiency. They described themselves as part of a movement stretching back to the first European settlers in New England—people who, they wrote, were like "the many young people of today who find no satisfactory way to exercise or develop their talents and interests in modern city or suburb."

Dan and Dory had been drawn to the Maine life the Nearings wrote about. Cult heroes to the end, they romanticized one version of American bootstrapping—not the suburban postwar version, something more akin to an updated version of colonial homesteading.

After World War I, which thrust the U.S. onto the international stage, Americans spent a lot of time thinking about who they were and building a narrative to fit their new superpower status. In the 1920s, John D. Rockefeller Jr. bought an entire Virginia town with a multitude of dilapidated colonial-era buildings. His enormous, decades-long restoration of Williamsburg fired up Americans' imaginations. Museums around the country opened "period rooms" rife with Chippendale chairs and Paul Revere serving pieces; the heirs of DuPont Chemical filled their Delaware estate, Winterthur, with 90,000 American antiques and opened it as a museum in 1951. Americans went crazy for colonial-style home design and furnishings, triggering a demand for domestic cabinetmakers and other craftspeople.

The Nearings encouraged their followers to go beyond the aesthetic and embrace the colonial pioneer mindset. They taught them how to clear their own land, build their own homes, dig and cultivate their own gardens, and survive by the sweat of their brows.

Native Mainers may have chuckled at the Nearings for making life harder for themselves, but the promise of honest reward for hard work attracted generations of people searching for a more authentic life. (It was later reported that while the Nearings certainly worked hard, they could not have supported themselves without their sizable inheritances.) Heavily subsidized or not, the Nearings lived one version of the American dream—a life based on rising early, soil-tilling, beekeeping, and animal husbandry.

To the children of suburbia who questioned their privilege and yearned for a stronger connection to the earth, there was honor in that.

A tamer version of the New England dream was captured in the pages of *Yankee Magazine*, the family-owned publication that hired Dan for ad sales in 1985. *Yankee* presented the gentleman farmer's take on New England. It ran essays that reveled in the moments when bumbling ex-urbanites intersected with their often savvier, occasionally bemused native Maine neighbors. *Yankee's* covers were indistinguishable from another Maine institution, the L.L. Bean catalog, which sold gear and clothing primarily manufactured in New England, first to outdoors people, later to fashionistas. The political and economic tension between old Yankees and parvenus made for great *Yankee* essay fodder, and attracted a slew of readers who didn't always know on which side their loyalties lay.

In 1987, Dory was pregnant with their third son, Josh, when the Waxman family moved into a ramshackle 150-year-old farmhouse with a massive timber-frame barn on the outskirts of Portland. The property was a fragment of what it had once been—subdivided so many times that the former field behind the house had been reduced to a thin strip of grass separating the property from a 1970s suburban development. A busy road ran in front of the house, just beyond Dory's bohemian garden of potted plants and wildflowers edged by a thick bramble and run-down arbor.

By the time Ben and Adam were in junior high, Dan was spending a lot of time on the road, traveling from Maine to Connecticut to Vermont selling ads. He was a natural salesman—voluble, laid-back, and easy on the eyes as they say, plus he was honest, the kind of guy who had to consciously remind himself that people sometimes did try to cheat one another. Buyers could tell he wasn't in it for the money per se, but to feed his family.

Dory earned income as a doula and a massage therapist, fitting in appointments between carpooling and school board meetings.

With three boys, something was always happening at the Waxman house; the old place creaked and groaned with kids running up and down the thick-carpeted steps from their tiny bedrooms to the front door. The Waxmans' doors were always open to their sons' friends, and as Ben grew older his crew expanded. Ben kept old friends close and, along with Adam, who now teaches special ed at Portland High, played varsity baseball, football, and basketball. (Adam would end up the tallest Waxman, standing six-foot-four.)

Ben was a fiercely loyal friend; some of his closest date back to grade school. From the beginning, they say, they saw something special in the pudgy kid with the "super precise" bowl cut. They say they were drawn to him because he never put down anyone and had a soft spot for underdogs. He'd been teased himself, and when he got big enough, Ben stepped up to protect kids from backyard bullies. He built a sizable following in high school. He became captain of the football and basketball teams. His popularity tripled when he reached six-foot-two, grew a beard, and could pass for twenty-one.

In private, Ben struggled academically. He worked twice as hard as the other students and earned half the reward. It wasn't a matter of discipline—when he wasn't playing sports, Ben was upstairs in his room, hunched over his books. Hearing him awake at all hours of the night practically broke Dory's heart. No matter how much time he spent studying, he never quite got it. His writing was tortured, his spelling even worse.

The teachers at Portland High School liked the eager, opinionated, politically engaged young man, and showed Ben Waxman mercy. They kept pushing him along. As a result, his learning disability went undiagnosed.

Dory focused on righting other wrongs. A zealous problem-solver and a social justice warrior, Dory had a compulsion to help whenever and however she could, and Portland was a complex city with complex problems.

While the media focused on the Rust Belt, the Coal Belt, and Appalachia, photogenic Maine was suffering from many of the same economic pressures, but the damage was mostly hidden away in remote inland towns. The state had been an industrial powerhouse in the nineteenth and twentieth centuries. Until the 1990s, it was the shoe-making capital of the nation. There were textile mills, paper mills, and fish-canning plants—you could tell you were getting close by the smell.

Wherever there were jobs, immigrants followed. Tens of thousands of Catholic Quebecois traveled south from their faltering Canadian farms in the nineteenth and early twentieth centuries to work in Maine factories. French-speaking, astonishingly poor, and uneducated, they found an uncomfortable peace alongside the Protestant settlers in small towns. Former Maine governor (and proto-Trump) Paul LePage was born in Lewiston, Maine, in 1948, but spoke only French when he started kindergarten.

As Maine's biggest city, Portland had the most ethnically diverse population in the state. It had nearly always been so. For four hundred years, the city served as the trading hub for northern New England. Furs, lumber, cod, granite, slate—and, after the Industrial Revolution, manufactured goods—traveled by road, rail, or boat to Portland's wharves, where they were loaded onto ships and carried down the coast to Boston and New York, then out into the world.

You can still climb the eighty-six-foot-high Portland Observatory on Munjoy Hill, built by Captain Lemuel Moody in 1807, more than a century before the invention of the two-way radio. Moody would climb the tower daily and survey the water with his powerful telescope to identify incoming vessels up to thirty miles out. He sold subscriptions to shipowners for his alerts. When he saw a ship heading to port, he would inform the ship's owner by hoisting signal flags so that the merchant could prepare for the vessel's arrival, reserving dock space, longshoremen, and stevedores.

The booming port supported countless businesses—boarding-houses, hotels, banks, taverns, sailmakers, shipbuilders, blacksmiths, mechanics, provisioners. All that industry offered hardworking immigrants a shot at financial stability. Seafarers from afar mingled with locals and sometimes settled down in the city; a multitude of ethnic neighborhoods sprung up.

When the interstate system was completed in the late 1950s, Portland's star dimmed considerably. The new highways ran north–south, funneling trade from Vermont and New Hampshire straight to Boston, Hartford, and New York City, bypassing Portland altogether. There was no work, there was no money. The city declined. Urban renewal and overzealous highway building in the 1960s and 1970s further sliced and diced the fabric of the old port city, leaving vast seas of open parking lots and highways and off-ramps that rendered the city's neighborhoods a disjointed mess of remote islands. The city's boom times were behind it, but Portland retained its middle-class pride.

At some point, Maine became the oldest state in the union, population-wise. Mainers were graduating from high school and leaving. When state legislators and business leaders finally began acknowledging these disturbing demographic trends, they realized that without an influx of new blood, Maine would age out of existence.

Who would keep the economy going if there was no one to do the work?

Portlanders like Dan and Dory were proud of the city's immigrant past and ability to integrate different groups. The Waxman kitchen table became the epicenter of Portland political organizing. In the 1980s, people from Laos, Cambodia, and Vietnam began to settle in Portland. To support New Americans, the city began offering a slew of services, including language programs, job-training programs, and housing to help weary travelers settle into their new Maine life. The next group to arrive in Maine was from war-torn Somalia. Then came Rwandans, Iraqis, and Congolese. About a third of the people in Ben's high school class had been born in other countries. Some of his classmates had spent years moving from continent to continent before landing in Maine.

The stress of moving to the U.S. sometimes made family life difficult. When Dory heard that one of Ben's teammates, Simeon Alloiding, an excellent soccer and basketball player and recent arrival from Liberia, was having trouble at home, she invited him to stay with them during the weekends. Those weekends stretched into weeks, then months. Ben now considers Simeon a brother. Another classmate, Jessica Ares, came from Puerto Rico, and when Dory got wind that she was having a tough time at home, she invited her to stay at the Waxman house in the loft above the kitchen.

Dan and Dory were just getting by financially. With so many mouths to feed, they served a lot of rice-and-beans and big pots of chili. The dinner table became a place for intense political debate. If you spoke up, you were expected to defend your position.

When Ben was twelve, Dory and Dan decided to try to build a business together, as a family. They hoped that the right venture would allow Dan to quit the traveling life. They wanted something that reflected their love of Maine and would further connect them to their community. They also thought a business could help teach their boys important lessons about the world as they understood it.

Their impulse was to make something—a fairly simple product that didn't require too much training to construct—and use materials they could source locally.

New England had a rich textile-producing tradition, and on New Year's Day 1992, Dory bought what she calls a "dead company" named Maine Maid Outerwear. The company had manufactured and sold capes made of the thick woven wool fabrics produced in local mills to wholesale buyers around the country.

Dory likes to tell people that she bought the business on a freezing day over warm apple pie. "I didn't have any money," Dory says. "The banks laughed at me." She negotiated a purchase price of $20,000, which the previous owner agreed to finance over three years, and founded Casco Bay Wool Works.

Dory's only sewing experience was in her eighth-grade home economics class, and the original company's sole employee, Geri, a Quebecois, "spoke three words of English," Dory says. Fully leveraged, Dory couldn't afford to pay Geri for more than ten days. Over that time, Dory used the French she'd picked up from her grandfather, a language professor at Bates College, to learn everything she could about using the Merrow crochet machine to finish the edges of wool fabric. (The Merrow family has continuously operated a mill and sewing machine factory since 1838, first in Hartford, Connecticut, now in Fall River, Massachusetts.)

Then Dory and Dan moved everything—the machines, the buyers' list, the patterns—from a warehouse on the Portland waterfront into the unheated post-and-beam barn next to their house.

Dory cared very much about the quality of the fabric she used for her capes. "I'm a wool snob," she says. "I believe wool's the best by every test. You don't have to feed sheep a lot of water to keep them alive. It's very sustainable."

Dozens of textile mills were still operating in Maine and around New England. Dory convinced two friends to lend her $1,000 each, promising to pay them back in sixty days, then ordered six rolls of cloth—totaling 3,600 yards—from Cascade Woolen Mill in Oakland, Maine.

Studying old photos of Cascade, it's clear that the person who designed the mill took great pride in the project. The four-story wood-clad building featured tall windows that let in natural light for up to 250 workers. The top floor was even brighter, with its additional row of clerestory windows, as was the fashion in that region in the nineteenth century. A large freight-elevator tower sat at the building's midpoint; capped with an ornamental cupola, it looked like a church spire.

Cascade Mill settled in along the Messalonskee Stream, which drove the factory's belt-driven looms. The stream also powered other mills in town, including several scythe- and axe-making businesses, but now it's just another picturesque Maine waterway (albeit polluted) quietly babbling by backyards and under bridges where anglers occasionally hook smallmouth bass or pike, then throw them back.

Cascade made a fabric called Melton, the finest felted wool in the world.

The story of Melton shows how community and industry once helped build an empire.

Around the year 1300 the European climate suddenly shifted. The period between 1300 and 1850, now known as the Little Ice Age, was marked by long, icy winters that heaped heavy snowfall on cities and fields; frosty summers cut growing seasons short. Across the continent, farmers suffered more frequent and prolonged droughts and deluges. Europeans were desperate for warmer clothing.

In this new frigid world, the bubonic plague decimated the human population while wool became a critical commodity. England's sheep population multiplied. Fewer people meant fewer fences and wide-open fields for grazing. Left free to run wild over the cool, wet countryside, the animals bred with abandon.

Widespread human death also led to a chronic labor shortage; plague survivors demanded higher wages. The Church tried wrestling down costs by setting maximum pay rates, but that wasn't easy to enforce. If a field needed to be plowed, a field needed to be plowed. Labor would dictate the price. For the first time in memory, capital (and power) was shifting from the elite into the hands of peasants. Something had to be done.

Pasturing sheep was easier than farming food crops and required fewer workers. Sheep urine and excrement nourished plants, and hungry sheep kept grasses short and tidy. The only thing the little wool factories needed was lots of land and a few folks to move them from field to field to allow Mother Nature time to repair the flora.

Bishops and barons alike drove farmworkers off their acreage and replaced them with enormous flocks. The image that we carry around of British wealth—the manor house on a thick carpet of manicured lawn—comes to us courtesy of the sheep economy.

A wool industry sprang up, involving people at every level of British society. Shepherds and farmers raised and fed the sheep. Carders, spinners, and dyers turned wool into yarn. Using handlooms, weavers magically transformed yarns into cloth. An array of middlemen sold wool fabric to shopkeepers and merchants. Cutters and stitchers fashioned cloth into garments and other textile products. Together, those involved in the textile industry formed such a powerful political bloc that they could push for political reforms, protectionist legislation, and even, in the case of Charles I, help overthrow a king.

By the 1400s, wool cloth was England's primary export. Thus, the British Empire was built on the backs of a small, rugged, four-legged ruminant with a voracious appetite for wildflowers. English townspeople pooled their resources to establish and maintain textile industries.

Melton was first produced in Melton Mowbray, a community northeast of Leicester. To make their unique fabric, townspeople would shear their sheep and distribute the bags of wool among the families. Using a pair of brushes with long, stiff teeth, family members would spend long days carding the wool, drawing the fluff back and forth between the bristles to get the fibers running in the same direction while removing bits of plant and small stones caught in the animal's hair.

The carded wool was then spun by hand into a continuous length of yarn and wound onto a spool. Using foot-powered looms, townspeople wove the yarn into a twill fabric. The fabric was then napped—roughed up with combs to create a thicker, warmer surface. Using shears, they would closely trim and clean the fabric. That last step, called scouring, required heavy-duty chemicals to rid the fabric of its natural oils, dirt, and insects.

(Fun fact: The Romans and medieval manufacturers soaked wool fabric in human urine, which is essentially ammonia, to clean it. Urine was such a widely utilized industrial commodity—used in cleaning, textile manufacturing, and tanning—that collecting pots were strewn around Roman towns and cities, and eventually collectors were taxed by the government to finance, among other things, the construction of the Roman Colosseum.)

The cleaned fabric was then pounded into a thick, dense cloth—a process called fulling—and stretched into shape on tenterhooks to prevent too much shrinkage while it dried in the open air. The result is a hardy wind- and water-resistant fabric. Melton townspeople did all the manufacturing work in their homes or in workshops, and built equipment as needed.

The two main classes of British people who used Melton were laborers, who clad themselves in natural-colored fabric to stay warm and dry, and the wealthiest, who wore beautifully tailored frock coats for fox hunting made of Melton dyed bright red.

Before the water-driven fulling machine was invented, this step was usually done by women wielding wooden clubs or using their hands or feet, who sang songs to set the rhythm. The songs typically followed a call-and-response structure. I found several Canadian examples, originally sung in Scottish Gaelic, including "Horo Once More I Would Shout for Joy" (edited here):

> Let us sing a chorus in praise of the tweed . . . for the coat that
>   is dear and closely woven.
> When my tweed is passed to the maidens, they praise it as they
>   do the milling.
> When they put it on the frame, every voice was heard to
>   praise it.
> May the sheep be always healthy, they produced the good
>   thick wool.
> When my tweed goes to market, I make good money on
>   the way.

Not a yard is sold for less than a crown. Every eye seeks it with
pleasure.
The people who wear it are in the height of fashion.

—Duncan Ban MacIntyre (1724–1812)

Once Dory acquired fabric, she spread her sewing operation over
the first floor of their Portland home and hired a couple of women to
sew the wool fabric into blankets and women's capes. She convinced
a retired fabric-cutter working as a janitor at Brunswick High School
to teach her how to cut. It was so cold in the attached barn where
they cut fabric that first year, she says, that Ben had to hold a hair
dryer to thaw the oil in the cutting machine while she worked. They
made eighty capes. Then it was time to sell.

Dory soon discovered that Maine Maid's wholesale customer list,
written on index cards, kept in a folder, was completely outdated.
She would have to rebuild it from scratch. She traveled to boutique
shows, selling to small retail buyers, and within a year and a half
had enough work that she could hire more neighborhood women to
come over to the house and learn the craft.

Dory ran her first print ads—tiny spots that simply read: "Wool
capes made in Maine"—in the *New Yorker* and *Yankee* magazines.
The first day the *New Yorker* ad ran, Columbus Day, 1994, they got
so many calls that she had to flip over the answering machine tape
to keep up. Dan and Dory printed a brochure with an order form
and paid their sons' Little League teammates in pizza to stuff envelopes with a brochure and swatches, which they sent to potential
customers.

Dory hired everyone she could and paid them $10 per hour, equiv-
alent to $19.50 in 2022. "I'd been a waitress and had a few good
employers and few bad ones," she says. "I wanted to make coming to
work a joy, not a trauma." She didn't want people sitting at a sewing
machine twelve hours a day, so she gave her employees flexible shifts
and unlimited sick time. "And their kids stayed healthy because their

moms had the time to take care of themselves," she adds. She paid off the $20,000 loan in two years. By year four, the Waxmans were doing $500,000 in sales.

Ben and his younger brother Adam both remember long rides in the back of the family's Dodge Caravan, surrounded by bolts of wool, preceded by hours spent following their mom around the local mills as she chatted with owners and foremen. "I remember old mills near rivers," Adam says. "We'd walk in and there was a musty, wool smell. Kids at school would sniff me the next day and say, 'You've been to a mill.'" He remembers stacks of inventory and giant machines. "You had to yell when you were in there," he says.

Eventually, Dory and the boys would load up the Caravan— sixteen rolls at a time. Back at the house, the boys would lug the heavy bolts into the old barn.

Two years after she started her company, Dory says, "NAFTA killed us. The big designers, everything went offshore with NAFTA. If they knew they could make a jacket for $2, they didn't care about the workers. It was about making money." She says nine mills closed in the space of two and a half years. "I went to Homestead Mill in New Hampshire, then Oxford Woolen Mill in Oxford. When that closed, I went to Carleton Mills in Winthrop. They went under."

"In hindsight," Adam says, "you could tell at that point the mills weren't doing that great. There weren't huge tractor trailers lined up on the street waiting to be loaded. You had this feeling they were holding on to the past a little bit."

Over a bottle of wine, Dory tells the story of the last days of Carleton Woolen Mill, a 150-year-old company whose big-ticket item was felted wool for pool tables. The mill occupied about four city blocks in Winthrop, Maine, outside of Augusta, the state capital. Everybody around there either worked in government or in mills or in the lumber industry.

"The best in the world came out of there for seventy years," Dory says.

Carleton was owned by a New York Garment District veteran

named Arthur Spiro who sold it to a U.K. textile conglomerate in 1994. In 1990, Spiro was interviewed by the *New York Times* about the state of the textile industry "amid a flurry of takeovers." The Q&A is a fascinating glimpse into textile manufacturing at a pivotal moment in history. Spiro said Carleton Mills was doing $45 million in annual sales; he'd fought off hostile takeovers by keeping the company privately held and maintaining a low debt-to-equity ratio. But, he added, the recent mergers and divestitures in retail were brutal for business, creating an increasingly unpredictable and confusing environment, which was disrupting even the healthiest businesses.

Most tellingly, he predicted that the American textile industry would "continue to shrink, giving way to imported garments as it eroded down to the few remaining, very cost-effective, commodity-type producers and a small group of niche-market, creative manufacturers of specialty designed fabrics."

Although he said this before NAFTA, he got that right.

Spiro was hopeful that opening up Asian markets would be good for business: "The opportunities are in the Far East and Eastern Europe where rapid social and economic changes are occurring and huge consumer markets will develop. All of these people want to emulate American lifestyles. They will want to learn fashion, technology and distribution from us."

Spiro was convinced that Asian buyers would siphon up his products, and wanted the U.S. government to free up markets so that America's manufacturers like Carleton could sell "our fabrics and know-how abroad." For this reason, he supported "reasonable tariffs" and the elimination of all nontariff barriers abroad "to realistically develop a level playing field. This will encourage efficient and creative US textiles manufacturers to competitively sell their fabrics in world markets now closed to us by protectionism."

The U.K. conglomerate Allied Textiles, which bought Carleton in 1994 (shortly after NAFTA passed), at first was bullish about

American manufacturing. The company invested hundreds of thousands of dollars in state-of-the-art, computerized Italian looms. Half the wool that wound around the warps was sourced locally; the other half came from New Zealand, Australia, and Uruguay.

The new billion-person Chinese market for American goods everyone hoped for didn't immediately materialize. It was true that the Chinese were eager to learn trades. And yes, Chinese workers made more money than ever before. But during the first decades of China's astronomical economic growth, its government encouraged its citizens to save, not spend, to strengthen the country's global position and keep yuan in the country.

Carleton continued producing beautiful woven fabrics, and Dory continued buying thousands of yards a year for her capes and blankets. But one night in August 1999, she got a call from Paul Koroski, a fifth-generation Carleton millworker and assistant comptroller. She remembers that his parents had both worked in the mill on the looms, in the carding room, or in the washroom, where the raw wool would come in and get ruched, carded, combed, and spun. Paul told Dory that the "auction people" were coming the next day. He said Allied had already told all six hundred workers that the mill was shutting down in two weeks, "which totally rocked that whole geographic area," Dory says. "It was a lot for a little town like that right on the river." He told her to come the next day and bring a flashlight and some Post-it notes.

The next morning, Dory drove up to the mill. When she got there, Paul told her to pull around back. The only other person left on-site was Roger, the mechanic who took care of the furnace and the boiler. She entered the bowels of the mill, expecting to see the people that she had come to love working at their stations. They weren't there. "It was tragic," she says. "The place was empty."

On the fourth floor sat thousands of rolls of thick, quality wool fabric. "I was climbing over all this wool. There weren't any aisles. I mean, shit was just thrown everywhere. And Paul said, 'Just put a tag on what you want.' So I was buying wool—beautiful, beautiful tweeds to make tweed blankets and scarves—for $1.99 a yard. The stuff sold for $30 retail."

Then Dory went down to one of the rooms where the looms had been kept. Roger opened the door and Dory couldn't believe her eyes. The Italian looms were gone. Paul told her, "Management sold the looms and the Chinese came and took them last night." They'd packed them up and sent them to Asia.

Dory was speechless.

Paul encouraged her to take whatever she needed, figuring most of the stuff left would end up in a Maine landfill. She grabbed a few tables and old mill chairs—stools with a back where women once sat, inspecting the wool at a light table. When she got home, she found Dan at the dining room table having a beer with John McVeigh, a lawyer for the town of Winthrop. The town had put a lien on the mill because Allied hadn't paid its taxes. Dory says she told McVeigh that the looms were gone. The deal between Allied and the new Chinese manufacturer had been done without the knowledge of the town, making it more difficult for Maine to recoup back taxes. "The management knew this," Dory adds. "And they all walked away with all the money and left everybody belly-up in the town of Winthrop and all those little towns around there."

John called the state cops and told them to seal off the area. "Seriously, they roped off the whole mill with hazard tape that night and nobody was allowed in," Dory remembers. But the looms were already gone. "And if I hadn't gone up there," she says, "no one would have known."

Carleton filed for bankruptcy protection the following year. In 2003, the union successfully sued Allied for $2 million to cover severance, vacation pay, and medical benefits to employees (union and nonunion) because the company had failed to give them sixty days' notice before closing the plant.

Dory had to work harder and harder to find good wool fabric at

reasonable prices to sustain her company. She says the events following 9/11 killed what was left of the business. "Everyone was afraid. No
one was spending money. Small businesses were getting wrecked."
She ceased operations in 2002.

Dory says, "You just move on."

THIS KID IS OKAY

In early December 1999, Ben was a sophomore at UMass Boston earning pocket money at a bagel shop in Harvard Square when he saw a flyer posted to a telephone pole: "Call this number and carpool with us up to New Hampshire to canvass for Bill Bradley." Ben was rooting for Bradley, the more progressive Democratic presidential candidate to Clinton's VP Al Gore, the party favorite in the 2000 race. He liked Bradley's quasi-outsider status because, as he says, "Fuck the establishment."

Ben called the number. In the Concord, New Hampshire, office, he met the campaign's young field director, Shaun Kelleher, who'd just left Cornell to run the ground game for Bradley's primary run. The two young men clicked. That night, in a packed gymnasium, Ben heard Bill Bradley and Paul Wellstone speak. Surrounded by kids like him—idealistic and energized—he was dazzled.

Caravanning around New Hampshire gave Ben his first taste of door knocking and strategizing, and he found he was cut from the same cloth as his mother. Friendly, gregarious, ever the social justice warrior, Ben thrived in the competitive environment of politics, where you always knew who was up and who was down. He loved the inside baseball and fierce debates.

Ben returned to UMass and finished out the semester, then spent Christmas break in Portland with his family. One Saturday morning as the Waxman family was sitting down to breakfast, the phone rang. Ben answered it. On the line, his former high school basketball coach calmly told him that Simeon, Ben's quasi-stepbrother, had been shot in the Old Port and was in the hospital.

Simeon would recover. But Ben saw the near death of his friend as a sign that he needed to stop sitting around and do something. "Society always told me: *Either go to college or be a loser,*" Ben says. He decided to hell with that and quit UMass to make a difference "in the snowfields of New Hampshire."

Dan and Dory were relieved that Ben had found something he excelled in. Not that they had a say in the matter. Ben did what Ben did. But it had been one big hustle trying to get three boys through Portland's struggling public school system. Ben's high school years had been particularly hellish, academically speaking, and there was little chance that college would be any better. Dory recalls nineteen-year-old Ben on the campaign trail, his auburn hair slicked back, wearing "an ugly maroon Goodwill wool jacket," looking every part the starving stumper.

Unfortunately, Bradley got smoked in New Hampshire. The former NBA star and Democratic senator from New Jersey lost to Gore by fourteen percentage points.

Failure didn't discourage Ben from politics. He took to it like a bear to honey. Ben loved hand-shaking and listening to people's stories. He also loved telling his own—always outsized—in a rough-and-tumble bass, inflected with tough-guy bravado, littered with f-bombs. He had a gift for the sound bite, and was usually the butt of his own tales, which often involved some poorly-thought-through thing he did that somehow turned out okay.

When Ben laughed, you could hear him from down the hall.

Who wouldn't want to have a beer with a guy like that?

Ben had strong ideas about right and wrong and realized that through politics, he could shape the world. That was a hell of a lot better than sitting passively in a classroom. On the campaign trail, Ben got in the habit of carrying around yellow legal pads where he wrote down the names and numbers of everyone he met, which he does to this day. The pages of scribble looked like an organizational affront, but Ben knew exactly where everything was. Dealing with his reading disability, he'd learned to keep a lot of information in his head.

And then, just like that, Bush was in the White House. Ben worked as a staff assistant on Capitol Hill for Maine congressman Tom Allen through summer 2001 then moved back into a Portland apartment on Federal Street with several roommates and tried to finish his B.A. at the University of Southern Maine. Meanwhile, he worked on and off for political campaigns.

By November 2003, Ben says he was "the eternal student, lost, anxious, and depressed, smoking pot and drinking beer." All his friends were graduating and finding jobs. "I was floundering." That's when he got the call that would set him on a decade-long journey through organized labor in America. He was sitting on the couch in his apartment nursing a drink when his Nokia flip phone buzzed. It was Shaun Kelleher from the former Bradley campaign. The two hadn't connected in a couple of years.

Shaun said, *Come work for the AFL-CIO.* The organization is a federation of unions across the U.S., representing 12 million workers. Growing up, Ben didn't know much about the labor movement. He knew his family was working-class, but he never linked politics to labor. "I always knew unions were a good thing but didn't know a lot about them."

Shaun said the AFL was building a campaign team in Pennsylvania for the upcoming presidential election—George W. Bush versus John Kerry—and told Ben that he could run a zone.

Then he told Ben how much he'd make: $48,000.

Ben had $130 in his checking account. He took a long drag on his Marlboro Red and thought, *Holy fuck, that's a lotta money.*

So on an icy morning in January 2004, Ben gassed up his Ford Taurus and hit the interstate, heading southwest. "I was piss broke, I was twenty-four years old, and I packed my bags and I drove to Harrisburg."

He told his parents he'd be back in a year.

The drive took him through the Appalachian Mountains, which, 270 million years ago, stood as high as the Alps. Over eons, the mountains folded over on themselves; millions of years of compression and deformation produced thick veins of coal throughout the rock.

At the New York–Pennsylvania border, Ben approached coal country and drove through a terrific snow squall, but he literally couldn't afford to stop.

He got to Harrisburg at 3 a.m. Six hours later, running on nothing but adrenaline and caffeine, he skidded his way through the icy city streets to the federation's headquarters, across from the state capitol. Waiting for the elevator, he says, "this big fucking Lebanese dude with a skullcap and leather jacket comes huffing behind me yelling, 'Hold it!' He was like someone straight out of *On the Waterfront.*"

The man shoved a meaty hand at Ben. "I'm Billy George," he told him. "This is my building. This is my state."

Billy George was the state president of the Pennsylvania AFL-CIO, in charge of the welfare of one million of the most entrenched and active union members, a job he'd hold for two decades.

The elevator door opened, the pair got in, and Ben says, "Billy lights up right in the fucking elevator."

While the car crawled to the eighth floor, Ben told Billy he was there to meet with Paul Lemon, the state director of the national AFL-CIO. Billy sized up the young, hungry kid standing next to him.

Ben's friends call him "the real deal," a true believer in the inherent goodness of people.

Billy had a superpower, too. He could read people. And he immediately liked this kid.

"Screw Paul," he told Ben. "You're gonna talk to me first."

Billy pulled the Mainer into his office and gave him a crash course on the labor history of Pennsylvania steel country while smoking half of Ben's pack of Marlboros, putting out the butts on the carpet behind his desk.

Billy told Ben that he had built his organizing chops with the United Steelworkers of America when he got a job in 1960 working at the Jones & Laughlin Steel Mill in Aliquippa, Pennsylvania. It was a fascinating place to start, from a labor history perspective. J&L was a massive industrial complex of blackened steel smokestacks, industrial shed buildings, and hellish blast furnaces that ran 24/7. The company had built a town around the complex in 1906 that included twelve planned communities—one for each ethnic group, complete with its own church—plus two adjacent neighborhoods for the mill bosses. Radical for its time, the town was segregated to ensure that successive waves of unskilled immigrants, including Serbians, Croatians, Ukrainians, Hungarians, Italians, Germans, Irish, English, Slovaks, Poles, as well as African Americans, could find their community in steel country. Even today, nearly forty years after J&L folded, neighborhoods are still referred to by their original plan number.

The company had no utopian aspirations. By keeping ethnic groups divided from one another, J&L management could restrict company-wide mingling, isolate dissent, and ultimately crush any attempts at unionization.

During the Great Depression, J&L sued the brand-new National Labor Relations Board (NRLB) in a landmark case. The steel company had just fired a hundred employees trying to organize their fellow workers, and the board ruled that this was an act of discrimination.

The events that led to the J&L lawsuit demonstrate the extreme tactics employers have used to silence their workforce, and the extreme lengths to which investigators sometimes have to go to uncover wrongdoing.

The troubles began in 1934 when a young economics professor from New England arrived in western Pennsylvania to study labor conflict. While stationed in Aliquippa, he observed the worst kinds of antilabor offenses. "Union men were shadowed, beaten, and discharged," he wrote. "Meetings were spied on and members of the audience were warned or fired." In spite of J&L's best efforts, he noted, union fervor continued to spread among steelworkers.

The age-old strife between laborers and employers had been escalating for decades in the United States, but up to that point American law focused on protecting property rights and taxation, certainly not on the rights of working people. They were essentially an unprotected class.

The Constitution had been written by men in a preindustrialized society where one in five people were enslaved and the majority of paid workers had been trained through an apprentice system that could be considered a form of indentured servitude. That's why in early America, the concept of workers' rights was unknown. Sailors who tried to desert their ships were hanged. Servants were beaten. Young apprentices might be underfed and abused.

The Constitution was also written when America was underpopulated—a skilled workers' market. Townspeople in remote areas were sometimes so desperate for a blacksmith or carpenter that they pooled their money to cover a craftsman's relocation and housing costs.

Most founders came from the moneyed class and fretted more about who could vote than whether a twelve-year-old apprentice shivering in a Philadelphia workshop had any rights. Instead, they fervently debated how to avoid what Alexis de Tocqueville would later call the tyranny of the majority. In other words, how could they shape the nation's voting system to avoid a populist takeover, which would no doubt result in laws devised to please the madding crowds rather than to create a more just land for all people? (More likely, they were concerned about property rights, but justice sounded better.)

To avoid a major showdown over voting rights, the Constitution shunted responsibility for defining the electorate to the states. Needless to say, most state legislators were certain that women and Black citizens (enslaved or not) should have no power. And initially, most white men were disenfranchised, too. Legislators reasoned that those who paid into the system, via property taxes, should have the most say in how their money was spent. Voting, therefore, was a reward for being rich and paying into the U.S. Treasury.

No doubt this argument resonated with early America's ten-percenters—the men who'd invested $75 million in a war to get out of paying taxes to the Brits to form a new country. But even today, Americans can seem a little too comfortable with the idea that a billionaire can buy a senator or two. Given our history, that's the natural state of things in a place where money and power have always been inextricably linked, by design.

So it's not hyperbolic to suggest that workers were an unprotected class in early America. Until a Massachusetts Supreme Court case in 1842, anyone trying to organize workers could be charged with criminal conspiracy, following British law precedents. Of course, that didn't stop folks from trying. Some of America's very first labor organizers were the young women employed in New England textile mills who rallied—with surprising regularity—against pay cuts, abusive bosses, and excessive attempts to speed up the production line. (The men in the mills, stationed as managers or higher-skilled, hence higher-paid, workers, often distanced themselves from their troublesome female counterparts.) Sometimes, the mill women got what they hoped for. More often than not, however, organizers were blacklisted, forced to scurry out of town and find new work under a false name.

The Sherman Antitrust Act was passed in 1890 to prevent corporate monopolies, which were antibusiness because their very structure could "restrain" trade. In practice, the act was wielded with great prejudice against unions, which, litigators argued, could be seen as monopolistic entities within a shop or industry.

When Franklin Roosevelt assumed the presidency in 1933, labor laws were thus woefully inadequate to mediate the interests of the powerful—who were indeed getting ever more powerful, thanks to rampant industrialization and consolidation—and the powerless, who were indeed overwhelmed, thanks to a tanking economy. Roosevelt knew that the problem wasn't going to magically disappear.

The country was deep in the Great Depression. FDR was aware that since the country's founding, ordinary Americans had banded together to protest low wages, long working hours, and unsafe working conditions. He also knew that factory owners had developed a dizzying array of tactics to suppress unionization efforts. They regularly hired spies to report on organizers so that they could be rooted out. Private security companies, including the notorious Pinkerton National Detective Agency, were hired to protect scabs and managers when workers did strike so that production didn't stop.

Whenever company leaders felt particularly aggrieved, they turned to the government for reinforcement. If you've ever wondered why there are so many brick armories built smack in the middle of American cities, here's one answer: to suppress labor uprisings. After the Civil War and the aborted Reconstruction, the U.S. military's role shifted from militia-at-the-ready to a military force poised to defend corporate interests. National Guardsmen were frontline defenders of economic "freedom," cheered on by the moneyed elite. All it took to get America's armed forces to defend your factory from striking workers was a call from your state's governor.

Newly elected FDR seized the Great Depression as an opportunity to create a more level playing field for America's 53 million workers, 20 percent of whom were, at that point, unemployed. He launched the National Labor Relations Board (NLRB) in 1933 and tasked it with adjudicating labor disputes and overseeing union elections. By doing this, he thrust the concerns of workers into the limelight.

Immediately, FDR was accused of betraying his class. Almost as immediately, conservatives got to work dismantling labor protections, which they claimed were harmful to business, by challenging the constitutionality of every single piece of New Deal legislation. The conservative media, meanwhile, got to work convincing Americans that Roosevelt's policies, crafted to salvage an economy in dire straits, were an undemocratic power grab.

After reading the professor's report of Jones & Laughlin's behavior, Pennsylvania governor Gifford Pinchot sent a member of the state's Labor Department to investigate. When the investigator arrived in Aliquippa, no one in town would talk to him. J&L had the town buttoned up. So the investigator disguised himself as a vagrant and hung out on street corners where he eavesdropped on townspeople. That's how he learned the story of George Isosky, a former millworker who was seriously injured in an industrial accident. After his injury, Isosky began organizing employees to fight for safer working conditions. In retaliation for his activities, writes Robert R. Brooks in his 1940 book, *As Steel Goes,* J&L "railroaded [Isosky] off to the state lunatic asylum at Torrence."

Isosky's wife refused to sign papers to commit him, so a special lunacy committee (ostensibly funded by J&L) executed the deed. The governor's investigator headed back to Harrisburg with his damning report. Pinchot was horrified by what his investigator had discovered. He immediately set Isosky free, then dispatched a state police force to open up the town. That's when labor lawyers learned the extent of J&L's antiunion efforts. They convinced ten men to file a complaint against J&L for violating workers' rights with the newly established NLRB, which then ruled in the organizers' favor.

J&L didn't like that answer and sued the NRLB over the decision. In J&L's lawsuit, which went to the Supreme Court, the company claimed that the National Labor Relations Act of 1935—the legislation that defined the board's broad powers over labor disputes while guaranteeing the rights of private sector employees to organize, bargain collectively, and strike—was unconstitutional. The company had every reason to think it would win. Prior complaints against the NRLB over its jurisdiction and constitutionality had been successful. It was looking like none of FDR's labor protections would be upheld.

But J&L's case arrived at the perfect moment for a decisive labor victory. The country was deep in the Great Depression; 25 percent of Americans were out of work. Antilabor conservatives were exceedingly unpopular. The public began to see the good created by Roosevelt's myriad public works programs, such as the Works Progress Administration (WPA), which used federal money to employ people to build infrastructure across the nation, including railroad stations, bridges, schools, and roads. The country was moving again; surely the economy would follow.*

J&L lost its lawsuit against the NRLB in 1937 and was forced to rehire employees it had fired, with back pay. Aliquippa steelworkers then overwhelmingly voted to designate the Steel Workers' Organizing Committee (SWOC) as their "exclusive bargaining agent," marking the first time that workers held a union election in steel history.

More broadly, the court's ruling in *NLRB v. Jones & Laughlin* made it clear that the U.S. government would finally throw its muscle behind America's century-old labor movement. Government by the people, for the people.

That was the history Billy George wanted Ben to know. When he was done, he released him.

Ben hurried into the hallway to find Paul Lemon. He got to the front desk and, this being Pennsylvania in 2004, the woman seated there, Judy Staker, was chain-smoking. Ben asked her for Lemon, and without looking up, Staker pointed to a door.

From inside the office, someone suddenly exploded, "We don't put up with this bullshit!" Ben turned the knob.

---

* Some of Roosevelt's programs employed photographers, artists, and writers who were paid to chronicle a changing landscape and a changing people. These artists were more vulnerable to conservative attack. Without these programs, however, we wouldn't have Walker Evans's and Dorothea Lange's striking photos. We wouldn't have John Steinbeck's *The Grapes of Wrath*. We wouldn't have the tremendous artwork created for municipal buildings, schools, and hospitals by thousands of WPA artists, including Jackson Pollock, Mark Rothko, Willem de Kooning, and Alice Neel. Any one of them might have ditched a career in art had it not been for the small grants they received from the federal government during the Depression.

Paul Lemon sat behind a giant desk yelling into the phone, ash-trays to the left, ashtrays to the right, and one on the coffee table. With him was Rich Barchiesi. Ben walked in.

Lemon regarded the skinny kid standing in the doorway and asked him, "You smoke?"

Ben nodded. Paul raised his eyebrows and announced to the room, "This kid is okay."

GREED IS A REAL THING

Ben's youth and idealism were just what the labor movement was looking for.

In early 2004, Lemon put him in charge of organizing the ground game for John Kerry's presidential campaign for a third of Pennsylvania—from Harrisburg to Lehigh Valley to Reading—that election year.

Ben had no idea what he was getting into. The labor movement "was like a funeral. It was like death," says Ben. "I mean, I touched it and I felt it."

This was early in the opioid epidemic, before anyone really had a handle on what was going on, and addiction was sweeping through former steel cities like Allentown and Bethlehem. Jonathan Burkhardt, who worked alongside Ben during the campaign, says, "I had lived in Third World countries. I knew poverty, but this was just crazy."

Ben and Jonathan were told to keep talking to people, "even if you don't like them," because even as union rolls were shrinking, labor leaders continued to see themselves as the voice of the underclass. They wanted to know what people were thinking, what they needed, and how to reach them. And they wanted to make sure their former members voted in their best interests instead of succumbing to the rage of the helpless.

As young labor advocates, Ben and Jonathan were expected to work twelve-hour days. They were going door-to-door in forgotten towns with grass growing out of the paved street, asking questions like *What's the most important thing to you? Health care? The war in Iraq? Jobs?* "You get someone talking," Jonathan says, "they're going to say some pretty tough things. There were some very angry white people."

It was the best education a young idealist like Ben could get.

Ben had a one-year contract with the AFL-CIO and hoped that if he did a good job, they'd keep him.

Ben got good fast. "He's just one of these guys who picks up the phone, knocks on doors, talks to anyone," Jonathan says.

For the first time in his life, Ben felt like he was making a difference on a large scale. The AFL-CIO had a team of researchers who did the hard work of exposing antilabor politicians and ensuring that those who promised to support workers followed through on that pledge. Organizers like Ben were like apostles, spreading political truths to people who didn't always have access to good information. Going door to door, he could help steer conversations away from divisive rhetoric and back toward constructive action. He was community-building in a very real way. Organizers like him were a bulwark against misinformation and hateful narratives. Thinking back to those grueling days, Ben says, "We worked eighty hours so America can work forty."

One day while Ben was phone-banking—trying to convince union members that George Bush was bad for working people— Rich Trumka walked into the room. He was built like a truck and wore a big brush of a mustache. The only thing Ben knew about the then secretary treasurer of the national AFL-CIO was that he had his roots in coal country.

"You could tell he was a leader. Everybody wanted to touch him," Ben remembers.

Word was getting around that the Maine kid had a knack for organizing. Trumka walked up to him and said, "So, you're Benny." Ben stood up and shook his hand.

After the election, Trumka called Ben to the AFL-CIO headquarters in D.C. The monumental marble-clad building on Lafayette Square was dedicated in 1956 by President Dwight Eisenhower when nearly 35 percent of the working population carried a union card. (It's now close to 8 percent.)

"Labor is the United States," Eisenhower told the crowd. "The men and women who, with their minds, their hearts, and hands, create the wealth that is shared in this country, they are America." He ended his short speech with these words: "Free trade unionism . . . has continued to make equal opportunity available to all people, free—under a free nation—the United States of America."

It was an unequivocal endorsement of working people and collective bargaining.

"Think about this," Ben says. "There are only two nonfederal buildings around the White House: the AFL-CIO and the Chamber of Commerce. Talk about what has driven America for a hundred years, right? Business and labor, right there."

The first thing Ben noticed walking into Trumka's office was that his window shades were drawn. Trumka's office overlooked the White House and he kept the shades down throughout the Bush years. "Rich never missed an opportunity to make a statement," Ben says.

To the young starstruck organizer, Trumka was the direct link between D.C. and one of the roughest, meanest labor battles ever fought on American soil.

It was the battle over coal country, and it ended in murder.

Rich Trumka and Jock Yablonksi had both worked in the Appalachian mines in their teens, four decades apart. Both got their start in the United Mine Workers of America (UMWA). Both were reformers.

Yablonski began organizing after his father was killed in a mine explosion in 1933. His popularity and intelligence caught the attention of UMWA's then president, John L. Lewis, another labor icon. It was the bulldog-faced Lewis who founded the Congress of Industrial Organizations (CIO), which later merged with the AFL to become the country's largest federation of unions. And it was Lewis who supported Yablonski's rise up the union ranks to president of his district in 1958.

When Lewis stepped down from the UMWA presidency after running the union for four decades, he appointed Tony Boyle, a former mineworker from Montana, as his successor. Boyle, like Lewis, ran the UMWA like a ruthless mob boss, but without his predecessor's charm. Boyle controlled every election and every leadership appointment. He was unlikable and unpopular. Chip Yablonski, son of Jock, says, "[The UMWA] was a corrupt institution from top to bottom."

At 5:30 a.m. on November 20, 1968, a mine shaft in Farmington, West Virginia, exploded, sending up massive plumes of smoke and flames and shaking the foundations of buildings twelve miles away. Coal mining releases highly flammable methane gas, which can build up in the shafts while men work. The mine burned for days, preventing rescue workers from reaching the seventy-eight men trapped inside. A decade later, after a heroic recovery effort, nineteen miners were still lost, sealed inside their coal coffin.

For years leading up to the accident, mineworkers had complained about safety violations at Farmington, but Boyle refused to champion their cause. Instead, he called it "an unfortunate accident" and praised the mine company's safety record while refusing to meet with the miners' widows. Two years after the tragedy, an inspector discovered that a safety alarm that activated a ventilation fan had been disabled before the disaster.

Boyle's callousness in the face of disaster caused union members' resentment to boil over. Boyle had lost any connection with his people; it was clear he was in the pocket of mine owners.

Sensing Boyle's time was up, Yablonski ran against him for the UMWA presidency in 1969, but lost two to one in what everyone knew was a rigged election. Boyle's henchmen had quite literally stuffed the ballot box. Yablonski wouldn't leave quietly. He filed a complaint with the Department of Labor and multiple lawsuits in federal court against the union for fraud.

Boyle decided to take out his opposition the old-fashioned way: he ordered a hit. Through an embezzlement scheme and phony education fund, Boyle was able to funnel $20,000 to three drifters in return for Yablonski's head. On New Year's Eve, the hired gunmen shot up the Yablonski house while the family slept, killing Jock, his wife, Margaret, and their twenty-five-year-old daughter, Charlotte.

News of the triple murder rocked the quiet Pennsylvania town where the Yablonskis lived. When large news outlets picked up the story, the nation at large finally learned about the abject corruption at the UMWA.

Overnight, Yablonski went from reformer to martyr, and a new coal country union emerged—Miners for Democracy—to take up his cause. The new union hired several young lawyers, including Yablonski's two sons, to battle Boyle and pressure the UMWA to reform.

One young lawyer-in-training working with Miners for Democracy was a guy built like a bull with a thick black mustache and a head for facts and figures. He'd worked in the mines while getting his BA at Penn State. His name was Richard Trumka.

The things Trumka would learn during that period would forever shape him.

During Boyle's murder trial, a pioneering documentary filmmaker in New York City hired a crew, packed cameras and lights into a van, and drove to Harlan County, Kentucky, where 180 miners were striking against the Duke Power Company–owned Eastover Coal Company. The miners—white, Black, and Latino—lived in company housing in appalling conditions; many homes lacked running water.

Barbara Kopple's film, *Harlan County U.S.A.,* would end up

covering the thirteen-month-long strike, interspersed with shots of Boyle's trial. Her powerful film also revealed how the women in the community came together to support the men. While the miners struck, their wives, mothers, and daughters organized, waking before dawn to block the road with their bodies to prevent the company from trucking in strikebreakers, and rallying the community to support each other.

One particularly moving segment captured the performance of Florence Reece, a coal miner's daughter born in 1900, who had written the famous union song "Which Side Are You On?" during the Harlan County War in 1941, a song that Pete Seeger would later make famous.

Forty years after she had written her anthem, Reece sang it once again for hundreds of miners during a union-wide rally for Harlan. Wearing a red-checked dress and cat-eye glasses with thick lenses, seventy-three-year-old Florence stood at the microphone. In a thick Tennessee twang, she told the crowd, "I'm not a coal miner as you well know, but I'm as close as I can be not to be one. My father was a coal miner who was killed in the mines, and my husband is slowly dying of black lung. We were in the Bloody Harlan strike in the '30s, and when I say bloody, I do mean bloody. And I hear the miners are gonna stick it out and refuse to sign that contract until hell freezes over. The men know they've got nothing to lose but their chains." The audience roared.

Reece then adjusted her glasses and began to sing in a gravelly voice seasoned by years of toil and heartache: "My daddy was a miner/And I'm a miner's son/And I'll stick with the union/'Til every battle's won/Don't scab for the bosses/Don't listen to their lies/Us poor folks haven't got a chance/Unless we organize."

All that autumn, Harlan County simmered with the threat of violence; when strikebreaking vigilantes began openly wielding guns, strikers responded in kind. The tension was palpable. One morning, nearly a year into the strike, a young miner was murdered in a predawn scuffle with hired agitators. After his death, Duke finally agreed to work with the miners' union leadership.

In the midst of the Harlan strike, Tony Boyle was sentenced to three consecutive life prison terms for the murder of the Yablonski family.

Trumka became the president of the United Mine Workers union in 1982.

By 2004, Trumka was the secretary-treasurer for the AFL and asked Ben to take the field director position in D.C. for the federation's Alliance for Retired Americans. He said the department needed new energy, new ideas.

The following day, Ben drove back to Harrisburg, packed his bags, and moved to D.C. A year later, Trumka began putting Ben on political campaigns for the federation across the country, supporting pro-labor Democratic candidates in increasingly Republican districts.

It was a "stressful but meaningful job," says Ben. "There were wins, there were losses." But he was learning invaluable things about his country, manufacturing, corporations, and the plight of American workers. When Ben first started campaigning for the AFL-CIO in 2000, the U.S. easily had the biggest economy in the world, even if the union's power was slipping.

From 2004 to 2012, while Ben worked for the largest labor federation in the United States, representing 12 million workers, American companies, forever on the hunt for bigger bottom lines, cheaper goods, and bigger executive bonuses, offshored their economy, one million pairs of socks at a time. Economists, lobbyists, and politicians cheered them on.

Ben spent that time standing between business and workers, the powerful and the underrepresented, big money and wage-earners, legislators and picketers. While the nation's political rhetoric crept closer to authoritarianism, Ben was trying—and often failing—to convince union members to ignore the culture wars designed to stoke racial and social divisions, and to vote blue.

By 2018, the U.S.'s annual trade deficit to China was $419 billion.

It's critical to recognize that what happened to American manufacturing over the past two decades was not the organic by-product of free market policy. The Chinese government, in particular, eager to get a foothold in the lucrative American market, subsidized every step of the way so that its producers could sell their exports for less than they cost to make, a process called "dumping." Foreign goods were cheaply transported to the U.S. on government-subsidized ships that sailed from government-subsidized ports.

That China ruthlessly flaunts international rules to dominate global manufacturing is now common knowledge. In November 2022, the Information Technology & Innovation Foundation (ITIF) released a report encouraging American policymakers to revive Depression-era tariffs to save domestic industry from "China's unfair trade practices."

Economist Robert Atkinson summed up current thinking: "The last decade has seen a growing consensus that China's economic, trade, and technology policies and practices pose a significant threat to U.S. economic and national security. For the most part, the debate is no longer about whether China poses such a threat, whether its practices affecting trade and investment are mostly legitimate, or whether China is getting in line with its World Trade Organization (WTO) obligations. The new Washington consensus is that China is a threat, Chinese government trade policy actions are *mostly unfair and predatory* [emphasis added], and it is moving away, rather than toward, its WTO obligations."

The report argued that Congress should slow down Chinese imports by strengthening Section 337 of the 1930 Tariff Act, which was passed to protect domestic industries from harm due to unfair competition.

But that's 2022 economics.

In the early aughts, American companies were elated to find a cheaper source of labor. By the end of that decade, fully one third of American manufacturing was exported to other countries.

In *Factory Man,* journalist Beth Macy tells that saga through one family-owned, hundred-year-old Virginia furniture business. In the early aughts, the third-generation owner of Bassett Furniture Company, once the largest wood furniture manufacturer in the world, traveled to China to explore the possibility of shifting his manufacturing over there. He toured facilities throughout the country with a Taiwanese fabricator.

During one of these tours, the Taiwanese businessman confessed that he was confounded by Americans. He'd worked with buyers from all over the world, including Europeans, Asians, Middle Easterners, but he said that the Americans' greed was beyond anything he'd ever seen.

Fearing copycats, foreign buyers from other countries tended to give foreign manufacturers just enough information to make parts of things. But the Americans had no such fears. The Chinese fabricator marveled at the Americans' willingness to sell out each other and freely give away their own corporate secrets. In just a few years, he said, he'd watched as Americans exported entire industries to Asia, gutting their domestic workforce, destroying their own tax base, and exposing their products to knockoffs or the black market. He'd never met people so hungry for profit that they were willing to export everything—not just their labor but all their manufacturing knowledge—to reap bigger payoffs.

Indeed, the American furniture exec eventually shut down his North Carolina plant, laid off hundreds of employees—destroying the entire town his family's company once supported in the process—and sent all the physical work of crafting his furniture line to China.

Economists, lobbyists, and politicians celebrated offshoring. Suddenly, goods in the U.S. were more affordable than ever, somewhat mitigating the drop in real wages. Even if Americans' paychecks were stagnant, their buying power stayed strong. Container ships got bigger; America's ports got busier. Each vessel arriving from Asia was another nail in the coffin of American manufacturing.

But what would Americans do once the Chinese monopolized all industries and decided to raise prices?

Trumka believed that the best way to rescue the labor movement was to pour the AFL-CIO's precious resources into realigning the Democratic Party's agenda with the needs of working people and domestic industry. Most of the party was still under the spell of neo-liberals. In contrast, Trumka was ardently anti-free-trade, a position that made him seem a radical. But he had history on his side.

The last time Americans had been so chronically dependent on imports was when they were a colony of the British Empire.

Modern American-style trade policy started as a way to contain Soviet influence and open foreign markets to American-made goods after World War II. American policymakers and industrialists wanted to build a framework that would support a new U.S.-centric world economic order. The world was up for grabs as regions, torn apart by war or liberated from the fetters of colonialism, raced to establish governments and economies.

Unlike nineteenth-century imperialists, however, Americans wouldn't amass power through occupation. Instead, the U.S. would use its economic might, and foreign lending, to steer governments toward capitalism. The world's biggest economy would control other countries by shunting money to "good" countries while withholding financial access to punish "bad" (read: communist) ones.

Cheerleaders of a quasi-globalization argued that investment in mini-capitalists around the world would create new markets for American products and ideology. Imagine all those Japanese, Indians, and Cubans spending their money on U.S.-made cars, grain, and weapons.

Lowering trade barriers and allowing the free movement of capital among democratic nations would inextricably tie together their fates, forging an everlasting peace. In 1944, the U.N. held an economic conference in Bretton Woods, New Hampshire, just ninety-three miles from Portland, Maine, to codify global stabilization through lending. The goal of the 730 delegates representing forty-four nations was to foster international economic cooperation and a new financial world order, planting the seeds for the "open market." The International Monetary Fund (IMF), an organization that set the rules for international lending and borrowing, began taking shape.

Which is how peace, debt, and free trade became intertwined in the American century.

One country that Americans worried about in 1944 was Japan. Would the Soviets try to take over the country in its weakened state, triggering a chain reaction of communist coups in the region? Even before the end of the war, policymakers proposed to prop up Japan's textile industry to stabilize the country. To get buy-in from the southern states, policymakers agreed to send American cotton to Japan, subsidized by American taxpayers. Production experts, trained by the military, would teach Japanese manufacturers techniques to boost their efficiency. The U.S. would also extend credit so that the Japanese could purchase industrial looms and sewing machines, made in the USA, naturally.

When American textile manufacturers balked at these policies, they were accused of being unpatriotic or, worse, communists. But they knew of what they spoke. Soon, Japanese-made textiles—sold cheaper than the cost of production, thanks to subsidies—were flooding back into America, replacing domestic cloth.*

Large American corporations have always had outsize power over foreign policy, but during the Cold War, fear of Soviet incursion united policymakers and corporate leaders as collaborators in an unholy war against socialism. When elected leaders in Congo, Cuba, Nicaragua, Argentina, and Chile enacted socialist-leaning policies to create more equitable economies, these progressives triggered right-wing violence and coups seeded by American operatives, supported by American industry.

* Textile manufacturing had been one of the first major American industries to unionize. It was also the first to be sacrificed in an effort to contain Soviet influence—and socialism—around the world. Was the decision to offshore the strongly unionized industry a coincidence?

A quick look at what happened in Chile demonstrates the horror that "free trade" unleashed on the world. When Salvador Allende was elected president of Chile in 1970, he instituted the most progressive agenda in the world. He wanted his people to benefit from their rapidly industrializing economy. Shortly after taking office, Allende nationalized major industries, including copper mining, and used the funds to finance infrastructure, education, and health care. He set a minimum wage, expanded public works programs toward the goal of full employment, and bolstered the voice of labor.

In the context of the Cold War, Allende's agenda sounded like dreaded socialism. In Chile, U.S.-owned Anaconda, then the largest mining company in the world, owned the Chile Copper Company, which owned the most productive mine in the world. If Allende returned ownership of the mine to the people of Chile, Anaconda would lose a fortune. Another American company, ITT, had invested $200 million in Chile's communications infrastructure. Was ITT's profit threatened as well?

At the time, the U.S. was actively fighting an exceedingly costly war in Vietnam to assert its market dominance in Asia. Thus a covert, right-wing takeover of Chile, justified by free market theory, would be an easy sell to President Nixon. While U.S. corporations, including ITT, used their private army of spies and police to intimidate Allende's supporters, corporations like IBM and Exxon, along with the CIA, granted young Chilean economists full scholarships to the University of Chicago's school of economics, where Milton Friedman held court. Other acolytes of the "Chicago School" were sent to teach at Chilean universities.

After a couple of years spent fomenting a free market revolution, the Nixon administration gave General Augusto Pinochet the green light to invade the capital city of Santiago and seize control of the government. In the wake of a bloody military coup, hundreds of thousands of lives were destroyed. Pinochet's military government immediately removed tariff protections for local industry, banned trade unions, and privatized social security and hundreds of state-owned enterprises. Some of the government properties were sold below market price to politically connected buyers, including Pinochet's son-in-law. Chile bought Anaconda's copper mine from the company for $250 million.

The result was an economic miracle, but one that benefited only the rich. In 2021, Chileans boast the highest income inequality in the world; the top 1 percent owns nearly 59 percent of the nation's wealth. (For reference, the top 1 percent of Americans own 19 percent of the wealth. In France, that figure is closer to 10 percent.)

Reflecting on the capitalist coup fifty years later, the British Parliamentarian Jeremy Corbyn, who had spent time in Chile before the coup, observed, "Understand that the power of international capital and global corporations . . . will be used against any progressive government. The only way forward is to have strong labor movements, and a strong cultural movement goes with it. That unites people in the . . . expectation that we don't have to live in a world of global inequality."

Richard Trumka knew his labor history and chose to devote the AFL-CIO's resources to building alliances with policymakers who might be open to the idea that domestic manufacturing and organized labor would continue to be the foundation of a healthy citizenry. He argued for bringing the money back into the U.S., supporting domestic workers, and focusing on policies that sheltered the American economy from bad trade partners.

Ben had enormous respect for Trumka, but working under a massive figure like him had its challenges. The future AFL-CIO president had a "brain like a sponge," Ben says. "He was one of the smartest human beings I've ever met in my life." He was tough, compassionate, thoughtful, and bold. "And he never shot from the hip," Ben says. "He was strategic." But Trumka was also demanding.

It wasn't easy arguing for organized labor in the first decade of the twenty-first century. There was plenty to distract Americans from the gutting of their manufacturing economy—9/11, the Iraq War, New Orleans and Hurricane Katrina, the Great Recession, issues of data privacy, the rise of white supremacy and hateful rhetoric. Meanwhile, some 60,000 American factories shuttered. At the same time, foreign-made goods bearing major American labels began flooding into U.S. ports. Overseas labor was enriching shareholders and executives, but at least everyone's 401(k)s were growing.

Over that same period, academia abandoned manufacturing, too. To many highly respected economists, making stuff in America had lost its luster. Why compete with workers in China, Honduras, or Vietnam, where things could be made for a fraction of the cost?

Trumka knew that the labor movement needed to grow, and to do that, it had to confront its racist and sexist history. Just before he took the reins of the AFL-CIO, he gave a rousing speech to thousands of United Steelworkers members at their annual convention in 2008, telling them that the Black presidential candidate was the one who would support their cause. These were mostly working-class white men, who'd been drifting ever further to the right for more than a generation. They were losing jobs to offshoring. They were the aggrieved.

In America, captains of industry frequently exploited race and gender differences to splinter the workforce into fearful, angry sects, driving wedges between rich and poor, native and immigrant, urban and rural, white and Black and Indigenous. Black workers in particular were used over and over again as strikebreakers to reinforce the divide.*

Exploit differences—divide and conquer the workforce, pit white workers against Black, immigrant, and female workers. Who took your job? This Black man, that Syrian, this Italian, that Jew. Why

---

* There are many bright spots for labor as well. In the 1920s, the UMWA under John L. Lewis recognized this tactic and successfully pulled non-white workers into the union. Let's also remember that the 1963 March on Washington for Jobs and Freedom, which culminated in Martin Luther King's "I Have a Dream" speech, had been sponsored by the United Auto Workers.

are we cutting your paycheck? Because all these foreigners are driving down wages. Such labor-suppression tactics were astoundingly effective at building a grateful-for-anything workforce—united by race or cultural group against the other. These tactics also ensured that racism would work its way deep into the core of Americans' psyche and sometimes corrupt the labor movement. Racism was a big, red button that anyone could push to atomize the workforce.

"I mean, there's a reason Donald Trump happened," Ben says. "Donald Trump is completely full of hypocrisy and lies and misinformation and all of that. But when you're getting kicked and you're getting the crumbs from the table, I don't care if you're union or nonunion, as a working person, you want to believe somebody that's telling you something you want to hear."

Trumka recognized that unions were imperfect. They had a checkered history. Persistent racism had crippled even the strongest attempts to organize. Sometimes unions were willing to lose labor disputes rather than admit people of color and strengthen their ranks. It was a weakness business leaders would exploit again and again.

So many race riots in America had started as someone's effort to suppress workers' demands for higher wages, better safety standards, or better living conditions through racial vilification. With enough time and prodding, anger and resentment against "the other" will burn white-hot. The only thing needed to ignite a labor conflict into a holocaust of rage was an "incident," real or imagined.

For example, while many historians attribute the Tulsa Race Massacre of 1921 to false allegations about a Black man attacking a white woman, the truth is even more revelatory. In fact, white supremacist, antiunion messaging had been stoking a white grievance narrative in Tulsa for years.

In the early twentieth century, Oklahoma had a large Black and Native American population, many of them farmers, many of whom were socialists. When oil was discovered on the Osage reservation, tribe members became very wealthy, an affront to the white people who had come to Tulsa looking for work in the oil boom town. After much lobbying, the state government decreed that the Osage weren't sophisticated enough to handle that kind of money and assigned white "handlers" to assist tribe members with their affairs. Dozens of tribe members would be murdered in the early 1920s by contract killers, leaving their land and oil rights to their white caretakers.

White supremacists found a powerful ally in these profiteers. Together, they united against a common enemy—socialism—and branded it as dangerous, anticapitalist ideology imported by the loathsome Eastern European Jews. In 1917, some seventeen white members of the International Workers of the World—labor organizers all—were rounded up in Tulsa, flogged, tarred and feathered, and released on the prairie by Knights of Liberty dressed in black robes and masks.

A few years later, a white mob ripped through the Black section of the city, burned it to the ground, and killed hundreds of Black citizens, including women and children.

The KKK went mainstream in 1925 when an estimated 60,000 members marched down Pennsylvania Avenue in D.C. in a claim for respectability. The men—yes, all of them were men—wore pointy hats instead of full hoods, so you could see their proud white faces.

Against that background, Trumka stood in front of thousands of United Steelworkers and shocked just about everyone when he told them to vote for Barack Obama. Yes, he told them, the Black candidate is labor's friend.

"There's no evil that's inflicted more pain and more suffering than racism," he told the crowd, "and it's something we in the labor movement have a special responsibility to challenge. It's our special responsibility because we know, better than anyone else, how racism is used to divide working people."

WITNESS

Hoofing it from state to state, campaign to campaign, Ben bore witness to the offshoring of American manufacturing from a rare and precarious place in American culture. He knew that insidious, often deliberate, forces were deconstructing the economy from the top down, and within companies. "I learned what bad trade deals, greed, and shortsighted economic and business strategies had done to communities," he told me.

Ben spent that pivotal time on the ground, standing shoulder to shoulder with working people across America as their jobs evaporated.

Ben covered Bethlehem, Pennsylvania, just one year after the American steel giant lost its long battle against foreign competitors and declared bankruptcy. In an instant, more than 95,000 employees and their dependents lost their pensions—money some workers had spent decades earning while risking their lives to do their jobs. Ben moved on to North Dakota, where he watched union workers at sugar beet processors get locked out as their employer demanded concessions from their workers, threatening them with plant closures. Ben arrived shortly after Delphi Automotive closed its auto-parts plants in Dayton, Ohio, sending thousands of men and women from middle class to unemployed.

He told me about the day in 2010 when the AFL-CIO went to the Whirlpool refrigerator plant in Evansville, Indiana, in a last-ditch effort to prevent 1,100 workers' jobs from being sent to Mexico. Whirlpool had just received $20 million in stimulus money from the federal government and was about to use that money to send the entire plant to another country.

Whirpool was controlled by the Chicago-based Crown family, early and ardent investors in Barack Obama's campaign. The connection between the Crowns and Obama was a big deal for the AFL-CIO, Ben says, "because we had all worked our asses off to elect him and [his administration] wasn't doing anything to stop [the off-shoring of the plant]."

Rumors began to circulate that the company was shutting down Evansville. "By that winter, you started hearing that collective bargaining fights were coming to Indiana, Wisconsin, Ohio," Ben says. "There were some big job issues happening. NASA was fucking with the machinists in Cape Canaveral. And then there was this fucking Evansville thing."

Trumka sent several AFL-CIO staff members to Indiana to organize and put pressure on the company not to shut down the plant. But they were failing. In a last-ditch effort, the AFL-CIO decided to organize a massive day of action. "I didn't know what we were walking into, but the local organizer kept saying, 'It's going to be big. This town is fighting for its life.'"

Ben remembers Trumka saying, "We gotta go. We gotta go. We gotta go. This is what it's about."

When they landed, Trumka immediately got into the car to be briefed. He always carefully planned all his moves, Ben says. He knew that labor organizers like him had a big target on their backs. Ben and Trumka drove to the IUE-CWA electrical and communications workers' hall the back way, "and we pull in the parking lot and it was just a sea of cars, people came from all over," he remembers.

Trumka held a press conference with the local union, where a few workers told their gut-wrenching stories. After two hours, they went outside to formally launch a march to the plant, about a mile and a half away.

Ohio brought delegations. Kentucky brought delegations. Indiana brought people. "They were coming because . . . this was about money. This was about greed. This was like, *Fuck people. We can make more money, pay people less money, make higher margins, and move this plant to Mexico.*" That's when Ben saw a group of old men wearing camouflage mineworker shirts from the historic 1989 Pittston Coal Strike. Back in 1989, as UMWA president, Trumka had deftly led striking mineworkers to the bargaining table after a year of sometimes violent confrontations and was able to negotiate the restoration of workers' health and retirement benefits. The miners never forgot.

"When Trumka asked [the Pittston mineworkers] to cover the backs of people they didn't know, they came," Ben says. "That's what the labor movement is. That's why corporate America hates the movement. Because for all of its internal struggles, the labor movement is the only economic voice left for working people. They'd driven to Evansville from Kentucky and from Pennsylvania because Richard Trumka had had their back."

Trumka was ushered up front to lead the march. Outside the factory a huge crowd had gathered. Whirlpool called in government protection. "They got state police, town police, county sheriffs, rent-a-cops, all suited, blocking the entrance to the factory," Ben says. "Richard just went right up to that fucking door and started banging. Nobody came. They shut the factory down."

As of 2022, the Crowns are the thirty-fourth-richest family in America, estimated at $20 billion, and own a major stake in military supplier General Dynamics, the fifth-largest weapons contractor in the world.

In 2011, Trumka was profiled for *Esquire* magazine. When journalist John Richardson asked the labor organizer what he was fighting for, Trumka answered: "Better world. Better life for everybody, every worker. Poor kids oughta be able to go anyplace their brains will take them. Not where Daddy or Mommy's pocketbooks can send them.

Everybody oughta have health care, everybody oughta have some retirement security, every American. Every one. Everybody oughta have a decent good job. That's what I believe in, and that's what I fight every day to try to achieve."

Ben remembers Trumka saying on the plane home from Evansville, "Greed is a real thing. It doesn't care about people."

SHE'S OUTTA
YOUR LEAGUE

On February 14, 2010, Ben boarded a plane in D.C. and flew back to Portland for his middle brother's thirtieth birthday. When he got to the party, he knocked back a few drinks and started working the room. In typical Waxman fashion, it was a huge affair featuring a live band in a storied waterfront restaurant that had supported the local fishing community for generations.

"The place was rocking," Ben remembers. But he'd changed a lot since he'd left his hometown. He'd been working the political ground game for more than a decade and looked like the world he inhabited: thicker than before, his suits cut wide, his hair slicked back, swearing like a union boss.

While he sipped a Jameson, in walked his former Federal Street roommate "with a beautiful brunette on his arm." The roommate introduced his date to Ben as Whitney.

Ben considered himself an expert schmoozer. But he was a union man, not James Bond. "Like a total schmuck, I handed her my business card and said, 'If you need anything . . .'" Whitney took it, smiled inscrutably, and walked away.

When she had disappeared into the crowd, Ben's friends, who'd watched the whole awkward exchange, gave him hell. "What the fuck, did you just give her your card? This is Maine, not D.C.," they teased him. Ben didn't care. The only thing that mattered to him in that moment was that the stunning woman with the lion's mane of chestnut hair knew how to get in touch with him.

Whitney Reynolds was used to random encounters with tongue-tied men. Tall and athletic, the spitting image of the actress Minnie Driver, she got that reaction a lot. When she got home, she studied Ben's card, and saw it said something about the AFL-CIO and "Office of the President." She didn't know much about labor unions or politics, but the blue-eyed, red-bearded guy from Washington seemed important, so she slipped the card into her wallet and kept it there.

Maybe Whitney held on to it because she believed in fate. Over her thirty-two years, she'd let life carry her from New York to Florida to Melbourne, Australia, to Oregon to Pennsylvania to Maine. She'd learned to keep moving while making the most of whatever fate threw at her. She'd been a competitive skier, a New York City bartender, a real estate agent, and a wife. She pursued everything she did with determination and dedication. She always had to be the best. But none of the roles she'd tried so far had been a perfect fit. She was still searching.

Whitney had been raised in a comfortably upper-middle-class family, with two parents who she says "started at the bottom of the ladder and worked their way up." Her mother, Mary Ann Lawson, grew up in a tiny town in South Georgia, population four hundred. Mary Ann was one of eight children of the so-called "Watermelon King of Georgia." The family had a long agricultural history. "My grandmother used to pick tobacco," Whitney says. "There's this family story about how when my grandfather went to escort her to the church to get married, her hands were stained with tobacco."

Mary Ann was the only member of her family to leave the state. She was working as an X-ray tech in Atlanta when she met Whitney's father, Tod Reynolds, at a convention in 1976. The handsome, square-jawed northerner was recently divorced and had full custody of two young daughters. When they married, Mary Ann gained an instant family. Whitney was born two years later.

Tod was from upstate New York, and was a freshman at the University of Rochester in the early 1960s when his father died. That's how Tod ended up working for the local company, Eastman Kodak. He says, "I had to get a job because I needed to eat."

Tod excelled at Kodak during the peak years of America's industrial supremacy. Kodak made film, photographic paper, and cameras. Later, the company got into medical diagnostic equipment. At its peak, the company had manufacturing plants across the U.S., as well as in East Germany, Paris, London, Mexico City, and Brazil.

Photography had become integral to the human experience. Precious memories were stored in shoeboxes and family albums and passed down from generation to generation. What was more American than a "Kodak moment"—an event worth capturing on film? (A strange concept in today's obsessively documented world.)

Tod was also an avid skier and passed his passion on to Whitney. She was fast and nimble and loved competing in downhill events. As a teen, Whitney spent a lot of dad-daughter time driving from event to event, bonding with her father over her wins and occasional losses.

In the 1990s, Kodak began making a big push into Asia and Tod took an executive position in Melbourne, Australia, to oversee manufacturing plants there. Whitney was halfway through her sophomore year in high school. She didn't want to go. "It was a hard time for me to leave," Whitney says. "I'm midway through creating solid friendships and then my parents say we're moving across the world."

Tod told his youngest daughter that she could stay behind and attend boarding school in Lake Placid, and Whitney agreed. She could keep skiing, but she'd be on her own. The Reynoldses sold their Rochester house and gave the dog to Whitney's aunt and uncle for the second time. (They'd relocated to Florida for a few years when Whitney was in elementary school.)

Then Tod and Mary Ann changed their minds. They knew high school was a tough time for kids—Tod's daughters had struggled in their teens—and decided to keep their baby, Whitney, close. Tod convinced her to come with them. Give it six months, he said. If she hated it, she could go back.

Moving to Australia, Whitney says, "was a defining moment for me in so many ways." Her insular world was blown wide open. The Reynoldses lived in the middle of Melbourne, where Whitney got her first taste of big-city life. She found a small ski community a few hours outside of Melbourne where she could continue competing while finishing her high school diploma. She ended her career placing twenty-seventh in Giant Slalom at the 1996 Junior National Championships at Sugarloaf, Maine.

But Kodak was about to get hit hard. When Japan's Fujifilm began exporting cheaper photographic products into the American market, Kodak began losing market share. In retribution, the company petitioned the U.S. to file a claim against Japan with the newly formed World Trade Organization, claiming that Japan's government had artificially rigged its domestic system to favor Fuji and prevent Kodak from establishing a market there.

The WTO rejected Kodak's suit with prejudice, stating there was no evidence to support the U.S.'s claim. The decision came as a major blow to American policymakers who had supported the formation of the WTO, hoping it would pry open new markets for American products under the guise of free trade. The concept of "equitable trade" suddenly seemed elastic and difficult to define.

For many policymakers and businesspeople around the world, the decision, coupled with NAFTA, also made it clear that a six-decade period of international legal preference toward American industry was over, ushering in a new era of borderless capital.

After the WTO decision, Kodak began to collapse. The Chinese and Singaporean governments had just invested billions of dollars to develop a massive industrial park and port in Suzhou, China, a former silkworm-producing city, to attract foreign manufacturing, and Fuji was setting up a huge plant there. (Suzhou is now home to more than 12.7 million people and generates $352 billion annually.) The largest untapped workforce in history—735 million Chinese—left their rural communities and flocked to heavily subsidized industrial cities where they labored for exceedingly low wages under sometimes brutal conditions.

Kodak couldn't compete with Fuji's rock-bottom prices. At one point, the company was losing $60 on every camera it sold. In 2012, Kodak finally off-loaded its entire manufacturing operation, eliminating 27,000 jobs in the process, and filed for bankruptcy. By 2023, the company had shifted focus to manufacturing high-end inks and printers. Emerging from the pandemic, Kodak announced that it would add reagent and pharmaceutical manufacturing to its product line.

Tod retired in 1998 with his pension intact and moved with Mary Ann to Sun Valley, Idaho, for the skiing. Politically conservative, wary of unions, Tod considers himself a self-made man who worked hard and can now enjoy retirement and the fruits of his labor.

Tod always told his three daughters to dream big. But what did that mean in the 1990s, at the beginning of America's big sell-off?

Whitney started college in 1996 at University of Oregon, a "hippie girl among dreadlocks and Birkenstocks," she says. In her sophomore year, she stopped skiing—the sport had lost its appeal.

Whitney thrived in challenging situations where she had to figure things out; that attitude had served her well. Now she dragged her feet through spring semester. "My whole life had been in constant flux, on a two-year cycle. I didn't feel invested in my school or my classes anymore," she says. Looking around campus, she realized she wouldn't find answers in Oregon. She finished the semester and moved back in with her parents for the summer in Sun Valley, planning to relocate to New York City in the fall to study dance.

Life had taught Whitney to bend, not break. When things no longer felt right, she moved on. "There's a part of me that has a hard time settling down," she says.

She'd been the baby of the family, her father's favorite, a child of privilege, a fierce competitor. Now all she wanted was independence and her own money in her pocket. She wanted to feel the grit of real life. On New Year's Day 1999, Whitney packed her bags and boarded a plane for New York City under the guise of following a boyfriend studying film at NYU. She enrolled at Hunter College and moved into a sixth-floor walk-up on MacDougal Street in Greenwich Village with a bunch of strangers. "It was the worst," she says. "You'd walk in and right there was a toilet. You had to sit on it sideways to pee. We brushed our teeth in the kitchen."

Soon Whitney was bartending at an Upper West Side country-themed bar. "I was working at complete dives with all female bartenders, selling shots and Bud Light $5 pitchers. I'd never made so much cash in my life and I was essentially on my own, in the city. I was doing it, I was making it."

She bounced from school to school while falling in with the actor-dancer-restaurant crowd, learning to navigate big-city life. She moved in with a friend on 105th between Columbus and Amsterdam, a transitional neighborhood she grew to admire. "I loved the guys sitting on the sidewalk playing dominoes with their folding table and boom box. I loved the freedom of being able to live by myself, right next to Central Park West."

In her spare time, she danced in Central Park with drum circles and started dating a man from Haiti.

One night, he became physically violent. Whitney was able to get away from him before she was seriously injured, but she was emotionally shaken to the core. In an instant, everything she thought she knew about humanity suffered a tremendous jolt. "It was at that moment that my trust was knocked out of me," she says.

When Mary Ann called her daughter that night, she immediately sensed that something was wrong. "Come home," she told her. "Bring everything you can."

Whitney spent that summer at her parents' house in Idaho but refused to let the incident break her. Overcoming her fear, she returned to New York and continued bartending while completing her BA in anthropology from Fordham.

When the two planes slammed into the Twin Towers a year later, Whitney didn't even consider abandoning her adoptive city. In a way, she says, 9/11 made New York City feel smaller. Lots of people left. Those who remained formed deeper ties. They were survivors in a world gone mad. New Yorkers became tribal.

Because she'd spent her formative years Down Under, Whitney had missed many American rites of passage. She'd never studied U.S. history (though she knew U.K. history cold) and always felt a little disconnected from her own culture. Shortly after 9/11, she heard about an opening at the fabled biker bar Hogs & Heifers, a tiny joint at the corner of 13th and Washington Streets, and decided to give it a shot.

The interior of Hogs was Americana on overdrive. The bar was just two rooms—a small main space and a cozy back room with a beat-up bar-size pool table under a dim Pabst Blue Ribbon–branded lamp. Every square inch of the place, including the ceiling, was covered in symbols of American industry and patriotism. There were stickers and flags—the Stars and Stripes, Don't Tread on Me, POW-MIA, plus signs of iconic brands of working America: Miller Lite, Mobil, Red Bull, Jim Beam, Mack Trucks, Yuengling. Someone had copped a yellow Arizona U.S. 66 road sign; it found a home here. Hard hats and cowboy hats filled in the blanks.

Hogs & Heifers was a New York institution, one of those rare places where leather-clad bikers, steelworkers, and pipefitters mingled with bewildered tourists and slummers from uptown. After Julia Roberts famously tore off her bra while dancing on the bar one night, thousands of customers did the same, burying the stuffed swordfish on the wall in 18,000 pieces of cast-off lingerie. The place had a cult following. Patrons would line up around the block and wait for hours in the rain and sleet for the bouncers to nod them in. Inside, the vibe was New York–style antagonism, confrontational, in-your-face. Anyone who paused to take it all in risked an earful of insults from a bartender's bullhorn.

Hogs embodied everything Whitney missed while coming of age in Australia.

Because the bar was in the Meatpacking District, it attracted a union crowd, including cops and firefighters. Post-9/11, the Hogs scene was more intense than ever. Everyone seemed to know someone who'd died in the World Trade Center tragedy.

Whitney knew how to pour a drink but this gig demanded a lot more than that. Job-seekers had to audition. One by one, she watched hopefuls in cowboy hats hoist themselves onto the bar and clog to the honky-tonk blasting from the sound system. When it was Whitney's turn, she sprang onto the bar like a cat and did her best sexy cowgirl dance. Above the crowd, letting loose, showing off her moves, she got a huge rush and landed the job.

In the middle of Whitney's audition, Michelle Dell entered the bar. Michelle had been present at Hogs' creation in November 1992, and set the vibe with her tough New-York-City-broad-meets-daughter-of-rich-Texas-steer-rancher schtick. Whitney watched the way Michelle, blond and booted, commanded the room without saying a word. She possessed the kind of innate power that twenty-four-year-old Whitney craved.

For two years while working at Hogs, Whitney studied Michelle's every move. "She was running the show with a bunch of ironworkers and bikers and all kinds of dudes. They were all under her watch," Whitney says. "Michelle taught me how to not only regain my strength after what I'd just been through, but to find a strength I didn't know I had."

Whitney learned how to be fearless and never take shit from anyone. She learned to grab a bullhorn and razz customers, and how to artfully fend off would-be suitors. To this day, Whitney wears a clip of keys on her belt loop, an homage to Michelle.

But Hogs was a brutal place to work. Upper management was hard on the women behind the bar because they were the reason the crowds came. They had to be constantly on, keep things moving, keep up the party. "Michelle led by example, but I wouldn't say she was nurturing or comforting or understanding—these weren't top qualities," Whitney says. "She's a badass, grew up in New York. She just has that mentality that she's not gonna fail and not gonna let anyone else take anything away from her."

As a manager, Whitney learned not to coddle new hires. It was sink-or-swim. On Julie Griglio's first day on the job at Hogs, she remembers being "totally intimidated" by Whitney, who barely looked at her during their shift. Julie followed Whitney's lead, trying to keep up without getting in her way. After a few months, the two women found their rhythm and became Hogs sisters-in-arms. Even so, Julia was genuinely surprised when Whitney called out of the blue a few years later and asked her to be a bridesmaid. She hadn't heard from her Hog sister in a long time. She didn't know Whitney considered her a close friend.

Working dusk to dawn, Whitney and her fellow beer-slingers did a lot of drinking; patrons were always buying them shots. She started dating Richie, a friend of Michelle's who was also a recovering alcoholic. Richie encouraged Whitney to quit drinking and she began living the AA lifestyle—sobriety, meetings, and black coffee—while bartending at night. It was quite a feat.

Whitney was always looking for ways prove that she was strong. One day, she took a ride with Richie to a Harley dealership in Long Island City to look at motorcycles for herself. She'd decided she "wasn't suited for the back of a bike." In the center of the showroom sat a massive Harley-Davidson Softail, custom-made for a Victoria's Secret photo shoot, tricked-out in glittering chrome. Whitney went right up and settled into the wide leather saddle. She leaned over and gripped the handlebars, electrifying the dealership. With her long legs, long brown hair, and mischievous smile, she looked like she was born to ride that bike.

Everyone in the showroom told her to buy it. But Whitney was reluctant to spend $25,000 on something she didn't know how to drive.

On the ride back into Manhattan, Richie goaded her: "You don't have the balls to buy that."

"Turn the truck around," she ordered him. She bought the bike.

Whitney learned to drive that Harley in midtown Manhattan traffic. If there was an easier way, it wasn't for her. She married Richie in 2005 and they moved to the Poconos, where they could ride together along country roads and Whitney could ski in the winter.

By 2008, following a miscarriage and divorce, Whitney found herself living alone, working at a small Pocono ski lodge. She'd considered nurse midwifery and real estate, marketing and event planning. But she didn't feel passion for the things she was doing.

When her sister's husband invited her to help him open a bar in Portland, Maine, she packed up her house, loaded the Harley onto a trailer, and drove ten hours north to a city she knew nothing about. A few months after she arrived, he backed out. Whitney's sister was pregnant and he decided working nights and weekends wouldn't be compatible with a baby.

She'd always tried to steer her fate; now she was determined to stay put for a while and let life shape her. She got an apartment and took a job at the hottest bar in town, Brian Boru. Within a few years, she was managing the place.

REBOOT

Traveling across the U.S., Ben had seen that unchecked trade was deconstructing the economy from the top down, and within companies, destabilizing Americans' sense of themselves and their relationship to work. Unlike Tod Reynolds's Kodak, companies rarely felt a responsibility to take care of their employees over the long term. Outside of union jobs, pensions went the way of pay phones. They were replaced by 401(k)s, which bound more workers to the market. Americans' financial security was now directly tied to stock values which fluctuated wildly. America entered a new era of bloat. So many hands were now grabbing a cut in service of the knowledge economy, adding astounding complexity to health care, insurance, and financial services. Workers' entire life savings were at the mercy of mutual fund managers who charged high fees regardless of performance. Executive pay skyrocketed and C-suite managers earned fantastic bonuses whether or not the companies they oversaw got stronger under their leadership. Higher education followed, adding expensive administrative levels to payrolls. While workers' real wages flatlined, the idea of the "business" president took hold, and a Harvard Business School grad named George W. Bush landed in the White House.

Ben spent that pivotal time on the ground, standing shoulder to shoulder with working people across America as their opportunities evaporated, but he was slowly killing himself in the process. He'd battled depression on and off all his life, and D.C. living was chronically unhealthy—lots of young go-getters clawing over each other to get ahead. "I think what got him was that it's a one-industry town where everyone is doing the same motherfucking thing every single day," says Jonathan Burkhardt, the young labor organizer who had worked with Ben in Pennsylvania. "They're looking at spreadsheets, yelling into the phone, making bulleted MS Word documents. Maybe they're doing it for a think tank or a legislative office, but they're all kind of doing the same thing. It feels pretty vapid to live like that."

Oh, and everyone was doing coke. "It was a social drug," Ben says. "We'd go out to party and it was just everywhere."

In a vain, destructive attempt to ignite his energy and optimism, Ben shacked up alone in his apartment and snorted fistfuls of cocaine, enough coke to "kill a horse," he says. When he got too up, Xanax brought him back down. A pill doctor in Washington kept him supplied.

Ben wanted to fix injustices everywhere, but politics moved slowly. As a D.C. operative, he began to internalize the hopelessness of the situation. He needed a break from the frustration of working for people who often couldn't, or wouldn't, save themselves. He needed a break from the grim reality for many of America's workers.

He needed to sober up and rethink his life.

On a January morning in 2012, Ben walked into Trumka's office and told him he felt like he was underwater.

Trumka took a long look at his protégé, studying the deep lines in the young man's face.

He told Ben to take off as much time as he needed.

Ben flew out to a residential rehab center in Seattle the next day. Later, he transferred to one in Huntington Beach, California. Official word went out that Ben Waxman was taking time to deal with some health issues. Back then, he points out, few people openly discussed recovery.

Although Ben had been using drugs, he never thought of himself as an addict. He was just a workaholic who self-medicated. Six weeks into rehab, the counselors started describing the addict's double life—how users go to great lengths to hide their habits from family, friends, and coworkers. That hit Ben like a freight train: he'd spun a web of lies to conceal what he was doing. He'd just about cut off his closest, oldest Portland friends. He avoided too much contact with his own family. None of them had any sense of what was really going on.

In short, he finally realized that he was an addict.

Rehab was transformative. For the first time in his life, Ben learned how to be fully present. He'd worked nonstop for a decade and found religion on the other side. It wasn't about God and church. Ben's faith was rooted in humanity. "I'd seen faith in workers, people who lost their jobs, who said, *Everything's going to be all right, I'll get through this.* But I didn't know what faith was—getting through the tough times—until I went to treatment."

His higher power? Community. Ben's family, friends, and the generations of fighters who'd come before him.

He had to get home, back to Portland.

Ben didn't know what was next, but he felt an insatiable drive to create the world he knew was possible, a world based on making. "There's no difference between the women and men who walk into this country with nothing more than the shirt on their back and my ancestors who came through Ellis Island," he says. "The American dream got lost and we need it now, more than ever. America's just got to look in the mirror and say, *Okay, we can do this. We can make paper here. We can make steel. We can make cotton. We can do those things.*"

Ben wasn't the only person thinking about how the U.S. had lost its way. While he was in rehab, Bruce Springsteen released *Wrecking Ball,* which Ben played on repeat.

Springsteen's album focused on the collapse of the market in 2008. The biggest hit on the album was "Death to My Hometown," a

major-key anthem with a fist-pumping chorus backed by a muscular
horn section and tin whistle riff, like a Revolutionary fife-and-drum
band on steroids.

The song's message was dark, capturing everything Ben had been
thinking about during his time at the AFL-CIO. It didn't take a war
or a dictator or famine to destroy Main Street, the song's storyteller
says. Instead, "the robber barons" and "greedy thieves . . . destroyed
our families, factories, and they took our homes." Springsteen's final
verse laments the Obama administration's lack of will prosecuting
those who "brought death to our hometown."

The subprime lending fiasco that Springsteen wrote about had
been the result of deregulation. About a decade earlier, financial
institutions lobbied Congress to repeal what remained of the Glass-
Steagall Act, Depression-era legislation that prevented commercial
banks from making risky investments with depositors' money. Once
Congress cut the brake line, big banks began finding increasingly
creative ways to juice their profits. Some started bundling good
mortgages with risky ones and selling them as AAA mortgage-backed
bonds to pension funds, hedge funds, and mutual funds, the main
investment vehicle for 401(k)s. Rating agencies looked the other way.

Because the highly rated bonds were considered safe investments,
they were in high demand in an increasingly unstable environment.
America's manufacturing sector was crumbling; financial products
were all the rage.

To maintain a constant supply of the mortgage-backed bonds,
banks unleashed cheap loans on developers, which triggered a building boom. Flush with inexpensive cash, developers built tens of
thousands of single-family homes in sprawling suburbs across the
nation. Speculators bought up the bulk of the new housing stock,
which seemed like a solid investment. The speculators borrowed
and bought, creating artificial demand, and across America housing
prices spiked.

Homebuyers also took advantage of low-interest mortgages. Even
if they were a credit risk, banks were eager to lend. So eager, in fact,

that they introduced new mortgage products to rope in more buyers. Big mortgages could be had for little money down and very low monthly payments—fixed for a few years—or variable rates, but with a caveat: one massive balloon payment at the end of the loan's term. These were complex financing instruments that many homebuyers didn't quite understand. If they did worry about how they'd manage the balloon payment, they were assured by their brokers they'd be able to refinance before the payments were due, or sell and pay it off.

Because home values in America always go up, right?

When all those sketchy mortgages came due, the speculators defaulted, banks seized properties and tried to flip them for pennies on the dollar, and the entire American housing market crashed. Actual homeowners found themselves holding mortgages worth twice the value of their homes. Or less. That made refinancing impossible. Foreclosures peaked in 2010—1.2 million of them—nearly ten times the number in 2001. In Miami, the foreclosure rate hit 20 percent. It was a catastrophe that set off a chain reaction in every market. No one was immune.

Ben could relate to Springsteen's rage. The stories felt real enough. He'd seen the impact of terrible policy, driven by greed, with his own eyes.

On his first night out of rehab in April 2012, Ben got two tickets to see Springsteen at the Los Angeles Memorial Sports Arena and invited a grade school friend, Kevin Kane, then working as an architect in the city. When the band launched into "Death to My Hometown," with Rage Against the Machine's Tom Morello on lead guitar, Ben says he was "on the floor." Played live, the song cut even deeper.

"Those songs defined every reason why I needed to build something," Ben says. "Every reason why it's not impossible to bring back manufacturing. Every reason why, no matter how tough it gets, I will not stop until the last drop is bled."

The next day, Ben boarded a plane heading to *his* hometown— Portland, Maine. He didn't have a plan, but he was energized and his head was clear. A few hours later, he found himself stooping under the angled ceiling of his tiny childhood bedroom. He studied the familiar lamp. The dresser. The bookcase. He watched the curtain blowing in the afternoon breeze. Everything felt too small; his heart was big and open.

He dropped his bags, pulled out his cell phone, and called his grade school friends Derek and Pete.

And so began what his friends affectionately call "The Summer of Ben."

That first night back, Ben and his crew went to their old Portland haunt, Brian Boru pub. They sat at their favorite booth in the back, a place where they'd plotted and planned high school hijinks, nursed breakups, drank to wins, drowned losses, back when they were just kids.

"Then she goes flying by," Ben says.

Ben watched the tall, elegant bar manager in jeans and a white tank top command the room without saying a word. She moved like an athlete, her keys jingling on her belt loop, in total control.

There was something familiar about her.

Ben turned to Pete and said, "Who the hell is *that*?"

"That's Whitney," Pete told him. "Don't bother. She's out of your league." One by one, she'd rejected all of them. They downed their beers and told tales of the good old days.

But Ben was under Whitney's spell. He couldn't take his eyes off her. "And they're laughing at me because she's *way* outta my league," Ben remembers. He didn't care. At the end of the night, he asked her for her number.

Whitney vaguely remembered her previous brief encounter with Ben. She did a quick calculation to assess the threat level of the boisterous redhead built like a Maine black bear and decided he was harmless.

Harmless, but relentless. While he was doing outpatient therapy in Portland, Ben went into that bar every Sunday afternoon for the next four months straight, like clockwork.

At first, Whitney put off Ben. But the union guy who dropped f-bombs everywhere was growing on her. She decided that he was genuine and agreed to a date.

She'd watched a sea of humanity from behind the bar at beer-and-shot joints in New York City; she'd seen people at their best and worst. And she decided that Ben was the real deal. His belief in the good in humanity was so strong and pure that even the most cynical person, like her, was drawn into his orbit. "There was something so captivating about him," she says. "He made me happy."

On their second date, Ben told Whitney about his struggle with addiction and announced that he was four months clean.

Whitney had been through AA and had spent years around people in recovery. "No, you're not," she told him. "You're sitting here having a beer."

To this day, Ben says he wanted to walk out on her. But he didn't.

"I think that was the beginning of me challenging him," Whitney says. "And I think that's part of what he loves about me."

In courting Whitney, Ben wasn't just selling himself; he was inviting her to join his family and huge circle of Portland friends. She was enticed. Throughout her twenties, she'd moved from place to place, trying to claim her independence from addiction, from bad relationships, from her sheltered upbringing. Here was Ben, inviting her to finally come home.

The morning after their first night together, Ben tried to close the deal. "Are we going to do this or what?"

Whitney said no.

Ben understood. She wasn't ready. He returned to D.C. in July, but began feeling strong pangs to settle down in Portland to build something in his home state. In January 2013, Trumka reluctantly let his protégé go.

Back in Maine, Ben formed a political consulting group with a few colleagues and got pulled into the union effort to support Marty Walsh's campaign for mayor of Boston. The future secretary of labor, a man who'd come up through the trade unions, had bonded with Ben over politics and addiction when they helped elect Elizabeth

Warren to the Senate the previous year. Walsh won his own campaign and Ben returned to Portland.

And he kept coming by Brian Boru. Whitney continued playing it cool. But truth be told, she couldn't get Ben out of her head. "There was something about him," she says. "I just knew." When she went to Seattle that October to visit her sister, she told her, *I've been seeing this guy on and off and I'm probably going to marry him someday.*

Early that December, Whitney found herself without a date for an annual fundraising gala in Portland and, on a whim, invited Ben. They spent the night together after the event. The next morning, Whitney drove Ben back to his apartment.

As they pulled up to his place, he told her, "I'm falling in love with you. And I can't take this on-and-off anymore. Are we gonna do this or what?"

Whitney said she still wasn't ready to commit.

"If we can't be together," Ben told her, "then I can't do this. I'm out."

For two weeks, they didn't speak.

Once again, Ben traveled down to D.C. for business, then flew back to Maine just in time for a friend's Christmas party. He had a strong hunch that Whitney would be there. Why did he want to see the woman who was breaking his heart? "Because I was in love with her," he says simply.

As soon as he walked into the party, his brother Adam buttonholed him. "You're fucked," Adam said. "Whitney's here. You're done. Hang it up. You're off the market."

When Ben ducked outside for a smoke, Whitney taped a "Wanted" poster she'd made to the wall. It featured a photo of Ben and said, "MISSING: BEST FRIEND, most likely found on the dance floor with a Jameson on the rocks. Call this number if found."

Whitney surprised herself. "Normally, I don't do things like this," she says. "I make them come to me."

But that did the trick. They've been together ever since.

LET'S MAKE SOMETHING

Ben moved in with Whitney in the spring of 2013. They were in their mid-thirties, seasoned by lives fully lived. Ben's idealism still knew no bounds. He dreamed big. Whitney kept him grounded. She was a realist. But his optimism was rubbing off on her. She never thought of herself as a crusader, but being around Ben sparked a desire in her to leave the world a little better than she'd found it. She was considering leaving her lucrative bar job. She was ready for the next thing.

The dream of reviving American manufacturing consumed Ben. He was passionate about manufacturing because he'd spent more than a decade with people who once made things and felt pride in producing. When those jobs were shipped abroad, they would never feel fully whole again.

Ben felt that unionized manufacturing was the best way to create opportunity and rebuild community. Unions had always offered workers much more than bargaining power. At their best, they were sources for thoughtful political analysis, job training, language instruction for non-native speakers, and social events that celebrated cultural differences. Unions squirreled away dues to support workers during strikes and take care of injured workers' families. Some unions even built co-op housing available at affordable prices. Union membership could mean so much more than a card and a pension, but the prevailing rhetoric painted them as cesspools of corruption.

At night, Ben stayed up late brainstorming business ideas on yellow legal pads, confident that somewhere in his ADHD-fueled scrawl lay the kernel of a brilliant entrepreneurial idea. No proposal was too ambitious. "I didn't want to go to the party," he says. "I wanted to throw it." After watching Ron Howard's Rockyesque *Cinderella Man* about an underdog fighter who uses his boxing winnings to build a construction company during the Great Depression, Ben even considered shipbuilding, which Whitney summarily nixed.

One sweltering August day in 2014, everything came together.

Dory had restarted her cape and blanket business after spending a few years on the Portland City Council, and in a fit of nostalgia, invited Ben to join her on a fabric run, this time to Uxbridge, Massachusetts, where one of the last remaining wool mills in New England continued to produce high-quality fabric. It would be like old times—Dory and Ben driving around New England in a hot van stinking of wool. Ben's memories flooded back—watching his mother in heated conversations with eccentric mill owners, their words drowned out by the clacking of looms.

He said yes, and invited Whitney along.

Dory pulled the van up to a nineteenth-century brick mill complex, once the Stanley Wool Company, along the Blackstone River, thirty miles upriver from Pawtucket, Rhode Island, where the first cotton mill in America began operation in 1790. Inside the mill, it was dark and airless. As their eyes adjusted, Ben and Whitney saw just one loom clacking away. At peak production, dozens of looms would have been operating.

Whitney was transfixed by the sight. She watched the long pair of heddles bopping up and down at a rapid clip, separating the strands of warp yarn to clear the way for the shuttle, which whizzed back and forth, meting out the weft like a spider on a rocket. Every part of the machine moved at great speed, but the fabric grew inch by inch, one shuttle pass at a time.

Nearby, four women wearing owlish glasses sat at their crochet machines edging thick wool fabric to make throw blankets. They occasionally peered over their thick lenses to study Ben and Whitney while keeping up a conversation that had been going on for decades.

Whitney observed the old canvas rolling carts that once moved raw wool and woven textiles from looms to the fullers, where the fabric was beaten, and to finishers, where it was napped and snipped. She surveyed the unused power looms idle in the dim light, covered in cobwebs and dust.

Surrounded by the materials of the manufacturing age, Whitney felt something inside spark to life. She had a visceral sense of the industrious people who once created textiles here, their dreams for themselves and their children. Whitney's thoughts wandered to her family's agricultural roots. She envisioned fields of cotton under the southern sun and herds of sheep on the coast of Maine. She loved thinking about how she could become part of the life cycle of an ancient tradition.

A small, unassuming man in his seventies wearing jeans, a button-down shirt, and a lopsided smile approached Dory. She introduced him to Ben and Whitney as Strickland Wheelock.

Strickland's family, the Wheelock-Tafts, had founded the mill in 1803. Stanley Woolen Company once dominated New England's textile industry. The mill produced top-quality woven wool fabrics and cotton-wool blends, which the Wheelocks had pioneered. They manufactured the indigo-dyed cloth the Union Army wore during the Civil War and the olive drab wool that American soldiers wore in France during World War I.

In their day, the Wheelocks had been innovators. They devised America's first completely vertical wool operation—starting with scoured wool stock—which they ran through the entire process, from dressing and weaving, to finishing. By controlling nearly every step along the way, they eliminated middlemen and uncertainty from their production line.

"This was my parents' life," Strickland later told me as we stood in the dusty parking lot outside the five-story mill complex, now dark and empty.

As a schoolboy in the 1960s, Strickland spent his summers in his family's hot, dusty mill cycling through every department. Two hundred highly skilled workers were working there at the time—generations of Uxbridge residents, most of Portuguese or Italian descent. From them, Strickland learned carding and spinning, weaving and napping, and spent long hours apprenticing with the mill's designer, who taught him the complex art of blending warp and weft weights and colors to produce everything from fine men's suit cloth to thick, fuzzy blanketing.

Strickland's father did all the stock-dyeing, yarn-dyeing, and piece-dyeing. His grandfather was a soft-spoken leader whom he admired very much. In Strickland's youth, his grandparents lived in the magnificent Queen Anne manse his great-grandfather had built half a mile down the road. The ornate house was filled with art and antiques, paid for with the fleece of sheep and thousands of hours of work by generations of textile professionals.

Strickland is also a direct descendant of Ralph Wheelock, the English-born, Cambridge-educated Puritan who sailed to Massachusetts in 1636 and is believed to have been the first teacher of a public school in the colonies. Ralph's grandson was the founder of Dartmouth College.

Strickland is shy about discussing his family's history—either from a sense of modesty or slight embarrassment. His brother went to Williams and Harvard and became a curator at the National Gallery of Art, but Strickland's heart stayed at the mill. "I absolutely loved what I was doing here, making beautiful products," he says. Before Stanley Wool shut down, it was the longest-running family-owned woolen company in the United States.

But Strickland was an artist, not a businessman. By 1988, he realized he couldn't keep his family's business operational. He told me flatly: "A mill this size—all the expenses that keep it heated, and all the people and their families—we couldn't afford to keep it going. Just couldn't make enough money to cover all the expenses."

The company's board and he both agreed to shut down the mill. It has sat nearly empty ever since, a relic along a bend in the road leading to the center of town. Strickland keeps a handful of older women busy making custom blankets for a few high-end customers around the country.

Strickland attributes the end of Stanley Wool to a generational shift. "The people who had all those high skills and knew how to repair machines, they got old and retired, and the younger generation didn't like doing the machinery jobs the older folks had no problems with."

He adds that he preferred to focus on design, quality, and selling over management. "I don't know how to inspire someone to come to work every day."

Had Americans changed since Stanley shut down? In 2021, had they realized there was something magical about making? Standing in the old mill, Ben and Whitney felt a rush. They believed there were other people like them out there, too—people who wanted to make things, create goods, people who didn't find satisfaction in serving coffee or racing around an Amazon warehouse packing random things into a box.

Ben says, "I'd been in a lot of shut-down factories in my life. But when I saw the looms covered in cobwebs, I looked at Whitney and we both felt the thrill at the same time. It was—*Let's do this. Let's build this. Let's make something, revive something, be a part of something.*"

GAME ON

In the winter of 2015, Ben quit political consulting to focus on his dream of building a business that made things. Dory asked him to join her company. Ben could sell while she put her energy into developing new products and training employees. Ben thought that sounded "as exciting as watching paint dry."

Whitney continued managing Brian Boru and used her savings to put a down payment on a house in Westbrook, close to Ben's parents' Portland home. To keep the money coming in, Ben started plowing driveways.

One night, after fourteen hours of plowing following a massive snowstorm, Ben pulled the truck over to chug a tepid Dunkin' coffee. The heat was cranking and the cab was stuffy. Ben peeled off his fleece vest—swag from a political campaign he'd worked on.

"Where the hell was this thing made?" Ben said aloud, tugging at the tag sewn into the seam. The vest was from L.L. Bean, but that didn't mean it was locally produced.

"Jesus Christ," he growled, reading the label. "Made with U.S.A. fabrics," it said in big letters. In much smaller font, it said: "Assembled in El Salvador."

That was the closest to American-made that L.L. Bean could

muster in 2014. At least the vest was made of PolarFleece, still manufactured in the U.S., but apparently, there was no one left in America
to actually stitch the vest together.

When Ben got home that night, he woke up Whitney and told
her they were going to make fleece vests. Then he called up Dory
and asked if she knew anyone at Polartec. Dory said she'd make
some calls. She added that the owner of the Massachusetts-based
mill was an incredible man, Aaron Feuerstein, and told Ben to watch
the *60 Minutes* segment about him called "The Mensch of Malden
Mills." Ben grabbed his laptop, sank down on the basement sofa with
hot chocolate, and found the 2002 clip on YouTube.

The episode told the story of Feuerstein, the third-generation
owner of a textile factory who invented PolarFleece.

Feuerstein was one of those rare industrialists who deeply cared
about the fate of his workers, and he used his brains to protect them
from the vagaries of global commerce. After graduating from Yeshiva
University in New York in 1946, he joined his father's struggling
knitting mill in Malden, Massachusetts, and immediately tried to
innovate. "I felt an obligation to help [my father], assist him, and
save the family business heritage," Aaron told me when I visited him
in 2019.

The original Malden Knitting Mills was not a progressive company, though the workers were represented by the International
Ladies Garment Workers Union (ILGWU). Samuel, Aaron's father,
made just one style of button-down sweater for the workingman,
made of coarse wool, dyed navy blue, gray, or burgundy. After the
First World War, that kind of sweater fell out of fashion—people
wanted more variety and style—and Malden Knitting Mills lost its
market.

Cotton fleece and synthetic fabrics were on the ascendancy.

Aaron says his father was "a very stubborn man" who knew his business was sinking but refused to adapt. When Aaron turned twenty-
three, his father gave him a $100,000 loan to start a new factory. "In
spite of what I said about my father's lack of resiliency," Aaron says,

"he felt deep down in his bones that he wanted me to stay, but not in the same business." Aaron launched a yarn factory in Malden and ran it for several years. In 1956, he decided to get into the textile-making business and bought the sprawling Arlington Mills complex in Lawrence, Massachusetts, "at a fraction of a fraction of a penny" because the town was "completely bust."

The city of Lawrence was once the epicenter of American textile manufacturing, as well as the birthplace of America's labor movement. It was founded in the mid-nineteenth century to harness the power of the Merrimack River to run machinery. Boston's best-known nineteenth-century industrialist-philanthropists, including the Lowell family (major benefactors of Harvard University), made a fortune in Lawrence's textile mills.

The seven-square-mile factory town became the destination for immigrants willing to work in the city's dangerous mills for meager pay. First came the Irish, then the Germans, then the Poles, Russians, Italians, and Lithuanians. Each ethnic group built its own churches and synagogues, clubs and homes. Each group worked hard to support their children, who at first worked in the mills with their parents. After child labor laws passed, millworkers' children were able to receive an education and often left the city for better opportunities elsewhere. Leonard Bernstein and Robert Frost were both raised here.

Driving through the city today, you can see the entire life cycle of American manufacturing—the huge Gilded Age factories (now struggling to find tenants), the imposing Victorian houses built on hills (too expensive to maintain, many are in shambles), the grand public common (now a forlorn expanse of grass), the triple-decker houses (crammed with families), the small postwar suburban enclaves, the gaping holes—most now parking lots—where theaters, stores, and churches once stood.*

---

* Lawrence is working hard to reinvent itself as a technology hub, drawing start-ups to the same mills that once produced textiles.

In the wild days of unregulated industrialization, disaster sometimes struck. In January 1860, the Pemberton Mill, a five-story brick and iron building, collapsed under the weight of new industrial machinery the owners had piled onto the second floor in search of greater profits, killing at least eighty-eight people in what would be deemed one of the worst industrial accidents in American history. The twisted iron, piles of broken bricks, and massive machinery trapped more than six hundred women and children in a scene of horror. As evening approached, rescuers built bonfires to aid their search, revealing "faces crushed beyond recognition, open wounds in which the bones showed through a paste of dried blood, brick dust, and shredded clothing," recorded an observer. The year before the accident, the millworkers earned their shareholders the equivalent of $42 million.

Fifty years later, workers were still fighting against dangerous working conditions, appallingly low pay, and line speedups. On a frigid Friday in January 1912, some 20,000 textile workers, the majority female, many of them children, opened their weekly pay envelopes and saw they were short 32 cents. They were living in chronic poverty; the reduction in pay sent them into the streets in protest. The millworkers hailed from fifty-one nations and spoke nearly as many languages, but whether Italian or Ukrainian Jew, their average life expectancy was less than forty years; many died within a decade of taking the job. Respiratory infections were endemic; workplace accidents took lives and limbs.

Anger quickly spread throughout the city and workers walked off the jobs. The giant looms ceased running. Out of frustration, some strikers sabotaged mill equipment, slashing drive belts and scattering bobbins. They marched through the streets chanting lines from a popular poem, demanding both Bread *and* Roses—bread signified decent wages; roses signified work with dignity. Female textile workers made rousing speeches and marched in the icy streets of Lawrence, drawing national attention to the horrendous conditions New England's millworkers were forced to endure.

Factory owners hired agents to infiltrate the movement and divide the workers of many nations. When that failed, they appealed to the city and state to send police and militiamen armed with rifles and bayonets to guard the factories, protect strikebreakers, and intimidate the workers into submission.

The threat of violence hung in the air. Two weeks into the strike, a stray bullet killed a woman. The following day, a young man was killed by a militiaman's bayonet. Perhaps inspired by Mother Jones's Children's March of 1903—a multicity parade featuring several hundred child millworkers demanding labor laws and protections, Lawrence parents loaded some of their children on a train bound for Grand Central Terminal. News spread through the city and when the children arrived, they were greeted by 5,000 cheering citizens.

President William Taft could no longer ignore the Lawrence strike. He requested that his attorney general open an investigation. On March 2, Congress held a hearing. Millworker Carmela Teoli, just fourteen years old, gave moving testimony about the working conditions in the mills. She had irrefutable evidence of the dangers children faced while working long days among the factory's giant spinning belts and gear: a mangled scalp where a machine had caught one of her braids, landing her in the hospital for seven months. Teoli's speech, combined with other workers' stories, gave many of the nation's lawmakers their first glimpse of the horror of unchecked, unregulated industry.

Cowed by the public's outrage once the facts came to light, Lawrence's factory owners agreed to negotiate with workers. Shortly thereafter, a quarter of a million New England textile workers received a bump in pay.

The Bread and Roses Strike was a rare success in the world before FDR, the Occupational Safety and Health Administration (OSHA), the National Labor Relations Board, and the minimum wage. But it proved that unlike most lawmakers, the American public cared very much about how working people were treated.

One of the largest textile factories in Lawrence (and the state of Massachusetts) was Arlington Mills, which would supply Melton and shirting flannel to the U.S. Army. Government photos commissioned during World War I show a massive factory with enough machinery to transform cotton and wool into yarn on an industrial scale. In an enormous wool-sorting room, the fleeces were sorted. There was a giant carding room, a combing room, a weaving room with hundreds of power looms, and a room with huge belt-driven fulling mills.

After the war, Arlington Mills struggled during the Great Depression, never recovered, and finally closed for good in 1952. Aaron Feuerstein bought the complex four years later. "The textile industry had left the North for cheaper labor down south," he told me before he died in 2021. "And then God punished them because from the cheaper labor down south, they lost it all to China."

When industry left Lawrence, so did the money, but the blocks-long brick factories, with their daunting clock towers, still dominated the landscape on both sides of the river. Likewise, immigrants continued to arrive, at first hopeful, then resigned.

Feuerstein bought the mill at a time when many residents still believed in Lawrence. They were proud of its immigrant and manufacturing heritage. Although the mills were shutting down, a new group of arrivals was landing in the city: Puerto Ricans. Like all new groups, they encountered discrimination from those who'd come before, and had trouble finding jobs.

At first, Aaron's company made the wool cloth used to line raincoats and jackets sold by JC Penney and Sears Roebuck. His fabric was knit rather than woven, and machine-napped, just like the cotton fleece in a sweatshirt. But new fibers were entering the market, including viscose rayon (invented in the nineteenth century, derived from wood pulp), as well as nylon, acrylic, spandex, and polyester—petroleum-derived fibers developed after the war. By the 1960s, synthetic "miracle" fabrics were all the rage.

In the cutthroat, high-tech industry of textiles, Aaron needed smart, driven people to help Malden Mills stay ahead of the curve. He hired "anyone who wanted to work, and could contribute, and had intelligence," says Aaron's son, Raphael. Aaron dedicated himself to creating and producing new textiles and nearly lost the company in the early 1980s after betting on the fake fur and velvet trend, which petered out too soon for him to cover his debts.

In 1979, he was experimenting with various polyester textiles when he invented PolarFleece, a napped fabric that wicked away moisture while keeping the wearer warm, even when wet. It was much lighter than wool and cotton, didn't wrinkle, and was super soft to the touch. PolarFleece came at the perfect time to appeal to a burgeoning class of white-collar, outward-bound enthusiasts. There was nothing like it on the market. A few years prior, Maine native and avid outdoorsman Yvon Chouinard founded Patagonia to outfit this new class of hikers, campers, and mountain climbers. When he learned of PolarFleece's incredible properties, he began buying up bolts as fast as Malden could make it.

PolarFleece saved Malden Mills. Eddie Bauer, Lands' End, L.L. Bean, and Ralph Lauren soon followed Patagonia's lead—using the miraculous fabric in a rainbow of colors for zip-ups and pull-overs. In 1993, Malden Mills' sales hit $340 million. Aaron invested most of his profits back into the company to maintain his dominance in the high-tech textile market—$20 million a year in research and development—and another $20 million on computer-aided manu-facturing equipment.

Malden became one of America's most innovative textile labs. Aar-on's engineers created undergarments for NASA and sled dog booties for the Iditarod.

Aaron also set out to prove a point about business and labor: "If you plan your business right and you think it out intelligently, you can succeed up here in the North, even though you have to pay the labor a decent wage."

But on an icy night in 1995, Aaron became a modern-day Job when Malden Mills went up in smoke in the hottest, biggest fire anyone had ever seen. The plastics used to make PolarFleece were extremely flammable, though it's unclear how the fire started. Later, Aaron learned that the wood floors of the old factory were saturated with ancient cottonseed and machine oil, which further fueled the flames.

When the insurance check arrived, Aaron could have retired to Palm Beach in style, but he didn't. Guided by years of studying Jewish ethics and the Talmud, he opted to keep all his employees and pay them their full wages, to the tune of $10 million a month, while he rebuilt the factory. He borrowed heavily over the next decade to keep the business going and sustain the next generation of predominantly immigrant workers while fending off creditors and competing with cheaper PolarFleece copycats.

"The Mensch of Malden" ended on a high note, suggesting that Aaron, then seventy-six, had overcome impossible odds.

Aaron's message that capitalism could be a force of good got Ben off the couch. It was time to prove every goddamn Milton Friedman–loving, trickle-down, supply-side Harvard MBA wrong. He was all fired up and told Whitney that he wanted to ensure that every stitch and component of their vests was American-sourced, from the threads to the fabric to the zippers. "If Feuerstein could get through a fire, pay his workers a living wage, union jobs, good union jobs, middle-class jobs," Ben said, "then we can do it, too."

Thanks to Dory's expertise in the industry, they could begin making PolarFleece vests soon, without a huge initial investment. They'd get the material from Malden Mills in Massachusetts, sew them in Maine, and send them out to a local company for custom embroidery.

Ben already knew who he'd sell their vests to: the unions representing America's transportation workers, service workers, carpenters, painters, laborers, pipe fitters, and nurses looking to buy ethically made swag for their members. Their buying cycle was tied to the state and national conventions held throughout the year where delegates from local affiliates gather to elect leadership, learn, and strategize how to defeat antiunion legislation, elect pro-worker candidates, and support democratic causes, including justice reform, voting rights, and fair immigration.

Every four years, the AFL-CIO threw a large weeklong convention where affiliated unions sent their delegates to work with Federation leadership to set the longer-term national labor agenda and develop strategies to support it.*

Ben knew that all those unions regularly bought custom-embroidered and printed clothes for their members, who wore their union-branded tees and hoodies with great pride. It was an important part of community-building. He also knew that there weren't a lot of union clothing shops left in America, and he suspected that none of them were 100 percent American-sourced. There were several unionized print and embroidery companies in the States, which is how the Democratic candidates could sell swag sporting a "union-printed" label. But embarrassingly, most of it was actually stitched in Central America.

That left an opening for Ben and Whitney.

Whitney listened to Ben's pitch. She was captivated by his vision for a better America based on strong unions and domestic manufacturing. She could envision how it could all work. They'd collaborate with Dory to launch a training program to prepare professional stitchers.

---

* In 2022, with a union-friendly president in the White House, the convention's efforts focused on pandemic recovery, as well as preserving workers' rights by lobbying for a fully financed and empowered National Labor Relations Board and Occupational Safety and Health Administration. Organizing action sessions covered topics ranging from dealing with Amazon's problematic labor practices to developing young workers to engaging the tech community in the movement.

The name of the company just came to Whitney: they'd call it American Roots.

In October 2015, Whitney and Ben, along with Dory and Dan, founded American Roots with a simple plan. Together, they would bring apparel manufacturing back to America. They would be uncompromising in their commitment to domestic sourcing and the welfare of their employees. They would never pay themselves more than four times their lowest worker's wage. They would build a legacy company that they could someday bequeath to their employees or perhaps their own children. They would build a community around making.

Making things simply made sense to Ben and Whitney. They felt in their bones that the American spirit was defined by inventing and producing, and they knew that no nation could function for long without domestic manufacturing.

So Ben's pitch to friends and potential investors went something like this:

It's time for Americans to be able to take two weeks of vacation a year, retire with dignity, work with their hands, or work with their brains, or work with both. People want to have a voice at the workplace, they want to earn a living. Health care in this country went from a right to a privilege. Now it needs to be a right.

And you can put this on the record: Look out Walmart, we're coming. Because Americans want high-quality stuff at an affordable price and they want to feel good about what they're wearing. Nobody wants to wear a T-shirt that's made by a twelve-year-old. Nobody. That was a choice that people in a boardroom made.

Ben's friends listened to his pitch. Then they told him he was an idiot. Making things was so twentieth-century. They said that manufacturing jobs weren't worth reviving. Americans had better things to do, like serve coffee, answer customer-support lines, or file health insurance claims—solid white-collar service economy jobs.

Besides, some pointed out, the margins in the apparel industry were too slim. U.S.-made textiles and apparel couldn't compete with

Vietnamese or Bangladeshi factories on price. Nearly all the manufacturing infrastructure was gone. And most American policymakers
didn't see anything in the textile industry worth fighting for, either.
Especially sewing, seen as a particularly lowly profession—the realm
of poor women and illiterate immigrants. Ignoring the skill and
stamina it takes to mass-produce clothes, it didn't feel like real American bootstrapping if you "made it" by setting sleeves into a dress eight
hours a day.

Policymakers and pundits often deemed male-dominant jobs like
coal mining and automaking (and investment banking) worth heroic
rescues, even if saving those professions again and again entailed killing renewable energy initiatives or billions of dollars in government
bailouts. But a bunch of women hunched over sewing machines?
Who needed that? Of course there was also the constant refrain on
the right that women shouldn't work outside the home, another reason to save men's jobs.

Ben says he knew his friends were right: "Who the fuck starts a
clothing company today? No one. Mostly crazy people."

But Ben and Whitney believed in each other and ignored the
doubters. They would make it work, damn the odds.

Straight out of the gate, they'd give their employees the same things
they wanted for themselves: the chance to work hard, earn money,
enough to send their kids to college and retire comfortably.

What Ben loved most about the concept was that his power as a
business owner would be his own; it wouldn't depend on favors or
political appointments. Manufacturing sure felt better than the dubi-
ous highs and lows inside the Beltway. Here, he could actually see the
progress they were making. He'd know that across the country, their
Maine-sewn clothing was keeping steelworkers, airline mechanics,
and laborers warm and dry.

They cashed in their retirements, mortgaged the house, and
accepted small short-term loans from a few close friends and family members to get their business off the ground. In the fall, they
took the $150,000 they'd raised and bought thousands of yards of

PolarFleece, built a website, and squatted in Ben's mother's tiny store-front factory with eight sewing machines.

"What could be better than this?" Ben would say to visitors. "Pulling yourself up by your bootstraps, having no idea what the fuck you're doing and doing it anyway, that's the American dream, right?"

NEW AMERICANS

Whitney and Ben filled Dory's downtown Portland space with sewing tables and a sales desk and contracted Ann Russo, a professional patternmaker in Quincy, Massachusetts, to coordinate the design of their fleece line.

Ann was a seasoned second-generation apparel-maker. She says her Italian grandparents, saddled with eight kids, were too poor to keep their children out of the labor market, so her mother skipped high school and learned tailoring from the local nuns. "In those days, all immigrants learned how to sew," Ann says.

When Ann was ten, her mother taught her sewing basics and Ann took to the trade. After graduating from the School of Fashion Design in Boston, she spent six years working in a local apparel factory, "sewing her brains out."

"This industry is brutal," she says in her sandpapery five-pack-a-day alto. "I knew I didn't want to work like that anymore, so I said screw it, I'm gonna start my own business." In 1986, at the age of twenty-six, she sank all her savings into a computer-aided design system. The computer helped her lay out patterns on fabrics virtually so that she could quickly calculate yield, a critical part of production.

The best patterns, combined with the deftest cutters, can squeeze every square inch out of a bolt of cloth. When you're running high volume, a good cutter can save a manufacturer lots of money.

Ann contracted out her patternmaking services to apparel businesses and designers around New England. There was plenty of work; at one point, she was cranking out fifty patterns a week. She invested her profits in launching her own cutting facility, too, where her employees unrolled miles of fabric on hundred-foot-long tables and cut pieces—sleeves, cuffs, backs, fronts of the garment—to be sewn elsewhere. She says she helped a lot of apparel businesses get their start.

She got a thrill out of helping other businesses grow and thrive. "I've never been married, never had kids. My customers were like my children."

When an apparel-maker like American Roots called Ann for a pattern, she'd have them send over a concept drawing, which she then discussed in detail with them. She'd ask tons of questions. The answers would help her construct the most appropriate garment for the job. The first thing she wanted to know was what fabric the piece would be made of. Then she'd get into more details. What was the skill level of the sewing staff? What would the garment be used for? What kinds of people would wear the garment? A fleece vest designed for telephone linemen would be built very differently from a vest designed for desk workers. Both would be different from one worn by day hikers. The cut would be different. The location of the pockets would be different. The design and location of the seams would be different. She had to make decisions about how the garment was edged, how the zippers were finished, and how much room to leave around the waist for beer bellies.

All these decisions would define that particular garment and determine its comfort and usefulness.

Once she determined the garment's construction and size and shape of the cut pieces, she'd make a prototype. The model would tell her more than whether the garment met the manufacturer's stylistic requirements. It also told her how difficult the thing was to actually sew together.

To test her patterns, Ann works with an eighty-one-year-old Belgian woman who sews a sample of every design with the actual fabric a manufacturer will use and gives her feedback. Ann then tweaks her patterns to ensure they're easy to make on a production scale, factoring in how the specific manufacturer likes to work. Some are very precise and cut her patterns carefully. These kinds of producers probably work with high-end, expensive fabrics, which they don't want to waste. For clients like these, Ann builds a quarter-inch seam allowance—the space between the cut edge of the fabric and the stitching—into her pattern. Other manufacturers cut sloppily—"like chopping linguini," she says—so she gives them bigger seam tolerances. They'll have to buy more fabric than they need, but with more forgiving patterns they can work faster.

NAFTA killed the garment industry; Ann kept going, but she found she had more time on her hands. In the aughts, she began teaching advanced patternmaking at her alma mater. On the first day of class, she asked her students if they liked making patterns, and they all said no. They *hated* it. Ann was surprised. She'd dedicated her entire career to the detailed technical process of making; to her, the construction of the garment was integral to its design. In contrast, her students were interested in fashion only on a visual level. She was flabbergasted.

Then she asked her students, *Who likes to sell?* Ann knew the hustle required to survive in the garment industry. She says they answered that they didn't hate that as much. All her students wanted to be fashion designers, but none had the drive to sew and sell their wares.

Ann concluded that her students were missing the point of the profession. She wondered: Was there something fundamentally different about this new generation? They didn't really seem to want to *make* anything.

Ann's business was rescued from the brink by the film industry in

2011. Wes Anderson was shooting *Moonrise Kingdom* in Rhode Island and needed 350 Cub Scout uniforms. The costume designers were great at creating one-offs, but didn't have Ann's factory experience. "The assistant designer guy was a wreck," she says. "They weren't used to that kinda volume. I said, 'Don't worry, buddy, this is what we do.'"

Word got around that Ann had expert knowledge and deep professional experience. Costume designers appreciated that her patterns made real, wearable garments. They were easy to construct and the pieces fit well, moved beautifully, and didn't need tweaking. Ann ended up designing pieces for Johnny Depp in *Black Mass,* the pattern for Maleficent's dress in the movie of the same name, and the incredible period pieces in the *The Marvelous Mrs. Maisel.*

To save money, Ben and Whitney decided not to outsource fabric-cutting to someone else, which could cost up to $2 a piece and eat into their profits. Instead, Dory taught them how to use a fabric-cutting machine to carve the components of Ann's vest pattern from a thick stack of layered fleece without losing a finger.

Ben and Whitney thought they would hire stitchers from Lewiston-Auburn or Biddeford, experienced people who'd worked for local apparel companies that had shut down. But it was too late. All those people were working elsewhere or retired.

So in July, they worked with Dory to set up a sewing training program, financed with some of their own money as well as grants from nonprofits, including Coastal Enterprises and Goodwill. They posted ads for the school. In came a flood of New Americans— predominantly political refugees arriving in Portland from Africa and the Middle East.

Wearing brightly printed dresses and head scarves, or jeans and T-shirts, unadorned or blinged out, the women learned how to use industrial lockstitch machines to lay in zippers, set sleeve, thread drawstrings, pop in rivets, and follow patterns. Most important, they learned to trust Dory and Whitney enough to reach out when they needed help.

The school also provided language and math training through Portland Adult Education (because the rest of the world works on the metric system), helped students and their families navigate the American health care system, public schools, and housing, and provided other crucial assistance so that students could adapt to their new Maine home.

It was through the training program that American Roots found its first employee, Anaam Jabbir. Anaam was the first person to apply to the school. She was in her mid-forties, barely five feet tall, but exuded strength and intelligence, her hair concealed under a hijab, her bright green eyes outlined in kohl.

Anaam had experienced much tragedy in her life. She was born in Baghdad to progressive parents who sent all eight of the children to college. "When you're educated," Anaam's mother had told her, "you'll have more opportunities."

Anaam's father had quit school at age ten and made a living manufacturing and designing shoes for women at a Baghdad factory; her mother completed high school and earned money doing custom tailoring for friends and family.

Making clothing was a family tradition, passed down from mother to daughter over generations. Anaam's mother taught her how to use a machine and make simple patterns.

Anaam's marriage was arranged. She met her husband, Saeed Hassoon Saeed, twice before she agreed to become his wife in 1992. Anaam's mother designed and sewed her wedding gown, basing the pattern on a photo they'd seen in a magazine. After Saeed graduated from community college, he couldn't find a job, so he opened a takeout restaurant in Baghdad selling falafel, shawarma, and hamburgers.

Anaam graduated from a four-year college with a degree in agricultural engineering and worked in a lab for six months until she got pregnant. Her husband wanted her to stay home and live a traditional life, raise their three children, cook, and do the shopping. She readily embraced that life. Her sisters and her mother had chosen the same path. They were a close-knit family and were happy.

"Then the war," Anaam says. "They came to Iraq and everything changed." She says that in 2003, life in Baghdad became untenable. The water was cut off, then the electricity. The city was repeatedly bombed. Friends and family began to flee the country. Her husband's restaurant suffered for lack of business, but they stuck it out, thinking Iraq would recover in a year or two.

Desperate for customers, Saeed began serving food to the Iraqi army. One day, he received a letter that read, "If you serve the army, we will kill you." It wasn't an idle threat. The family closed up their house, packed everything, and fled to Jordan, where they waited for three years, watching Iraq, hoping things would improve.

They didn't. When Saeed learned that his two brothers had been killed, he applied for asylum in the U.S.

The family landed in Atlanta in July 2008, and in October, the Great Recession hit. "It was bad," Anaam says. "No one let us work." Asking around their community, they heard about Maine—that it was a good state that cared about families and offered general assistance to those who had trouble finding work. Living in exile had wiped out their bank account. The state would help them with rent and food stamps, they were told.

They moved their family north, where the children completed their schooling. But they still would have to pay for their kids' college.

Heeding her mother's warning, Anaam began attending adult education classes in pursuit of a degree. Then she heard about American Roots. "They said they were offering training, and if you finished the sewing classes, they would hire you." Anaam immediately liked Dory and Whitney. "People can be very complicated. Whitney and Dory were simple. I could talk with them like a friend, not like managers and employees." She also liked that American Roots was a family business; it reminded her of home, and the six women she trained with— two Iraqi, two from Congo, two from Mexico—became her friends.

In that way, Anaam was like millions of American immigrants who had come before her and entered the great maw of manufacturing. They had given up everything, including their homes, their savings, and their community, to survive. Anything beyond that—a job, a house, a car, or an education—was a precious gift.

The New Americans came to Maine with talent to spare. Some of their children became star athletes, leading Portland High and other regional schools to state championships in track and soccer. Other immigrant children in Maine threw off the grading curves in math and science with high scores. Anaam's daughter graduated high school with the highest grades and scores in the state and is now getting a master's degree in psychology at Boston College. Anaam's oldest son works at a tech company. After graduating from the University of Southern Maine, her youngest son followed in his father's footsteps and opened a restaurant in Portland.

In 2017, Dory left American Roots to focus on training stitchers full-time. She called her school Common Threads; it received nonprofit status in 2019. Dory and her team screened applicants for English-language skills, sewing experience, and a willingness to learn and work, which made Makenga Tshibwabwa another excellent candidate. She was fluent in English and had sewn before.

Makenga had an impressive stature and broad features that belied her gentle nature. She wore big gold hoops and had a stunning crown of curls.

Just three years before she applied to Common Threads, Makenga and her husband, Robert Mbaya Biaya, arrived in the U.S. with their four children from the Democratic Republic of the Congo by way of South Africa. As soon as they adjusted to Maine life—finding housing, acquiring warm clothes, and enrolling their kids in Portland schools—Makenga saw an ad for the school. After she was admitted, Makenga spent five days a week for three months learning how to use the industrial sewing machines at Common Threads and getting familiar with American manufacturing terminology.

To graduate, each student was required to make a custom pattern and sew it. They could use cloth from the fabric room, where shelves overflowed with brightly patterned cotton weaves, including a variety of so-called Dutch wax prints (also called Ankara fabric) favored by

West Africans. These featured big, bold designs that originally imitated Indonesian batiks, rendered in every imaginable color.*

Many students chose to make a child's dress. On graduation day, family members joined the students to celebrate. A joyful array of child-size colorful garments, designed and handmade by the graduates, hung on the walls. The new professional stitchers felt pride in their work. After spending years on the edge of survival, it was such a gift to have the time, space, resources, and skills to create something unique for the next generation—little girls who would grow up as Americans.

Common Threads also offered job placement to ensure that graduates earned the income they deserved. Fresh out of school, Makenga was hired by American Roots, where she and Whitney immediately connected. They were the same age, the same height, and had a similar demeanor—quiet but commanding—which made Makenga a natural leader among the Central Africans already working at American Roots. Ben and Whitney needed someone with her background to help manage the production floor. Makenga could also speak French, Swahili, and Lingala. She was soon promoted to floor manager.

Makenga and her husband, Robert, had gone through a harrowing twenty-year journey to get from the Democratic Republic of Congo

---

* The most popular wax fabrics are still produced by the Dutch company Vlisco, founded in 1846, created almost exclusively for West and Central African markets. Their latest patterns, designed and named to appeal to local buyers, include "Michelle Obama's Bag," "Kofi Annan's Brains," and "Mama Benz"—the last named after the enterprising West African women who dominate the cloth markets, some getting rich enough to afford their own chauffeured Mercedes-Benz. Vlisco is now threatened by Chinese knockoffs. Perhaps equally interesting, when another Netherlands-based company tried to produce its own Africa-designed prints in Rwanda in 2013, Vlisco threatened a lawsuit. In 2020, an African consortium called Made in Africa (MIA) tried to buy Vlisco from the British private equity group that now owns the company. MIA's hope was to continue fabric-printing operations in the Netherlands but shift the cotton supply from Asia to Nigeria, to support the country's 87,000-plus independent farmers. Interestingly, the private equity group backed out of the deal at the last minute, selling to a European company for a lower price.

to Maine. When I met with the couple to discuss their journey from
DRC to Maine, Robert took the lead, perhaps to protect his wife
from having to relive the trauma. A friend who had immigrated from
Angola also joined us.

There were times during Robert's telling that Makenga's expression went blank; this was all too fresh. Four years in Maine had done
little to diminish decades of struggle.

Robert explained that after he and his nine siblings graduated from
school, they found themselves living in their parents' house in DRC
with no job prospects. "We started thinking about the future. What
will tomorrow be? And the next day?"

Congo was a place of extreme income inequality. Colonialism
under the Belgians had been unspeakably cruel. At the turn of the
last century, millions of Congolese perished furnishing King Leopold
with rubber. When the country became independent in 1960, the
new government tried to pursue socialist policies and was immediately destabilized by the CIA. Between 1960 and 1968, the CIA spent
the equivalent of $80 million in Congo beating back "communists"
and installing Mobutu, a brutal autocrat leader (famous for his trade-
mark leopard-skin fez and public executions of rivals) who embezzled
at least $4 billion before his death in 1997.

Congo was, and remains, resource-rich territory. Oil, copper, dia-
monds, and uranium abound, as well as half of the world's cobalt
reserves. It was mostly enriched Congolese uranium that wiped out
Nagasaki and Hiroshima during World War II. Congolese cobalt is
an essential ingredient in the new "green" economy, which depends
on lithium-ion batteries packed with the substance.

Mining companies may be the most destructive and corrupt entities on God's green earth, and they basically own Congo, which most
people would consider a failed state. More than half of the 100 million people living in Congo are under fourteen years old. Only 5 percent of the population lives past age fifty-five.

Robert said that he and Makenga separately fled their country in
search of a "place to get a job, to survive, and to help those who

remained behind." Robert moved to South Africa in 2000 and found a job running a printing machine, but the South Africans were hostile to foreigners. "They were not welcoming to us. Every day, they were asking us, 'When are you leaving? When are you leaving?' They were asking us all the time, 'When are you guys going home?'"

Makenga moved to South Africa around the same time for the same reason. "Go back home. Go back home," Makenga added quietly, staring expressionless at the floor.

"You have to go back to your country because you are taking our jobs," their friend from Angola added.

"You guys, you shouldn't be here. You have to go back to your country," Robert went on. "This is our country and this is our money. You are making money. This is our money."

"Our money," Makenga said.

Robert and Makenga were both Jehovah's Witnesses and met at a Johannesburg church. Their parents negotiated the terms of the marriage long-distance from Congo, and Robert and Makenga were married, though the South African government was overtly hostile to foreign workers and refused to officially acknowledge their union, forcing them to apply separately for work visas and keep their immigration statuses up to date, which took inordinate time.

"It was not safe," Robert continued. "Every day, I saw people dying. They kill people maybe for a phone, or for money. And sometimes for nothing. Almost every day, they pointed a gun at my head, especially before I bought the car. We used to walk and people would stop us in the road asking for money, pointing a gun at us. Pointing a gun at me because I am a man. Pointing a gun, asking for money, putting a hand in my pocket, pulling the earrings from my wife's ears."

Their Angolan friend leaned forward and spoke in a deep voice: "Everybody has things to tell about what we experienced. Like myself, I was on the border between Congo and Angola. I saw thousands and thousands of people coming from Rwanda crossing into Congo. There were a million people. And I'm telling you, they killed all of them. The military, they surrounded all of them, with babies, and killed them. All of them. This never ran in *The Washington Post* or on CNN. Nobody knows that story. But I was around. I can tell you. We saw people flee Rwanda, crossing Congo to get to Angola to survive. None of the population reached a city in Angola. They killed all of them. I saw the military from Congo and from Angola surrounding the people. They killed all of them, with their babies."

Robert and Makenga spent nearly two decades trying to build a life in South Africa, but it was too difficult. "We were not welcome there." All four of their children were born in South Africa, but the authorities refused to issue South African birth certificates to the first two, part of a general effort to discourage immigration. Robert had to acquire them from the Congo embassy. "My kids, they don't know Congo. They don't know my country. Sometimes we make fun of them and say, 'Kids, you're not Congolese, you're not South African. Who are you?'

"Stress after stress," Robert said. Makenga took life in South Africa particularly hard. Robert gestured toward his wife. "She's still struggling with high blood pressure much of the time," he said. "She gets scared about everything from the past when we were in Africa."

As if in a trance, Makenga added, "I saw things with my eyes that—no, it is not good. That is not life. Especially in South Africa. I had my own store and another lady her own store. Gangs were after her husband. Because they couldn't find the husband, they shot the lady in the store, her own store, her own clothing store."

I had heard that Makenga's brother and his family had been killed in a horrific home invasion in Congo earlier that year, but didn't mention it that evening.

"When you find a place, when you find a way to move or to run, you better go, because if you don't, maybe you'll be next," Robert said. "When I got the opportunity for asylum, I said, 'Let us go.' We came to the United States for security reasons. We felt unsafe, that's why we fled from South Africa. That is the only reason we came here."

Makenga, Robert, and their children first arrived in Dallas. Within a week, someone directed them to Maine, where the Greater Portland

Immigrant Welcome Center, which survives through state and phil-anthropic grants, is a thriving organization dedicated to helping new Mainers learn English, adapt to their new country, and access loans to build businesses.

"On the first day we got [to Maine], my wife could not stay at home because of everything—the past was always coming to her mind. She was always scared. Social workers tried to assist her at the clinic, help her remove everything in her head. She got help. She's not like when we first came."

"A social worker told me that I must not watch news about Congo because it is affecting me a lot," Makenga said. "Sometimes even now, I feel scared. I'm shaking when I open the door in the morning. I see it's dark outside, it's a new place, I don't know the area well. But in my mind, I say, *No, I'm in Maine. When you're in Maine, everywhere, it's safe.*"

Once they were in Maine, they began to feel like part of a commu-nity. "You feel safe, like a member, like you were born here," Robert said.

Freedom from fear was a lifesaving gift. "Our kids are safe," Makenga said. "When they go to school in the morning, I'm not worried that they will get lost or maybe somebody will kidnap them. My kids are safe going and coming back. Even when they come home and I'm not home, they're getting home. They're safe. I'll find them, they're good."

If New Americans were willing to do the work, Ben and Whitney would take them. They didn't understand the complex forces that had delivered these men and women to Portland, they knew even less about their cultural traditions and native languages, but they com-mitted themselves to helping their employees adjust to life in the U.S.

Like his father, Ben was a natural salesman. As soon as they had a product to sell, Ben began calling union contacts. "Get down here and show us the vest," a couple of Boston union leaders told him.

When they saw the American Roots fleece vest—made in Maine of Massachusetts-produced fabric—the orders started rolling in. Ben hit the road and sold and sold. He drove so much during the early days of American Roots that he killed two Ford Explorers. "Destroyed them," he says.

In 2015, American Roots sold $8,000 worth of vests with four employees.

By October 2016, they had sixteen employees and had closed nearly $400,000 in revenue.

On the morning of October 15, Dory poured coffee into her travel mug and threw some papers into her bag. She pulled on her cardigan, pocketed her car keys, opened the front door of her house, and fell six feet down onto concrete.

The carpenter had finally showed up to rebuild the front steps but he hadn't told her.

Lying on the ground with broken ribs, a broken leg, and a head injury, Dory stared up at the sky watching a red-tailed hawk circling. A good omen. She knew she would not die that day. Her recovery would take years, forcing her to delegate the everyday management of Common Threads to others.

Dory's brush with death confirmed to Ben that he'd made the right choice returning to Portland. Whitney was pregnant with their first child. Raising their own family in Maine meant that their kids would grow up knowing their grandparents.

Three weeks later, the morning after Trump was elected, Whitney stayed home, nauseous and exhausted following the official election results.

Ben was scheduled to drive down to New York for a conference, but he felt that he needed to talk to the American Roots team about Trump. He got to the factory before dawn. An hour later, he was coming out of the break room when Dua Khalifa approached him. Dua was the floor lead at the time—a hardworking, single mother from Iraq.

"She just stopped and burst into tears," Ben says.

The first time she ever voted in her life was that election.

"What happened to America?" Dua asked Ben through her grief.

Ben gathered his employees together. He told them, *There are more good people—far more good people—in this country than there are people filled with hate or anger.* "I still believe that," he says. "We're a good country. I'll disagree with Barack Obama on a lot of things. But I do agree with him, we are the last great hope of what the world can be if we work towards it. But it takes a lot of work."

Ben and Whitney's success depended on American-sourced fabric, and they'd bet on Malden Mills.

In December, Ben was feeling confident when he arrived at the Massachusetts AFL-CIO Christmas party in Boston. But as soon as he walked through the door, someone said to him, "Polartec's closing. What are you going to do?"

Polartec was the high-tech textile branch of Malden Mills that made PolarFleece. Since the documentary about Feuerstein came out, things had changed dramatically. China began dominating textile manufacturing and the banks called in Malden's loans.

Mired in debt, Aaron lost control of his company to a private equity firm, which promptly ousted him. Once the company's founder was out of the way, the firm announced that it was shutting down the Lawrence factory and relocating some PolarFleece manufacturing to nonunion Tennessee to maintain its government contracts,* sending the rest to Asia.

* The Buy American Act of 1933 requires that the federal government purchase American-made goods and materials whenever possible. The Berry Amendment (1941) goes further, requiring that the Department of Defense (DOD) purchase goods 100 percent domestic in origin. In fiscal year 2021, the DOD spent $2.3 billion on textiles and apparel, comprising 5 percent of the $49 billion textile and apparel shipments sent from U.S. mills that year. Although the DOD has serious spending power that could keep lots of American companies afloat, here's the cold, hard truth. Ninety percent of that DOD-purchased apparel was made by incarcerated people, bought through the Federal Prison Industries

Aaron was ninety years old at the time. He told *The Boston Globe* that Polartec's move to the South was a "disgrace." He added, "I considered workers stakeholders in the business. These people are only interested in making profit. . . . [Private equity has] no interest in the welfare of workers."

In a desperate attempt to save their jobs, UNITE HERE, the labor union representing four hundred Malden Mills workers, sent a letter to Patagonia pleading with the apparel company to consider buying Polartec. Patagonia never responded. Polartec's new CEO, Gary Smith, told *Outside Business Journal* in November 2016 that the California-based company would never consider buying Polartec because Patagonia "never [has] been and never will be in the business of making things." It was true: like most American brands, Patagonia designs garments, then contracts with producers around the world to make their goods. Smith also defended moving Polartec down south; it wasn't "a cheap labor play," he said, even though Polartec would be using less expensive labor. Rather, he informed the reporter, non-union workers in Tennessee would be more productive per hour.

In fact, Polartec sent most manufacturing abroad and kept a small division in the South to meet the Department of Defense's domestic manufacturing requirements. At that point, the majority of textile manufacturers in the U.S. depended on government contracts to stay afloat, but landing those contracts required that they produce most of the components in their products on American soil.

American Roots entire line was made of PolarFleece at the time. As a small shop, Ben and Whitney knew they'd be last in line for Polartec's domestic supply.

(UNICOR), a wholly owned U.S. government corporation. Setting aside the ethics of using prison labor to make uniforms for American soldiers, it's a very expensive way to produce apparel. According to a 2017 Prison Policy Initiative report, taxpayers spend $182 billion each year on the American prison system. The annual cost of incarcerating just one person in the U.S. (including room, board, health care, jail-building and upkeep, policing, corrections officers, and legal expenses) runs up to $79,000.

The clock was ticking again.

Ben ducked out of the party to call his Polartec rep. "When were you going to tell us this?" Ben fired at him.

The rep said it had been a PR nightmare.

Ben replied, "Well, that's a fucking understatement."

"I don't know all the details yet," the rep told him.

"Well, here's what I do know," Ben said. "Thanks for fucking us."

A BRIEF HISTORY
OF THE HOODIE

The offshoring of Polartec was an American Roots blessing in disguise.

Ben and Whitney had been making fleece vests because that was the garment that first inspired Ben to start the company when he was plowing driveways that frigid January. When PolarFleece abandoned them in the winter of 2017, Ben and Whitney looked around for a new material and decided to pivot to cotton fleece. The U.S. was one of the top growers of cotton in the world. They hoped that meant that their supply was secure.

And what, in the slightly modified words of architect Louis Kahn, did the cotton fleece want to be? A hoodie, that's what.

Experts agree that the hoodie is an American icon; Museum of Modern Art curator Paola Antonelli once called the hoodie a "humble masterpiece." It is the world's best-designed top, the paragon of form-meets-function. Its built-in hood is much warmer than a hat and guaranteed never to get lost. Flip it up to stave off the cold, cinch it tight to cloak yourself in celebrity-inspired anonymity, or let it drape down the back like a cowl. Rib-knit cuffs and waistbands lock in heat and prevent roomy sleeves from getting in the way of your hands. The broad single-piece back presents a tabula rasa for silk-screened designs or logos. In its generous kangaroo pockets (technically called a "muff"), you can stow a phone, a book, or your hands in the soft embrace of cotton knit fleece. Add a zipper and call it a jacket. Light enough to layer, heavy enough to protect against wind and rain, the hoodie is one of the smartest garments ever created.

Hoodie precedents abound throughout the ages. Ancient Greek and Roman art depicts people in hooded garments; Europe's monks and medieval ladies carried on the tradition. (Stone monasteries and castles were awfully drafty.) South Americans crafted woven hooded ponchos that served them well in the snowcapped Andes. In the Arctic, the Inuit designed the most beautiful hoodies ever made; parkas and anoraks were complex garments sewn together with tendons and featuring fur-lined and trimmed hoods. Expert Inuit tailors used contrasting caribou and seal furs and skins to create surprisingly modern designs; exquisite embroidery made these garments perhaps the most stunning workwear.

The best-known hooded figure is no doubt the Grim Reaper. Whether he wore standard reaper garb, a belted shroud, or a perversion of monkwear, Death always pulled his hood far over his brow to hide his skeletal features, tempting mortals to imagine what horrors lurked in the shadows.

But throughout the nineteenth century, workwear didn't evolve much and neither did the proto-hoodie. Women wore voluminous skirts, men wore woven wool breeches and rough button-down shirts and overcoats. In the West, some folks wore denim. All these things were cut from machine-made cloth and stitched, first by hand, later by machine. Manufacturing workwear depended on high volume and thin margins. There was little demand for innovation.

The modern sweatshirt, thus, would be birthed in a completely different ecosystem: college sports. Before the twentieth century, college athletics were barely a blip on the national consciousness. Few Americans finished high school, let alone college. In 1910, roughly 10 percent of fourteen- to seventeen-year-olds were enrolled in secondary school, and just 5 percent of white American males went to college.

Instead, children worked. They sewed clothes, mined coal, hawked newspapers, and monitored machinery in loud, dangerous, dirty factories. They were farming, baling hay, picking cotton, tobacco, apples, and lettuce.

Upper-class Americans turned a blind eye to the tiny laborers who brought them hefty returns, but in 1904, the most influential social welfare advocates of the day united to form the National Child Labor Committee. The committee hired investigators to study working conditions across America and hired photographer Lewis Hine to travel the country documenting children at work. Soon, disturbing photographs were coming out of mills, tenements, and fields; the appalling conditions under which two million children worked became impossible to ignore.

When women won the right to vote in 1920, the labor reform movement gained a major voting bloc, although a century later Americans have yet to constitutionally regulate child labor. Only twenty-eight states have ratified the 1924 Child Labor Amendment, which would require the federal government to regulate labor for people under eighteen years old. The Fair Labor Standards Act, passed in 1938, came close to banning child labor, establishing the right to a minimum wage and overtime pay, and prohibiting employment of minors in "oppressive child labor."*

Once children couldn't work, they went to school. The rate of Americans attending high school climbed to 70 percent over a few decades. The number of Americans going to college increased, too. Between 1920 and 1945, college enrollment went from about 250,000

---

* But of course, the fight for protections continues. When a 2022 Labor Department investigation revealed that the country's largest food safety company illegally employed more than one hundred children (most of them from Central America) to do hazardous work in meatpacking plants, several high-profile Republicans, including Arkansas governor Sarah Huckabee Sanders, got to work further loosening their states' child labor restrictions. Republican spokespeople say that rolling back state requirements will give parents more choice over their children's lives.

to 1.3 million—from 5 percent to 15 percent of Americans. Following World War II and the passage of the G.I. Bill (1944), college enrollment climbed to 3.6 million in 1960 and 7.9 million in 1970.

By mid-century, America was finally ready to mainstream the hoodie.

The first sweatshirt was born near the cotton fields of Alabama, where Benjamin Russell, a University of Virginia grad, had been cranking out all manner of cotton and wool garments at his Russell Manufacturing Company in Alexander City. Russell was an all-American entrepreneur who got into everything—roads, hotels, electric power, and real estate. He made yarn, he dyed the yarn, he knit the yarn, he sewed things. He also loved sports, a fondness he passed along to his son, Benny. One day in 1926, Benny complained to his father about the itchiness of his college's wool football jerseys. Maybe athletic gear should be made out of cotton, he suggested. His father thought that sounded like a fine idea. After developing prototypes, he bought a textile mill to manufacture cotton knit sweatshirts at the peak of the Great Depression. With that purchase, Russell's Southern Manufacturing Company became one of the few fully vertical fabric factories in the world. Russell focused on athletic gear for college sports teams, a niche market at the time.

In upstate New York, three sons of Russian immigrants were getting into athletic gear, too. The Feinbloom brothers started out as apparel salesmen and middlemen in Rochester in the 1920s. They traveled the country shilling underwear and wool sweaters under the Knickerbocker Knitting Company brand. On a sales call in the mid-1920s, they learned how poorly wool performed in college athletics. Players complained that it was rough and itchy, and athletic directors hated how much wool sweaters shrank when you washed them. Working closely with the football coach of the Wentworth Military College in Missouri, the Feinblooms refined their designs for a cotton knit crewneck sweater. Under the name Champion Mills, they applied for a patent for a cutting process that reduced shrinkage (called Reverse Weave) in 1938; they also introduced heavy-duty cotton fabrics into the line and added cotton fleece interiors for a softer, warmer product for those late-fall football games.

Champion and Russell competed for the growing college athletic market. Champion patented a way to adhere flocked lettering to sweatshirts, and Russell innovated industrial screen printing.

And the hood? That was Champion's idea. Former Champion president Harold Lipson, who started his career sweeping the factory floors in 1934, said that the company developed hoods in the 1930s for track and football teams, and "for coaches who had to stand on the sidelines in cold weather." The first company to see the hoodie's potential as workwear was a struggling Pennsylvania tree service called Asplundh, founded by three Swedish brothers in 1928. In the late 1930s, the company ordered Champion hoodies to protect employees who climbed trees to clear telephone and electric lines in all weather.

By the 1960s, more Americans were attending college and more were wearing their school colors on and off the field. But outside campuses, athletic apparel wasn't considered appropriate attire. Men and women wore hats, women wore gloves, jackets and ties were required at the office. Factory and farmworkers wore denim, woven button-down apparel, and jackets with long collars that could be flipped up to stave off the chill.

I'd argue that Rocky Balboa sparked the hoodie craze when he donned a plain gray hoodie for his famous run through the mean streets of Philly in 1976. With that one scene, the garment finally leapt from college campuses to, well, everywhere. Rocky wasn't just the underdog. He was the working-class schlub, the eternal loser. He was every child of immigrants who for whatever reason couldn't keep up and found himself stuck in the poverty cycle of the uneducated and unlucky. Even Rocky's grizzled boxing coach gives up on him. Then, randomly, Rocky gets one shot at the dream. Casting about for someone to fight Apollo Creed, the Black heavyweight champion, Rocky is selected not because he has talent, but because his fighter name, "The Italian Stallion," has a catchy ring to it. Apollo and his team assume that Rocky will draw a crowd and go down fast.

Street-smart, brutish, yet somehow also painfully sincere, Rocky is completely ignorant of the cynicism that got him into that ring. To prepare for the fight of his life, he wakes at dawn, drinks raw eggs, punches sides of beef, and sports that sweat-stained gray sweatshirt as the music soars.*

Round after round, his face purple and raw, his right eye swollen shut, Rocky won't stay down. Ultimately, he loses on the scorecards. But because he can take a beating, the gritty brute with the monosyllabic vocabulary becomes the hero. It's a fascinating commentary on 1970s American values.

From then on, the hooded sweatshirt embodied the endless, senseless, primal battle—against the odds, against conventional wisdom, against haters, against oneself—to stay upright in a brutal world.

The hoodie's significance continued to evolve.

During the Reagan years, the hoodie became an integral part of the streetwear uniform, in part because kids could buy factory seconds and personalize them, in part because hoodies were standard issue for professional athletes. Later, Americans couldn't escape the FBI sketch of the mysterious Unabomber, a homegrown terrorist in huge dark glasses lurking under the shadow of a hoodie.

Also lurking under that hood: the people systematically oppressed by white America's seemingly bottomless capacity for racism. The cover of the Wu-Tang Clan's first LP, *Enter the Wu-Tang* (1993), showed the group, faces blurred, wearing identical black sweatshirts emblazoned with the vaguely sinister Wu-Tang logo, hoods up.

In time, the hoodie became something like a uniform for Black men and boys trying to survive in a dangerous world where money is power, but hard work gets you neither. *"Cash rules everything around me—C.R.E.A.M., get the money. Dollar dollar bill, y'all."*

The hood had transformed from gym gear into a symbol of

---

* Ben works out to the *Rocky* soundtrack every morning. Also note that the Rocky Balboa character was loosely based on Olympic boxer Joe Frazier, who actually did train in slaughterhouses and regularly ran up the steps of the Philadelphia Museum of Art.

subversion. It gave the wearer a quick way to hide from surveillance, which was becoming ubiquitous. Plenty of people had a reason to want to obscure their identity in public. The hoodie was a practical choice, but because it worked well, it also threatened authority. You can't control people if you can't identify them.

Union men and women wore hoodies with their locals printed across the back, in solidarity.

Hoodie paranoia soon became a conservative obsession. Schools and businesses began to enact "no hoodie" policies. In the U.K., David Cameron, leader of Britain's Conservative Party, who would later, as prime minister, work to privatize social services, made his infamous "hug a hoodie" speech in 2006, designed to give his party the veneer of compassion for the working class. "We, the people in suits, often see hoodies as aggressive, the uniform of a rebel army of young gangsters," he said. "But, for young people, hoodies are often more defensive than offensive. . . . So when you see a child walking down the road, hoodie up, head down, moody, swaggering, dom-inating the pavement—think what has brought that child to that moment."

In the aughts, American tech entrepreneurs also saw themselves as youth warriors and took the hoodie from the street into the board-room. Plenty of ink was spilled over Mark Zuckerberg's dark hoodie when Facebook first began to gain traction in 2009. How could any-one take a sallow young dude in a zipped-up sweatshirt seriously? But when Facebook began steering elections and fomenting coups, no one cared what Zuck was wearing anymore. On second thought, maybe the analysts had reason to be concerned after all.

Trayvon Martin was a seventeen-year-old kid in a hoodie when he was gunned down in a gated community in Sanford, Florida, by a self-proclaimed vigilante. His murderer, George Zimmerman, told the 911 dispatcher that he'd spotted a "suspicious guy" in "a dark hoodie, a gray hoodie." Then he shot and killed the teenager. Geraldo Rivera told Fox News viewers that "the hoodie is as much responsible for Trayvon Martin's death as George Zimmerman was" and warned parents not to let their children wear them. He referred to the hoodie as "thugware," and said wearing it sends a malevolent message. "You cannot rehabilitate the hoodie," Rivera said. "Stop wearing it."

But communities of color refused to let anyone dictate who could wear what. Five months after Trayvon's murder in 2012, organizers led the "Million Hoodies March" in New York City, and thousands of supporters took to the streets wearing hoods in defiance.

In 2020, LeBron James promoted his WNBA sisters by prominently wearing their (imported, unfortunately) signature bright orange hoodie during warm-ups. The WNBA didn't have much of a choice as to where their garb was made—Champion had been bought by global conglomerate Sara Lee in 1989; Champion's corporate headquarters moved from Rochester to Winston-Salem, North Carolina, in 1992; in 1999, after the passage of NAFTA, all manufacturing was moved to Mexico. Russell Athletic, Champion's main competition, had been bought by Berkshire Hathaway in the 1990s, and its manufacturing was soon offshored, too.

Even now, the hoodie can cause tempests in a teapot. During his 2022 senatorial campaign, John Fetterman often appeared in a black Carhartt hoodie, which aroused plenty of pundit chatter. Would it affect his election odds? At the time, *The New York Times*' chief fashion critic, Vanessa Friedman, observed, "[Fetterman] looks real, an avatar of the American archetype of the working man who does an honest day's labor (even though he did go to Harvard for his master's degree, and his labor is mostly deskbound)."*

The world's hippest political leaders see something powerful in the hoodie as well. Ukrainian president Volodymyr Zelensky has been regularly photographed wearing a black hoodie screen-printed "I'm Ukrainian" in bold white letters across the chest. Not to be outdone, French president Emmanuel Macron was photographed working at his desk in the Gold Room of the Élysée Palace one Sunday morning

---

* Fetterman beat his Republican opponent, Mehmet Oz, by five percentage points.

in March 2022 sporting a black hoodie with the CPA 10 emblem, representing the paratrooper unit of the French Air Force. Fashion internet went bonkers.*

And in early January 2023, former CNN host Don Lemon reported the news wearing a gray hoodie (or a "hooded sweater") under a suit jacket, a sartorial ensemble that Stephen Colbert quipped made Lemon look like "a high school track teacher who went for a run" then tried to dine at a formal restaurant, so he "stole a jacket from an extra from *Guys and Dolls.*"

Lemon rebutted: "If Trayvon Martin can start a revolution in a hoodie, then Don Lemon can tell the news in a hooded sweater."

Perhaps more than any other garment in American history, the hoodie now transcends every cultural, economic, and political divide. You'll find it on Ivy League campuses, in recording studios, at protests, on yachts, on street corners, and on Zuckerberg wannabes. It's the one garment that all Americans—rich or poor, powerful or disenfranchised, white supremacist or Black hip-hop star, wildly popular or hiding out in a tiny cabin alone in the woods writing manifestos—have embraced.

Clearly the hoodie is an established American icon. And like the country that spawned it, the hoodie had a complicated past. Ironically, it was no longer made in the USA.

* Cette écrivaine pensait qu'il avait l'air très chic-décontracté.

JUST PULL IT AND
IT'S DONE

When Ben and Whitney decided to make hoodies, they weren't thinking about the garment's cultural significance. They were thinking about how they'd find homegrown components necessary to produce their goods. A big part of their mission was to help rebuild the domestic supply chain that atrophied when needlework was exported. They weren't going to settle for foreign-made parts.

Ben's union connections from his AFL days represented workers in physically demanding industries, so Ben and Whitney wanted to create a hoodie unlike any other in the market—solid, like the post–World War II vacuum cleaners that rolled out of factories originally set up to make B-29 bombers. Those 1950s appliances were built for battle, weighed five times as much as they needed to, and would probably still work if you oiled them up and plugged them in. The American Roots hoodie would be the apparel equivalent, the antithesis of the flimsy, disposable, fast fashion garb that Americans had grown accustomed to.

But first, they needed domestically sourced cotton fleece, drawstrings, zippers, and grommets. Was anyone making this stuff anymore?

The answer was yes, but they had to look pretty hard to find them.

The Waxmans bought their thread from a 125-year-old manufacturer based in North Carolina that has operations around the globe.
Their cotton twill tape, which they used to reinforce the seam between
the hood and the sweatshirt body, plus the seams that held the left
and right sides of the zipper in place, came out of a sixty-five-year-
old family-owned factory in Brooklyn, New York. Their heavy-duty
braided white drawstring was manufactured in Virginia by a subsid-
iary of the Wayne Mills Company, a 112-year-old family-owned and
-operated Philadelphia-based manufacturer of woven fabric tapes.

What most people notice first about the American Roots hoodie,
however, is its zipper—a massive thing with chiseled teeth and a
metal pull big enough to grab on to while wearing welding gloves.
You wouldn't call the action smooth—this isn't a silk dress, after all—
this zipper's got grit. You've got to wrestle with the thing the whole
way up, kind of like busting a bronco, but once those teeth sink into
each other, they won't let go.

Like all the components of the American Roots hoodie, the zipper
is made in the USA, at L.A.-based UCAN, likely the last independent zipper company in America. No surprise that it's a family affair.

Paul Lai never intended to get into zippers when he moved from
Taiwan to Los Angeles in the 1960s. He started at Carl's Jr., working
his way up from cleaner to manager. In the late 1980s, though, he hit
a fast-food career ceiling. Ambitious and affable with three boys at
home, Paul joined a family friend's six-person zipper-manufacturing
operation.

The service industry had taught Paul how to manage customers, a
skill that made him a highly effective zipper salesman. When Paul's
partners tired of the dog-eat-dog world of manufacturing and moved
back to China, Paul took over UCAN. He expanded the factory's
offerings—adding custom dyeing and sizing to coax fashion buyers away from the big guys like YKK who couldn't move as fast, or
handle small-volume orders, with the finesse that an independent
operator like UCAN could.

Paul invested in elaborate machinery (made in New York by a

now-defunct company) that made a wide range of metal teeth—from dainty and demure to big and bling-y—and added injection molding capabilities to make custom-dyed plastic teeth and pulls of any size. A New York buyer could overnight a swatch to UCAN and get a sample the next day; upon approval, they'd have the full order in their own factory a week later. In the apparel business, that kind of responsiveness was gold; no one wanted their stitchers sitting around with nothing to do because the zippers or buttons were stuck somewhere on a ship in the Pacific Ocean.

By the late 1990s, UCAN had three hundred employees; machines ran around the clock.

It wouldn't last. After China joined the WTO in 2001, less expensive imported zippers upended the business. UCAN's biggest customers, including Target and JCPenney, began squeezing Paul on pricing, forcing them to make it cheap or lose the contract. After practically killing themselves to deliver a massive order to Target in the early aughts, Paul crunched the numbers and realized they'd made a 1 percent profit. That was unsustainable. To survive, he'd have to court smaller apparel companies that appreciated quality, excellent customer service, customization, and rapid turnaround. UCAN was forced to go niche.

Malan Lai didn't plan to take over his father's business. Growing up, he and his brothers did time in their parents' factory to earn things they wanted, like a driver's license or use of the car. Paul sometimes brought home unpaired zippers (he called it "homework"), which the boys would have to zip together, bundle, and package. The boys were slow as molasses ("We did about a hundred a day," Malan says with a chuckle), but his parents didn't let up. They wanted their kids to appreciate the value of work and, more important, have a physical connection to the source of their wealth. Malan and his brothers just saw it as drudge work forced on them by their immigrant parents.

After graduating from college, Malan's older brother reluctantly agreed to try out the business, but lasted only six months. Paul would try again with son number two. In 1997, Malan graduated from USC with a BA in psychology, intending to go into child development, maybe teach, but his parents nudged him to give factory life a shot. Just try it, they said. He could live at home. They'd pay him.

Malan went on deliveries, stocked shelves, ran machines, and found he really enjoyed working side by side with the people, mostly Latinas, who had helped his parents climb the economic ladder. A year into his father's experiment, Malan looked around and saw his friends clocking in long hours, sometimes working around the clock, at finance or consulting firms, "slaving away" for capricious bosses who drove them hard for no good reason. Malan was working from 8 a.m. to 4:30 p.m. He wasn't making big money, but who needed it anyway? The cacophony of dozens of clacking machines running at once and the lingering odor of dye and machine oil—that was the sound of home. "Things started to click," he said. "Coming back in the business with my father teaching me, being with the crew who patiently taught me everything I know, it was a nice family atmosphere and I decided to stay."

Of course, the zipper itself is as American as, well, Malan. The contraption was first dreamed up by the same Massachusetts tinker who would solve the sewing machine conundrum that had plagued inventors for more than fifty years. Elias Howe was born to a family of inventors (his uncle William designed the Howe truss bridge—an easy-to-build, remarkably strong wood-and-iron construction; Uncle Tyler cooked up the box spring bed after a particularly arduous journey through the Drake Passage by ship during the California Gold Rush of 1848), and after working in various industries, Elias joined what we moderns would call an "innovation incubator" in Cambridge.

One day, a fellow came in who asked Howe to invent a knitting machine, which Howe considered a colossal waste of his time. But a sewing machine—that was another story. After spending considerable time watching Mrs. Howe hand-sew garments, and thinking long and hard about his experience in Lowell with the cloth-weaving machines, Mr. Howe patented his lockstitch sewing machine in

1846. His application wasn't the first such invention to reach the patent office. There was plenty of demand for a machine that actually worked. While textile production had been thoroughly mechanized by the mid-nineteenth century, sewing cloth into garments remained a painfully slow handicraft. In the nineteenth century, hundreds of patents were issued each year for devices promising to automate sewing, but like early computers, none of these contraptions worked well enough to go mainstream, and all of them were wildly expensive. Sooner or later, though, someone would figure it out. Howe hoped it would be him.

While waiting for riches to roll in, Howe patented an early rough draft of the zipper in 1851, a time when most garments, including shoes, were secured with buttons, buckles, and laces—all challenging to use, in their way. Perhaps the complexity of producing his fastener kept Howe from promoting it; instead, he focused on fending off sewing machine copycats. Later that decade, Howe discovered that a boisterous and bewhiskered former stage actor named Isaac Singer had made a few tweaks to his lockstitch machine design and was successfully mass-producing sewing machines. Howe dropped everything and sued Singer for a cut, which he eventually got. The Singer sewing machine became a household appliance, forever changing apparel manufacturing, and Howe and Singer both became rich men, while the marvelous zipper fastener languished in a patent office drawer.

In 1893, a midwesterner named Whitcomb Judson got tired of hooking together the fasteners on his boots. After much futzing, he patented a new kind of automatic hook-and-eye closure, which he showcased at the Chicago Columbian Exposition. That, too, failed to enchant the discerning public, in spite of the catchy tagline created for Judson's Universal Fastener Company: *Just pull it and it's done.*

It wasn't until Swiss inventor Catharina Kuhn-Moos patented a zipper in Europe that a Swedish immigrant working for Judson, Gideon Sundback, had enough information to make the whole concept work. Among Sundback's many improvements was the addition of a cloth strip onto which the components were permanently clamped, infinitely improving the manufacturing and functioning of what would become the modern fastener. Sundback won his patent in 1917; he first produced the fastener in Meadville, Pennsylvania. The Department of Defense soon came calling—there was a war on, and "hookless fasteners" looked like a great way to speedily open and close all kinds of gear.

Enter the "Zipper," originally the brand name for a 1920s line of Goodrich rubber galoshes that prominently featured the new fastener straight down the front. The insanely intricate fastener made closing things a cinch, an asset heavily marketed by the company. Just get a load of this somewhat tortured ad copy for "Goodrich Zipps" boys' sport shoes: "Off or on with 'Fireman' speed! Quicker than it takes to tell it, you can get these shoes off or on. Just like a fireman puts on his clothes. No laces. No knots. Just slip that hookless fastener up—they're on! Just slip it down—they're off again!"

And yet, the fashion industry resisted. Perhaps the zipper seemed too lowbrow, industrial, or utilitarian for use on fine apparel. Until 1937, that is, when a consortium of French designers declared the zipper-fly superior in every way to the button-fly. That settled the issue for the editors of *Esquire* magazine, who pronounced the zipper the "Newest Tailoring Idea for Men," one that, they wrote, would eliminate the "possibility of unintentional and embarrassing disarray."

Modern zipper-making at UCAN starts with two raw products: miles and miles of metal wire (brass, nickel, or steel) and white cotton tape—the component that's sewn into a garment or bag. To compete with overseas suppliers, UCAN offers full customization and quicker turnaround because the factory is located in L.A. The first step is dyeing the tape so that customers get exactly the color they're looking for. UCAN uses a spectrometer to analyze color samples and whip up a pigment formula from more than fifty different hues. UCAN's dye technicians won't simply follow the computer's recommendation. Cotton is a living fiber. It has good days and bad days. Countless variables determine how it will take a given dye, so the techs test and tweak the formula to ensure that the color is spot-on. Once they've got their match, techs measure out the white tape, roll it onto spools, and insert them in an industrial metal vat into which the dye bubbles up. The vats are pressurized to ensure the color adheres evenly to the fabric.

Dyes contain all manner of toxins and carcinogens. Before President Richard Nixon created the EPA, American dyehouses routinely dumped contaminated water straight into rivers. Environmental regulations enacted in the 1970s infuriated manufacturers. Many of them, fearing the costs of proper disposal, dumped ungodly amounts of lethal material into the ground ahead of passage of the legislation, creating numerous Superfund sites that towns are still contending with today.

The newly dyed tape comes out of the barrels dripping wet, so it needs to be rolled onto a drying drum, prepping it for the next step. If needed, the zipperheads are custom-painted to match. Once you've got the tape and zipperheads the right color, you can start making zippers.

An operator threads the dyed tape and metal wire into a machine that punches out 2,200 teeth per minute, clamping them onto the fabric with incredible speed. Another machine cuts the tape, adds reinforcement material to the bottom, and stamps the zipper base to the end.

Then the handwork really begins. For premium zippers, UCAN's operators clip the zipperhead to the pull by hand to preserve painted or polished finishes. Each zipper is zipped up, inspected, and bundled, packaged, and shipped out. That's a lot of handling, but makes all the difference in the look and feel of the finished product.

Plenty of apparel manufacturers care not one whit which zipper is installed in their products; it's just another component sewn into cheaper garments that might fail sooner or later. UCAN appeals to buyers who absolutely do care—luxury brands that want well-crafted, custom accents—and companies like American Roots that are committed to supporting domestic companies. For high-end fashion brands, quick turnaround of a small-run customized product is a godsend. It means that if a product is selling well, they can make more.

UCAN's supply chain is fairly resilient to the caprices of international shipping. They import the metal wire that their machines punch into zipper teeth, the plastic that they injection-mold into teeth, the cotton tape onto which zipper teeth are clamped, and all their paints and dyes. While these things might come from abroad, they can be regularly stocked to hedge against uneven delivery times and availability.

Labor costs are Malan's biggest issue. When the minimum wage in L.A. went up to $15, he had to discontinue certain lines because they were too labor-intensive. Thankfully, all his employees are on their spouse's insurance plans, which makes UCAN at all possible.

Now in his late forties with three children of his own, Malan has no regrets that he stayed in the business, but that doesn't mean he wants his kids to take over. It's been tough—UCAN is now down to twenty employees—and he isn't bullish about the future. Malan's fashion customers are faithful to his company right up to the point that they get bought out by private equity firms. That's when they change management, scale up, and begin scrutinizing the bottom line. "Price comes into play," Malan says. "They always find a cheaper product."

But he's learned that working with the bigger companies is infinitely worse. "I'm all for capitalism, but when they control your profits and margins, it's something else. Remember when Walmart had big advertisements saying they wanted to bring manufacturing back to the U.S.? I've worked with Walmart. They drove prices down so low, it was impossible for us to operate."

UCAN nearly worked with Toyota until Malan noticed that the contract demanded a 2 percent decrease in pricing year over year. "How do we, as a small business, make a profit with that?"

54 OPERATIONS

To make hoodies, Ben and Whitney also needed a pattern, so they called Ann Russo again, this time to spec the parts for a rock-solid garment. Ann gave Ben and Whitney her standard rap: *Did they have money? Did they have a size chart?* "You could go in two different stores, buy a medium shirt, and they'd be totally different, so you must know your market," Ann said. "You need to know: Are you selling to the tall, skinny gay guy, or are you selling to the beer belly guy who drinks a six-pack?"

Ben and Whitney knew their market—union men and women who needed heavy, warm sweatshirts that could take a beating on the job.

Ann designed the American Roots hoodie roomy enough to accommodate big shoulders, spare tires, and plenty of layering underneath. The garment had a complex construction that would make it exceptionally tough but expensive to make, requiring fifty-four operations and six different kinds of industrial sewing machines—each costing about $2,000. The machines had plenty of moving parts that sometimes needed to be tweaked or replaced, which meant Ben and Whitney would have to depend on a repair person to keep their operation going.

The pièce de résistance of the American Roots hoodie design was, of course, its hood, which bore little resemblance to the fast fashion hood—often just a single piece of folded fleece, the result being an amorphous appendage more akin to a slouchy head-pocket agnostic about staying in place. Instead, the American Roots hood would be tailored to wrap the head in warmth like a parka, without slipping down over your eyes; it would have so much weight and structure that when you flipped it up, it remained there, even in a strong wind.

To get that kind of result, the hood was constructed of six fabric panels—three for the shell and three for the lining—to ensure a good fit. Each of those pieces had to be precisely cut to match the pattern. That's a lot of work.

Ben and Whitney followed Ann's recipe:

Step one: Build the hood. Use a grommet machine to punch a pair of metal grommets—made in Massachusetts by family-owned, fifty-year-old U.S. Slide Fastener Corp.—into the side panels to create a reinforced hole for the drawstring. Then sew together the three hoodie panels—two sides and a top—that comprised the shell and lining with the heavy-duty 5-thread overlock machine (also called a serger), an impressive multitasker that simultaneously wraps thread around the raw fabric edges to prevent fraying while straight-stitching pieces together, a seam that doubles as a "lock" for the wrapper threads. It also has a blade that trims the raw edges of the fabric (called selvage) as it goes, ensuring a neat, straight edge.

Because the cotton fleece of the American Roots hoodie is so thick, the hood's panel seams would have to be topstitched with a double-needle lockstitch machine, which lays down two parallel rows of stitches, flattening out the connection.

Once this was done, the inner and outer hoods would be sewn together with the 4-thread overlock machine, which was a lighter-duty version of the aforementioned 5-thread. The drawstring was then threaded through the grommets and held in place where the inner and outer hood halves met while they were folded together like a clamshell. Using a single-needle lockstitch, a channel for the drawstring would be sewn into the rim of the hood.

Step two: Prep the waistband and cuffs. The stretchiest components of the garment were made of a separate rib-knit cotton-Lycra fabric that had enough give that the wearer could move without feeling confined but would bounce back into place. The cuff pieces would be folded in half and sewn into a wrist-size circle with a single-needle lockstitch. The long waistband piece would also be folded in half lengthwise, then the ends would be stitched to a double-layer two-inch-by-two-inch fleece panel to give it some extra strength where the waistband met the zipper.

Step three: Set the pockets and American Roots labels onto the left and right front panels. This required four separate operations using a single-needle lockstitch machine.

Now the hoodie could come together.

Studying the pattern, Whitney planned the order of construction like this:

1. Join the back to the left and right front panels at the shoulder (5-thread overlock).
2. Topstitch the shoulder seams (double-needle lockstitch).
3. Set each sleeve into the armholes (5-thread overlock).
4. Topstitch the armhole seams (double-needle lockstitch).
5. Attach the hood to the garment (4-thread overlock).
6. Topstitch the seam where the hood meets the body of the sweatshirt (double-needle lockstitch).
7. Add twill tape inside the neckline to reinforce the hood/ body seam (single-needle lockstitch).
8. Close the sides of the hoodie (4-thread overlock).
9. Attach the waistband to the bottom of the garment (4-thread overlock).
10. Set the cuffs into the end of the sleeves (4-thread overlock).
11. Stitch twill tape onto the front edges of the hoodie to prep for the zipper (4-thread overlock).

12. Set the left and right sides of the zipper (single-needle lockstitch).
13. Topstitch the zipper seams (single-needle lockstitch).

Once American Roots had a few trained stitchers, each sweatshirt would take about forty-three minutes of total work time to construct. As it came off the line, someone would have to go examine it carefully, looking for mistakes and stray threads to snip away. If a garment passed inspection, it would get a paper tag, then be folded and poly-bagged.

Whitney and Ben were almost ready to go into production. But where would they get their fabric?

Maybe, like me, you assumed there was a warehouse somewhere full of bolts of sweatshirt material, waiting for orders to come in. That's not how manufacturing works in the U.S. No one stocks that much fabric; it would be a huge waste of time and resources for a mill to manufacture and warehouse stock. Instead, most fabrics in the U.S. are made on demand.

The cotton fleece in the American Roots hoodie was literally built from the ground up, and it began in the fields of the American South and Southwest—Texas, Georgia, and Mississippi. When it's warm and the danger of frost has passed, cotton seeds are mechanically deposited in neat rows across millions of acres in the Sunbelt. With regular irrigation, the seedlings quickly branch and flower into low, scrubby bushes with deep roots. After eighteen weeks, fluffy cotton bolls (from the Dutch word *bolle,* meaning "sphere") emerge from the spot where the plant shed its flowers. These bolls hold seeds, but in genetically modified cotton, they can't regenerate because their offspring aren't exact genetic copies, forcing farmers to buy new seeds every year.

I've worn plenty of cotton in my life, but I'd never seen it in its natural form until mid-October 2020, when I went down to Noxubee, Mississippi, for the cotton harvest. I drove from Memphis east across

Mississippi to Tupelo and turned south along Highway 45 on a forty-nine-mile stretch notable as the first paved roadway in the South (completed in 1915 to ease transport of cotton). I drove past vast cotton fields, many already picked bare. In the distance, seven-foot-high round bales of raw cotton wrapped in yellow, blue, and pink (for Breast Cancer Awareness) dotted the fields; soon they'd be loaded onto flatbed trucks with a forklift and transported to the local gin.

Cotton farms in Mississippi run big, like Tracy and Bill Skinner's 2,600 acres in Noxubee, but with the help of modern equipment they need just a handful of people to manage. The three men who the Skinners employ keep the $50,000 John Deere 1705 planter and the $700,000 John Deere 770 cotton picker (with air-conditioned cab) in tip-top shape. Cotton is bathed with more chemicals than any other crop, though it accounts for just 2.5 percent of the world's farmland. During growing season, they oversee irrigation and aerial insecticide spraying of the crops. (Fun fact: Delta Air Lines got its start as an aerial spraying company in the Mississippi Delta.)

When it's time to harvest their cotton, the Skinners run their picker from dawn to dusk, for a couple of weeks, hoping to beat the rains, which slow down the harvesting process and degrade the quality of the cotton. Due to climate change, Texas and Mississippi are getting wetter, which makes timing a harvest more difficult. The 555 horsepower picker comes with a thumping sound system and a swiveling leather seat with a massage feature, and uses computer-aided technology connected to sensors to automatically run along planted rows, stripping four acres of cotton—twelve rows at a time—in ten hours.

The picker pulls up raw cotton and a lot of other plant material with it, and automatically bales the raw harvest, dumping wrapped bales on the field when they reach capacity.

Seed-sharing and exchanging knowledge about working with indigenous seeds were once the glue that held farming communities together. In the past few decades, seed companies like Monsanto have positioned themselves smack in the middle of that social structure, requiring farmers to buy new seeds from the company every year and use Monsanto's products and expertise, instead of their neighbors'.

In the natural world, variety nurtures the ecosystem. Native plants and animals establish mutually dependent relationships, called biomes, that support each other in good times and in bad. These biomes encompass all living things, including the birds, animals, insects, and plants that fertilize the soil, spread seeds, and minimize destructive organisms. Diversity makes systems more resilient and adaptable.

For these reasons, agricultural monoculture—growing a single crop in a region—wreaks havoc on the environment across the globe. Removing the natural variety of plants from an area destroys micro-habitats, throwing everything out of balance. To reestablish a semblance of order and protect whatever single crop farmers want to grow, they're forced to replace all those insects, birds, and animals with a chemical arsenal of fertilizers and pesticides.

There's another problem with building dependency on a single crop. If it does fail, which the potato crop did in Ireland when a mold destroyed half the harvest between 1845 and 1852, those dependent on that crop will starve. An estimated one million Irish died during the Potato Famine, and another million fled the country.

The monopolization of the seed industry has further threatened the earth's flora and fauna, as well as farming communities. In 2019, 41 percent of U.S. acreage was planted with Monsanto's Deltapine cotton seeds. In India, the number of farmers using genetically modified seeds is double that. India is the second-largest cotton-producing country in the world, and two decades ago Monsanto muscled its way into that market. In 1997, the company launched a campaign to convince India's hundreds of thousands of peasant farmers to swap their native cotton varieties for Monsanto's genetically modified seeds, promising miraculous insect resistance and high yields. With 88 percent of Indian farmers hooked on the GM seeds, Monsanto now collects more than $200 million from them for seeds and pesticides each year.

When advocates for India's farmers claimed that Monsanto's seed patents violated Indian law, the company went straight to the WTO, which ruled in favor of the multinational. Over a few generations, the GM seeds in India lost their resistance to pink bollworm, which led to poor yields and higher pesticide use. Some advocates claim that the seeds may also have caused widespread livestock death. Countless Indians incurred astronomical debt and loss of livelihood, which, as of 2019, has been linked to an estimated 300,000 farmer suicides in the country.

Farmer suicides in the U.S. have also gone up 40 percent in less than two decades, a phenomenon linked to mounting debt, social isolation, and climate change.

Before the invention of the cotton gin, cotton seeds were once the bane of the textile industry. You could grow the cotton, you could pick off the bolls, but extricating the hard bits of plant and seeds from cotton fibers was a major chore. Without an easy way to do this, cotton textile manufacturing depended on a lot of people putting in lots of hours, which is why cotton wasn't grown much in the colonial South. It simply wasn't a good use of time, money, and enslaved labor when tobacco and other agricultural products still fetched top dollar.

Farmers like the Skinners now pool resources to build tax-exempt ginning co-ops. Ginning produces USDA-graded cotton lint bales (500 pounds each) and cotton seeds. The seeds can be sold as animal feed and lubricant, which covers the cost of ginning and baling, and then some. One acre in California yields 1,250 pounds of cotton lint and 2,200 pounds of seed, worth around $176. Ginning is pretty much a break-even business.

Once it's ginned, baled, graded, and purchased, the Skinners' cotton gets trucked to U.S. mills, warehouses, or down to Mobile, Alabama, where it's loaded on ships and sent out into the world. The U.S. supplies more than 35 percent of the world's raw cotton and is the leading buyer of finished cotton goods. Most of those finished goods come from China—the world's biggest buyer and purchaser of cotton—with India and Pakistan running a distant second and third, respectively.

If you love to gamble, you can mess around with cotton futures on the New York Mercantile Exchange (QTT), but you won't be able to corner the market *Trading Places*-style because the Commodity Futures Trading Commission (CFTC), established in 1974, limits how much of one commodity a single investor can buy. (So many rules and regulations holding back the free market!)

But if you're just a mill owner like ninety-year-old Sintex Industries in India, you can buy American cotton through cotton co-ops or middlemen using the daily global commodities price index as a guide. American cotton quality is carefully monitored by the USDA, which analyzes and grades a plug from every single bale of cotton to be sold. Some buyers, like Sintex, are willing to pay top dollar for Uncle Sam's guarantee of quality. At least, they *were*. Sintex supplied fabric to high-end clients such as Armani, Hugo Boss, Diesel, and Burberry, until the market for these textiles tanked during the pandemic. In 2021, Sintex filed for bankruptcy.

So who buys American cotton in the U.S.? Oh, you've never heard of Trelleborg Engineered Coated Fabrics? The North Carolina–based textile company takes in $4 billion annually manufacturing a staggering array of polymer-coated fabrics for every industry under the sun, from automotive to defense to marine to apparel. American Cord & Webbing in Woonsocket, Rhode Island, makes, you guessed it—cord and webbing for use as seat belts and straps, as well as plastic and metal hardware like the click-together clips you find on backpacks. American Cord & Webbing also makes the flat cotton cord sewn into every American Roots hoodie, aka, the drawstring.

Big buyers = big demand = lots of leverage. Ann knew that a small company like American Roots would have a tough time finding fabric. The few mills left service only regular clients, which means relationships are everything in this business, especially when cotton is in such demand.

Ben and Whitney didn't know much about the fabric business and didn't have the bandwidth to thoroughly research the trade. Ben was selling. Whitney was managing their small cadre of stitchers. They were scrambling to master a new garment. They thought they had their guy—a fabric dealer in North Carolina they'd found after a vigorous internet search.

Then along came the Painters Union.

CAN YOU MAKE 5,000?

One of the first people Ben reached was Jeff Sullivan, the tough, progressive head of District Council 35 of the International Union of Painters and Allied Trades, representing 4,000 painters, glaziers, and maintenance trade workers in New England. Jeff's members did dangerous jobs. They scaled tall buildings, worked with toxic chemicals, and spent a lot of time on ladders. It took constant union oversight to ensure that job sites met OSHA safety standards to prevent accidents and injuries. Union members' jobs were also under constant threat of nonunion, and sometimes undocumented, lower-paid workers—people who might have less training and be more willing to put themselves at physical risk. Anyone could wield a paintbrush, right?

Jeff was passionate about protecting his union brothers and sisters. Through his organization, they had pensions, health insurance, and annuities so they could retire before their bodies gave out. But the opioid epidemic had hit America's construction industry particularly hard—workers therein were four times as likely to become addicted than workers in any other realm.

When Ben told Jeff what he and Whitney were up to, Jeff wanted to see the hoodie for himself, so Ben sent him a prototype, warning him that it was an untested product. Jeff was willing to bet on his former union colleague. He was impressed with the hoodie's design and construction and ordered 1,700 for an upcoming safety conference.

Ben could hardly contain his excitement. "Jeff Sullivan—I swear there'll be a room named after him at this company someday," he says. As soon as he got off the phone, he told Whitney they'd scored big.

"That's the pattern of this business," Whitney says, remembering that day. "Ben says to the client, *Yes. We can do it,* but then comes to me and says, *Figure this out.*"

Did their workers have enough training to pull it off?

Before they could even try, they had to get that fabric. Seventeen hundred sweatshirts would use up about 4,000 yards. Whitney also wanted plenty more for practice and mistakes. So Ben called their fabric guy and told him they needed 5,000 yards of heavyweight cotton fleece.

"The phone goes real quiet," Ben recalls, "and I should have known then that he was a middleman, but I was in a panic because I'm like, *If we don't get this fabric in, our workers can't work.*"

"Everything okay?" Ben asked.

"Yeah, we can do that," the fabric guy finally answered. "When you need it? Like two, three months?"

"I need it now. We've got to make 1,700 of these things."

The seller said the soonest he could get the fleece to them was four or five weeks.

Somehow, Ben says, he was able to get them the fleece within the week. "He drove up the fabric by himself. He literally drove all night from North Carolina. God bless him, he did. He drove it up, we made the sweatshirts. I think we finished the order at 1 a.m. the day before it was due. And I'm calling Lauren, Jeff's right-hand woman, and I'm saying, *Lauren, we got it. We're gonna be on time, I'm gonna deliver them myself.*"

The American Roots hoodies were a hit . . . with, *ahem,* the suggestion of adding a little more Lycra in the waistband because, you know, that six-pack.

Ben and Whitney had moved their factory to a larger space on Westfield Street to accommodate the sixteen people who were working for them. They were building the company, moving product, training constantly, but they were still broke because they were plowing every last cent back into their business.

Their first son, Arlo, was born in February 2017 when Ben and Whitney had just $147 in the bank. Tod and Mary Ann traveled to Maine to help with the newborn, and when Mary Ann saw that Ben's Ford Explorer's tailpipe was held in place with a coat hanger, she told him, "My grandson isn't getting in that car." The Waxmans owed $9,000 for payroll, due that Friday, so Ben went right back to selling the day after Arlo was born. He had to raise more cash.

Richard Trumka of the AFL-CIO had been watching Ben's business from the sidelines and liked what he saw. One of Trumka's top priorities for the twenty-first-century labor movement was engaging women and people of color, the latter projected to make up the majority of America's workforce without a four-year college degree by 2031. He knew that most of the American Roots stitchers were female immigrants and asylum-seekers—precisely the kinds of people he wanted to reach.

For Trumka's reelection celebration at the AFL-CIO convention in October 2017, he invited American Roots' union leader, Anaam Jabbir, to speak. He felt that Anaam would be an excellent representative of the new American workforce.

The event would be a four-day gathering in St. Louis, Missouri, of AFL-CIO bigwigs—key federation leadership and representatives of all the AFL-CIO affiliates, 4,000 people in all. The federation was preparing to launch a commission on the future of work to explore ways to become more resilient and responsive in a rapidly evolving economy.

The night before Anaam's speech, they brought her into the convention center to practice; it was a daunting space with high ceilings and a booming PA system. The next day, thousands of people would be sitting at the tables set up before her.

Anaam had never spoken to such a large group, and certainly not in English. She spoke into the mic and was surprised to hear her voice bounce around the room.

The following day, Esther López, the international secretary-treasurer of the United Food & Commercial Workers, emceed the event, which was strongly focused on inclusion and equality. Wearing a bright yellow jacket, the lifetime labor advocate addressed the crowd: "What is the role of the American labor movement in a polarized nation? I know that it is our unions that have the power to bring us together. When we invest in American manufacturing with good jobs and good union wages, America becomes stronger. There are examples from New York to California, and we'd like to highlight one of those today. Please, roll the video."

Ben, Whitney, and baby Arlo appeared on the huge screen to Esther's left. The video showed scenes from their Portland factory and included sound bites from workers.

"It's important to be part of something that's bigger than yourself," one young worker said to the camera.

"We always talk about providing a space where people can come in and fulfill the American dream," Whitney said. "Well, Ben and I are now able to do that."

One female worker wearing a blue hijab said, "When I say that I am an American citizen, it means a lot to me." Then she smiled and turned away, overcome with emotion.

"My mom and dad taught me and my brothers the value of hard work," Ben said in a voiceover. "I look at my son as potentially the third generation in the textile industry."

The video ended on Whitney. "This does work," she said with confidence. "Everyone thought we were crazy to go into this business. They said that manufacturing can't be done in America. We're here to say that it can."

Back on the stage, Esther introduced Anaam as one of the stars of the video, and Anaam emerged in a black hijab to the twanging guitar of a country music ditty blasting over the PA.

In spite of all the preparation, she was nervous. "It's hard to see yourself on the screen," she mumbled into the mic. The audience laughed, putting her at ease.

Anaam steeled herself and then began in a quiet voice. "I'm here today with a simple message. I love my job. I love my union. I am a proud new U.S. citizen. I'm strong and I'm powerful because I have a voice on the job. American-made, union-made, that's how we will bring this country together. Thank you."

People leapt to their feet. Anaam backed away, eyes welling up with tears of relief and gratitude. Esther reached out and enveloped her in a big, warm embrace as the audience—predominantly white men in suits and ties—cheered her on.

"I'll never forget that," Ben says. "Anaam gives her speech and I was like, *Holy fucking shit.* She got two standing ovations. People had tears in their eyes. I raced back to my sales booth, and there was a line fifteen people deep."

Ben started shaking hands and handing out cards. All the while, he was vaguely aware of a gray-haired guy lingering in the back corner of the booth, scrutinizing an American Roots hoodie. He waited until the crowd left and then approached Ben.

"I love your story," the stranger said. "This is what we need in America."

Ben stuck out his hand and introduced himself.

"I'm Gary Peterson, the head of TWU Local 591, Air Division— Dallas, Texas. But I'm from Chicago," he added quickly. "And I really like this sweatshirt."

TWU stood for Transport Workers Union of America, which represented more than 150,000 airline, railroad, transit, and utility workers. Like all unions in the 2020s, TWU was expanding with the new economy, adding museum curators, health department employees, and bike-share workers to its membership.

Gary himself was an impressive guy. He'd come up through the air force, then worked as an aircraft mechanic at American Airlines. He held a master's degree in dispute resolution.

Gary asked Ben, "Can you do 5,000?"

Ben tried to contain his cool while doing quick math in his head—5,000 hoodies could make or break them that year. It was an enormous number for their small shop. "We can do that, when do you need them?"

"Anytime next year."

So Ben figured, *Awesome. We've got time.*

They would need 12,000 yards of fabric—that's nearly seven miles, half the length of Manhattan. "We're talking thousands and thousands of dollars' worth," Ben says.

Ben left St. Louis "fucking high as a kite." (Metaphorically, mind you.) On the drive to St. Louis he'd gotten a speeding ticket in Connecticut, and on the way back he got another one in upstate New York.

When Ben finally arrived back at the factory, Whitney immediately ordered fabric so they could start making hoodies in January. When the fabric arrived—12,000 yards of heavyweight slate-gray cotton fleece—they had it cut to Ann's pattern, then stitched like hell and began shipping the finished hoodies to forty locals across the country.

"We're killing it," Ben says. "At least we *think* we are."

Two weeks before Arlo's first birthday, in February 2018, Ben was upstairs in his kid's room, putting the little guy to bed. He stood for a long time gazing at his son, gently stroking Arlo's tiny back. Outside, a light snow began to fall, and Ben watched flakes swirl around the streetlight at the end of the driveway. To the born-and-bred New Englander, snow meant sledding and skating, snowmen and snow days—all things his son would someday enjoy, just like he had. He inched the blanket farther over Arlo's tiny shoulders.

In his pocket, Ben felt his phone buzz, shaking him out of his reverie. He tiptoed out of the room and quietly shut the door, then dug out his phone. It was a text from Glenn Olsen, secretary-treasurer of TWU Local 591.

"Hey, we got a problem," it read. Attached was a photo of one of the hoodies they'd just received. There were holes in the pockets; the knit was unraveling at the sleeves. The fabric was literally falling apart.

It had taken American Roots six weeks to cut, sew, and ship 2,000 hoodies. And they were all seconds—hoodies that hadn't passed inspection.

Ben texted Glenn: "I'll call you shortly. I'm putting my kid to bed."

He walked downstairs to Whitney, who was lying on the sofa after a long day at the factory. "The blood had drained out of my face and my balls were sucked into my stomach," Ben remembers.

He showed her the text on his phone.

"It was like the end of the world," Whitney says. "I thought, *This is it. It's over.*"

THE FABRIC KING
OF 38TH STREET

Ben and Whitney had no financial backers. They had no deep-pocketed investors, no banks to extend a loan big enough to cover the loss. They'd already paid for the fabric. Half the order was already made.

Ben finally called back Glenn and said, "I don't know what's going on, but whatever it is, we'll make it right. We'll fix it."

Then he took a deep breath and called Gary Peterson of TWU.

Gary was firm but merciful. "This is not good," he told Ben.

Ben said that they'd take all the hoodies back and redo them. Keep in mind, Ben reminds me, "I didn't know how we were going to make the order happen. We'd spent all the money to buy the fabric and pay our people to make the hoodies." Would the union president give them another chance?

"This is the labor movement," Gary told Ben. "You're a company that's paying good wages. You're paying good benefits. You're trying to do the impossible. We're going to stand by you."

Hearing that, Ben thought he might cry.

But what had gone wrong with the first fabric? The seller was a middleman who cut and run when Ben told him about the flaws. The Waxmans could have hired a lawyer and sued, but that's not where they wanted to put their limited funds and energy. They also didn't want a lawsuit on their hands when they were starting to think about building a corporate board and courting investors.

They had to take the loss and figure it out themselves. Ben and Whitney borrowed $20,000 from friends and family to redo the order.

Then Ben called patternmaker Ann Russo for advice.

"Benny," she told him, "you gotta fucking listen to me. I told you, fabrics are a delicate thing. You can't just buy shit from anybody." She told him to get in touch with Ned Pilchman of American Fabrics, one of the last "fabric converters" in the country.

Ben didn't know what a converter was, but he called the number Ann gave him. When Ned picked up his own phone, Ben thought to himself, *Now this is old-school.* He felt that finally they were tapping into the ancient American textile network.

Ned *was* old-school. He and his partner in North Carolina didn't own any mills, cotton fields, or dyehouses. Instead, they acted like general contractors of fabrics. They custom-designed a textile according to a client's needs, managed its production every step of the way, and arranged to have it delivered to their customers' cut-and-sew factories.

Ben wasn't going to make the same mistake again and hire a fly-by-night fabric seller. Instead, he got into his truck and drove down to meet Ned in person at his rented office in New York's Garment District—232 West 38th Street.

The place looked pretty much the same as it did in 1949. On both sides of narrow 38th Street, twelve-story Deco buildings stared each other down, creating a shadowy canyon of a street. To get to number 232, Ben dodged sidewalk grates, double-parked trucks, and the steel latticework of temporary scaffolding, past the few storefronts still servicing the garment business. He glanced in shop windows and saw glittery synthetic stuff with sequins and spandex, plus a vast assortment of trimmings and notions—buttons, hooks, mirrors, rhinestones, and feathers—the last vestiges of a once-booming industry, now mainly supporting New York's costumers, boutique designers, and custom tailors. In shops overlooking the street, a few designers, stitchers, and patternmakers continue the clothing-making tradition.

There was a time when the Garment District teemed with people pushing garment racks loaded with locally produced apparel off freight elevators, up and down the avenues, onto trucks. That time has passed. The logistics of getting large trucks into and out of the city now makes it a terrible place to try to do any kind of fabricating on a grand scale. Instead, hair salons, bars, pizza parlors, and vacant storefronts fill the voids.

Ben rode the freight elevator to the eighth floor and followed a narrow hallway to a door labeled "American Fabrics."

"Come in," Ned hollered from his desk. Ben opened the door to a tiny, brightly lit museum of cotton fabric wonders. Hundreds of fabric samples hung neatly on racks or folded on tables, each labeled with an American Fabrics style code. In the back of the room by the window, sixtysomething Ned sat in a sagging and duct-taped office chair with two cell phones and a giant magnifying glass at his fingertips, no computer in sight.

"It's amazing you're talking to me, Ben," Ned began in a thick New York accent. "I'm a goddamn dinosaur. I should be extinct, under some headstone, someplace on Magic Mountain."

Ned had been in the business since he fled Nicaragua in 1980 just after the Sandinistas overthrew dictator Anastasio Somoza. He said he was teaching English there, though he gave off an *Our Man in Havana* vibe. Ben sat opposite Ned, who laid on his well-practiced schlub schtick. He quipped, "I came back with one suitcase and a banana."

Ned's father had made a living selling cotton knits, and when Ned landed back in the States he fell into the business. "I'm not that smart," he told Ben. "I was a mediocre student. I'm not a Harvard grad, I'm not an MBA. I hate sports, football is boring. I don't care about the Yankees. I'm up all night listening to talk shows. So I said, *What the hell, I'll try selling fabric.*"

The one thing that got Ned out of bed was cotton. Don't bother him with synthetics. "You put a crease in polyester pants and come back in a thousand years and it'll still be there," he said. "God didn't do that." He believed in natural fibers because they're environmentally friendly and can be re-extruded.

He said that it was patriotic to be in manufacturing: "I make stuff and I sell it, so I generate wealth." He added, "I'm not buying fabric made in China and just marking it up—I bought it for a buck, I sell to you for two—great goddamn deal. No, I'm the guy that went out and found the yarn at a good price and slammed it through some stupid-ass knitting machines."

But the complexity of making things and moving things in the U.S. was a constant headache, even for a veteran like Ned. "I ship it on some truck where they fuck it up, get it to some guy who forgot it's there. Tell some other guy that they dyed it wrong, made it the wrong color, forgot to compact it.* And I do all this without getting it to my customer five weeks late."

Transporting bolts of fabric was a particularly troublesome business. "It's heavy, heavy, heavy," Ned said. Because it's rolled on sixty-inch-wide bolts, fabric is also unwieldy, so shippers tack on a surcharge. Fabric can be crushed, so you can't stack pallets of it to the ceiling—you need scaffolding in the truck to lighten the load on the bottom bolts, all of which adds to Ned's woes.

"If I ship a roll of white fabric like that," he said, pointing to a bolt, "they seem to think it's fair game to throw it all over the truck. They're not happy until that plastic wrap is ripped. They're not happy at all. They haven't done their job until that fabric looks like shit. The bag gets ripped and my customer calls me. *Hello? How come my fabric's dirty?* I say, *Because they played basketball with the goddamn roll.*"

Ned rattled off the names of big mills that he used to work with in the 1980s—Burlington, Gilford, Cannon, Champion, Hanes,

---

* Compacting is a mechanical process that reduces shrinkage in the lengthwise direction of a fabric.

Russell Athletic. "Russell had a brand of sweatshirts called Discus. They could dye a million pounds of fabric a week. They were a vertical manufacturer. They would buy yarn, knit it, dye it, finish it, cut it, sew it, bag it, weigh it. They did everything. They even owned cotton farms. I think they had 30,000 or 40,000 employees sewing all day, three shifts around the clock. The company was so big, believe it or not, they built the factory around a railroad spur and every night they'd back up twenty boxcars and fill it with sweatshirts." They all went to China, he said.

"The thing about the textile industry is it's always been very movable. Hi. You can sew? Yeah. All's I need is electricity. You plug in a sewing machine, get a building, get some ladies, and sew."

Ned's analysis of the state of things in the U.S. was thus: "We didn't protect our industries. It wasn't fair. If you wanted to offshore, other countries charged duties, who knows what they were. But we didn't charge duties here. And it was just cheaper to sew in '07 in Haiti, Dominican Republic, Nicaragua. I had a lady who had a children's clothing company. They set up all these factories in El Salvador where they were paying 75 cents an hour. But you know what the going rate was in China? Fifteen cents an hour. Guess where it went."

Ben told Ned what happened to their hoodies and asked him what went wrong.

"Let me punch the fabric," Ned told him.

"What's that mean?" Ben asked him.

"I gotta punch it," Ned said. "I gotta see the weight of the fleece."

Ben handed Ned a sample of the flawed fabric, and Ned examined it through the huge magnifying glass he kept on his deck.

"This isn't good fabric," he told him.

The cotton fleece American Roots used to make the flawed sweatshirts had come from a mill in North Carolina. Ned suspected that someone had mixed different grades of cotton into the same batch, which prevented the plant fibers from twisting together properly. Maybe the mill operators had rushed the job; maybe they'd cut corners because the Waxmans' order was so small; maybe it was just a dumb mistake. Or maybe American Roots had been sold fabric seconds.

Ben said they were eager to cut their losses and move on.

Ned asked Ben, "What do you need?"

"I need 12,000 yards of heavyweight cotton fleece," he answered. "And I need you to cut me a deal because I can't pay the same price I did before."

Ned eyed the Mainer. He looked sincere. Ann Russo had vouched for him. "I'm going out on a limb here," Ned said. "I'm going to help you out."

And he did. He delivered 12,000 yards of top-notch cotton fleece, and American Roots shipped 5,000 perfect hoodies out four months later.

For Ben and Whitney's heavyweight hoodie, Ned designed a double-sided knit fabric with a thinner-gauge ring-spun cotton yarn on one side (for a tight, wind-resistant shell) and a thicker gauge on the inside that he knew would nap up nicely. Ned also specified a certain amount of Lycra for the rib-knit fabric that would be used in the hoodies' waistbands and cuffs.

He then called North Carolina–based Parkdale, one of the largest manufacturers of spun yarn in the world, and ordered the yarn weights he needed. Parkdale buys a huge amount of cotton from farmers, spins it, winds it onto eight-pound spools, and ships it by 1,000-pound pallets to fabric mills around the world. Ned prefers to use mills in North and South Carolina—keeping it close keeps his shipping costs down. Parkdale knit the fabric to Ned's specification, then napped one side and dyed it navy or black to match the approved samples.

After four decades working in the textile industry, however, Ned Pilchman isn't bullish on manufacturing in America. He says making things is simply too hard to stomach these days. Too many machines to maintain, too many workers to manage. He's learned how difficult it is to build a business that depends on people coming to work every day. "I mean, you have a group of people that's supposed to sew on the hems. If they don't show up, you got 10,000 garments with no hems."

When asked how the Chinese are able to do it, he says, "Because the Chinese have a knack, or maybe it's just a cultural thing. I don't know what it is, because we used to be able to do this. New York used to be the center of the garment world. There was very experienced people, experienced managers, you know what I mean?"

Gary Peterson got his new shipment of American Roots hoodies and became a loyal customer.

Four years later, he says, "Ben has such a good heart and really takes care of his employees. It's truly a family company. It means a lot to us that he's doing all-USA manufacturing because it's been hard for us to find products truly made here."

Gary says that a while back, he placed a huge order of backpacks from another union shop. He was assured that the bags were made in America. When Gary inspected them carefully, though, he found that they'd actually been made in China. Only the embroidery had been done by Americans.

He says that finding the real deal has been exhausting. "Companies will say, *We're a union shop,* but we get burned. We had a vendor cutting made-in-China labels out of their shirts. For leaders of unions, we're never gonna be successful if they're cutting labels out."

He was convinced American Roots was the real thing. "Ben and Whitney are doing all the right things from start to finish, there's no cutting corners with them. Their hoodies may cost a little more," Gary says, "but we'd rather support working families."

FOLLOW THE RIVER

In May 2018, with annual revenue closing in on $800,000 and a staff of twenty-seven, Ben and Whitney moved American Roots out of the cramped Westfield workshop. Working with a real estate broker who'd grown up with Ben, they found 20,000 square feet in the cavernous fourth floor of the nineteenth-century Dana Warp Mill Building.

The blocks-long brick edifice had been built to house industrial spinners, carders, and bales of raw cotton to make warp—thin, strong yarn used to thread looms for weaving fabric. During the peak of New England manufacturing in the late 1800s, Dana Warp put out more than four million pounds of the stuff each year. After World War II, Dana Mill struggled. Interest in natural fibers waned as chemical companies introduced synthetic fabrics into the market. Dana Mill ceased operation some six decades ago. Now the building is underused. The real estate company that owns the building divided and subdivided the seven-hundred-foot-long expanses with studs and drywall for office space and artist studios, but you can still find metal shavings from the heavy textile-making machinery, long gone, ground into the floorboards.

Ben and Whitney got married in July 2018. Their second son,

Wyatt, was born in October 2019. "We did everything backwards," Ben says. "We bought a house and started a business, had a kid, and then got married."

Each morning before dawn, Ben stuck his head into his sons' room. The warm, humid air, thick with their night breath, hit him straight in the heart. He inhaled and felt a rush of pride. His boys. Whitney's boys. Their boys. In the darkness of the room, they slept guileless, without fear, warm and safe, their tiny limbs poking out of blankets here and there, Arlo's blond wisps like a clump of downy feathers sprouting from the pillow. Ben closed the door silently, his heart full.

The boys were just two of the reasons Ben got into his big gray truck every morning and rumbled down the empty Westbrook streets to the factory.

His father was another.

In 2018, Dan Waxman became another casualty of the unraveling American system. Dan had sold ads for *The Boston Globe* since 1999, back when the paper was owned by *The New York Times*. Claiming hardship, the company froze pension contributions a few years after Dan started, greatly reducing his retirement earnings. In 2015, billionaire John Henry bought the *Globe* and, threatening layoffs, encouraged employees like Dan to accept early buyouts. Dan eventually accepted one in 2018 for a fraction of his pay, and only three months of COBRA health insurance. Dan is still bitter about that: "I tried to negotiate a better package with management but was told no," he said. "So I took what was offered me."

To Ben, Dan's tragedy was further proof that something was decidedly broken in the American system. How could a hardworking company man lose so much after nearly two decades of faithful service?

Ben rolled through the streets of Westbrook, once a mill town, now a suburb of Portland, as the sun crept weakly over the horizon. He passed modest clapboard houses with tiny lawns frozen under patches of snow and pickup trucks parked in short driveways. Inside were the working people he and Whitney wanted to energize for a new economy.

He drove past the sprawling SAPPI paper mill with its seventy-foot smokestack, red warning lights blinking against the sky. A few of the mill's original nineteenth-century brick structures were still intact, now dwarfed by the giant aluminum-siding-clad sheds built in the 1960s.

The Presumpscot River frothed down a waterfall dividing the old and new mills. In 1882, the paper mill's founder built a grand Queen Anne–style house for his family across the street from the complex at a bend in the river so he could wake up each morning and survey his papermaking kingdom from his front lawn. Within a year, he died, and the home, dubbed "The Elms," was used as a boardinghouse. Eventually, it was abandoned. Who'd want to live across from a massive paper mill?

Just past The Elms, Ben hooked a left onto Brown Street, following the river under a rusty steel railroad bridge—now an unused trunk of Maine Central. The line was finished in the 1870s to carry summer visitors northwest from Portland to the grand Victorian hotels at Sebago Lake, and farther along the Saco River into the White Mountains in New Hampshire, continuing into the Northeast Kingdom in Vermont where it once connected with the Canadian railroad. From the train, riders could glimpse the majestic Mount Washington Hotel in Bretton Woods, now owned by Omni.

After parking his car in the open lot next to Dana Mill, Ben took the freight elevator to the fourth floor. Occasionally, the elevator broke down, sometimes with their supplies or workers inside. Just another thing that could slow them down.

Walking the narrow, dimly lit corridor, Ben listened to the pitted, varnished wood floors of Dana Mill creaking and crackling under his weight. He passed framed-and-matted historical photos of Westbrook and the mill in its heyday. He'd never really studied them. No time.

Ben and Whitney shared much with the Civil War vet who founded Dana Mill in 1866, Woodbury Dana. All three of them strove to be stewards of their small Maine community. Dana led his mill for fifty-six years; in that time, he saw that his employees were treated well.

Under his leadership, Dana Mill offered life insurance and a generous homeownership program, enabling millworkers to invest in their town. By the 1950s, the mill provided accident and life insurance, a pension plan, six paid holidays a year, vacation pay, and workers' compensation insurance.

Likewise, Ben and Whitney started their workers at $15 per hour, with benefits, and made sure they joined the United Steelworkers Local 366. Anaam chaired the American Roots group.

At the end of the hall was the door to American Roots. Ben unlocked the factory and lumbered to his office. His windows overlooked the Presumpscot—like so many Maine waterways, a river that retained its Abenaki name, a reminder that the region had been under the stewardship of the Algonquin people until very recently, and the European descendants who took over learned local geography from them. Prior to industrialization, the river rushed over a dozen falls as it wended its way from Sebago Lake to Casco Bay, where fresh water churned with the sea. Then the colonists began building dam after dam along Maine's rivers. It became impossible for the once-plentiful Atlantic salmon to swim upriver to spawn. Populations dwindled to almost nothing.

Below Ben's window, municipal employees worked heavy machinery all summer, hacking away at the dam that once harnessed the fast-flowing river that powered Dana's mill. Deconstruction of the dam was a victory for the conservationists and fishermen. Thanks to similar dam removals a few years back, the Kennebec and Sebasticook Rivers boasted the largest annual river herring run in the nation, more than three million fish, plus large populations of shad and sturgeon, as well as one of the most impressive gatherings of bald eagles on the Eastern Seaboard, timed with the spring return of the herring.

Half of the exposed brick walls of Ben's office were lined with whiteboards where he scrawled sales figures and projections. Several copies of *The Wall Street Journal,* a gift from his father-in-law, sat unread on his conference table—two folding tables pushed together—the latest editions rolled up like paper burritos.

Gazing out over the Presumpscot while selling their wares or contemplating the great things they'd accomplish with a little more time, a little more money, Ben had witnessed all manner of avian drama. Seagulls regularly congregated along the edge of the mill building's roof, just above his office, and swooped into the thermals coming off the river, so close to his window they sometimes looked like people jumping to their death.

In those quiet moments before the official workday began, Ben's thoughts often turned to Whitney. She was Ben's rock. In meetings, she was a quiet, thoughtful counterpoint to Ben's occasional explosions and exhortations. She spent half her days on the factory floor solving problems like repairing broken machines or moving inventory. She spent the other half figuring out how to keep the factory supplied with the workers, zippers, fabrics, and the machines necessary to keep everything going.

If they had had the cash to build inventory, life would be so much easier. Their staff could sew steadily throughout the year toward evenly spaced goals. Upper management could pace the production schedule to accommodate sick days, vacation days—all the variables that affect a small and vulnerable workforce. Ben and Whitney would have a good sense of their annual labor costs because they wouldn't have to scramble to staff up when Ben landed a big order. They'd also know their supply needs and be able to negotiate early for better pricing.

But American Roots didn't have that kind of capital. Every new order that Ben and the small sales team landed was part victory, part trauma.

American Roots' model was business-to-business, and the bulk of orders came from local union leaders across the country who Ben happened to meet as he traveled from convention to convention with his quick-assemble booth and his samples. It was a demanding schedule. At the beginning of each year, Ben would sit down at his desk with pen and paper to log all the upcoming events. The result of his work was a string of acronyms and dates that his assistant would then decipher to create a spreadsheet.

On any given year, Ben's schedule might look something like this: In March, he'd travel from Maine to Malden for the two-day Massachusetts Building Trade Council convention (MBTC), then hop a plane a couple of weeks later for the International Brotherhood of Electrical Workers (IBEW) in D.C. June would be packed—United Autoworkers (UAW); the American Federation of State, County, and Municipal Employees (AFSCME); and the AFL-CIO. At the end of July, he was in Ohio for the United Steelworkers District 1 convention. August was a mess. In the first week, he was off to Las Vegas for the Ironworkers convention; two days later, in Indiana for UAW; then over to Atlantic City for USW DC 10; another 5,000 miles to San Diego for the United Association of Journeymen and Apprentices of the Plumbing and Pipe Fitting Industry of the United States and Canada (commonly known as the United Association, or simply UA); and back in Atlantic City for USW DC 4. Halfway through September, he'd be in Vegas again for the Transportation Workers Union (TWU). October was brutal. Wilmington, North Carolina, for the NC State AFL-CIO; Denver for the International Foundation of Employee Benefit Plans (IFEBP); New Orleans for Communication Workers of America (CWA); back to D.C. for a subcommittee of the USW. The last stop on his tour, in the first week of November, was Atlanta for the IBEW.

It was optimistic that he'd hit all those dates.

American Roots also had a few part-time sales reps, including Ben's dad, but they weren't as effective as he was because they didn't have that deep union knowledge or Ben's evangelistic made-in-America fervor.

Selling $80 hoodies—even if they were entirely American-sourced and union-made, even if the buyers were generally inclined to support unionized companies—took a lot of convincing. Union decision-makers weren't anything like corporate purchasing agents. They were dead-serious elected leaders who'd risen through their organizations by convincing thousands of their peers that they were tough but fair negotiators, dedicated to serving the myriad needs of their members, and strong enough to stand up to corporate leaders without alienating them. The best union leaders, like Trumka, were exquisitely well informed and brilliant at reading people.

That's why a Willy Loman–like sales pitch hit like lemon juice in the eye. No, to sell to these buyers, you had to be the opposite of slick. You had to be the real deal. Union leaders' bullshit meters were set on stun.

Ben also tried selling to companies whose ethics drove decision-making. Some Maine businesses, like the many local breweries gaining national attention, made excellent prospects. Because they were homegrown, they made the effort to support the local economy that supported them. Ben was always looking for ways to collaborate with these kinds of businesses to elevate both brands.

But life often got in the way. Ben, Whitney, or one of their boys might get sick. Flights might be canceled. The demands of co-running a factory sometimes grounded him. Ben kept a running list of people he'd met on his yellow legal pads, but it took time to translate those notes for his executive assistant. His voice-mail box was often full. He had tens of thousands of unread emails. So much to do.

The handful of people running the administrative end of American Roots were mostly twentysomething New Englanders with college degrees in design or communications or English. They'd signed up with American Roots because they were eager to make a difference; the company's mission resonated with their own vision of a worker-forward America. Start-up culture was also exciting—to be able to work directly with leadership and shape decisions as a young person was a powerful draw.

But tracking all of Ben's promises—sending samples, following up on queries, connecting with leads—plus executing all the other daily tasks of running a factory pulled them in so many different directions that they were often overwhelmed. There was so much to learn about manufacturing, so many ideas floating around that could strengthen the company's internal operations, and not enough time or people to execute properly. The more I visited the factory, the more I began to recognize a certain facial expression—the one that said, *I'm doing my best, but it got away from me and I'm not sure how much longer I can hang on.*

Whenever Ben scored a large order, the first person he'd tell was Whitney. If he happened to be at his desk, she could hear his triumphant "Fuck yeah!" from his office next to hers. Then she'd hear him leap out of his chair, bust open his door, and enter her office to share the details: this many hoodies, this price, this deadline. Whitney would immediately begin strategizing how to shuffle people and machines around to execute the order.

In the spring of 2019, the United Steelworkers magazine featured American Roots stitcher Hanya Al Taher in a royal blue hijab on the cover. Inside, a six-page spread told the story of American Roots thus far and featured photographs of Ben, Whitney, Khalid Al Kinani, Anaam Jabbir, and other employees. They were now a company of thirty people, about to hit $1.1 million in annual revenue.

Once again, Ben's phone began to ring. When the magazine came out, "it was unbelievable," Ben says.

Shortly after the United Steelworkers issue dropped, Ben took a plane to Wisconsin for a sales call, and when he landed he had three texts from Whitney asking him to call her when he landed. *We've got a problem,* she told him.

Whitney had received a voice mail: "We'll see you on chimpmania .com soon." Chimpmania.com is one of the largest white supremacist websites in the country. The caller was threatening to use the site to mobilize members to attack American Roots—and Ben and Whitney—for employing immigrants and people of color.

"It'll make you vomit, but you should go look at the website," Ben told me.

Ben and Whitney called the Westbrook police, who responded quickly to assess the threat level. "We're lucky," Ben says. "They're just a really engaged police force in the community. They know who we are." The police couldn't find out who the perpetrator was because "he pinged it off a bunch of cell towers," Ben says.

Then the hate began to seep into American Roots' social media pages: "Just going to ignore the terrorist on the cover." "Nothing says 'American' more than a hijab." "So is she making a burqa for the union wife at home?" "What age are you arranging your daughter's wedding, six or so?"

In the midst of all the drama, Ben wondered how the head of their shipping department, Dave Butler, was handling the onslaught. Ben had known him for a long time. "Dave is a hardworking blue-collar guy," Ben says. Dave inspired him with his anger. "When we met as a company about what was happening, Dave literally grabbed me and said, 'I hate fucking racism. I hope I never meet the people who said those things because I'd put my fist through their faces.' He was so angry about it. His eyes welled up."

The New Americans at American Roots put their heads down and kept working. They'd been hardened by recent events—the Muslim ban, occasional attacks in public, racist outbursts in the news and on social media.

At the recommendation of the police, Ben and Whitney installed an alarm system and cameras. They gave panic buttons to their senior staff.

Ben was grateful that the union immediately stepped up in support of American Roots. "It warmed my heart—not just Mike Higgins, the Steelworkers rep, but all the other Steelworkers and members who came out in defense of who we are as a company and who these workers are. Our sisters and brothers."

Historically, the United Steelworkers owed a lot to the needleworkers. While Andrew Carnegie was hiring the notorious Pinkerton private detective and security company to crush steelworkers' attempts to organize, a group of young men and women, many of them immigrants from Eastern Europe, were establishing one of America's first unions, the ILGWU.

Before they unionized, America's needleworkers spent long hours in packed, poorly ventilated spaces (tuberculosis was a constant scourge) and sometimes had to pay for their own machines, thread, and needles. If they missed a shift due to illness or a sick child, they could lose their job or, at the very least, their week's pay. Adding insult to injury, they were often cheated—bosses would skim their pay for tiny infractions. Sometimes at the end of the week, bosses would refuse to pay stitchers altogether, claiming poor workmanship or failure to meet impossible quotas set by the company.

After escaping tyranny and oppression in their homelands, they spent their days and nights in a new country sewing dresses, skirts, and undergarments. The stitchers made an exceptionally vulnerable workforce—desperate for employment and unfamiliar with their new country's laws and language. In short, they were easy to exploit. The bosses and owners were nearly always men, some of whom demanded sexual favors in exchange for the opportunity to work.

Hailing from Europe, some needleworkers were familiar with the unparalleled power of collective bargaining. They arrived in the U.S. with organizing chops, and once they hit the ground, they began developing techniques to build membership in this new multiethnic world. Organizers knew that to be effective, they had to reach all workers, which meant meeting people where they were. They translated leaflets and speeches into Yiddish, Italian, Russian, and other languages in the community; they recruited organizers from within different ethnic groups; and they provided constant training, ESL education, and social events to ensure that the union was a critical part of daily life. The ILGWU advocated not just for better pay in an industry that was notoriously exploitive, but also for safer working conditions, shorter workweeks, and better equipment.

The most powerful thing the ILGWU did was build the idea of

"American" into the labor movement. Founding members grew the movement by making the case that strengthening workers' rights strengthened the nation as a whole by broadening the concept of freedom to include freedom from exploitation, freedom from physical danger, freedom to work with dignity, and freedom to earn a living wage to support your family and community.

In 1909 and again in 1910, at least 20,000 ILGWU workers in the city walked out to demand improved pay and safer factories. Their long strike, played out on city streets, drew the empathy of the National Consumers League, an organization of middle- and upper-class women concerned about the plight of their working sisters. The ladies-who-lunch met with impoverished workers, listened to their horror stories, and organized nationwide boycotts of nonunion shops. For bad bosses, it was the stuff of nightmares.

The ILGWU was the first union to offer health care (1913) and academic scholarships to its memberships. The union even got into New York real estate, raising money to build affordable and cooperative housing, plus a vacation property for members in the Poconos featuring murals by Diego Rivera.

No strike would shape the labor movement in the following decades more than the one following the Triangle Shirtwaist Factory fire in 1911, which took the lives of 146 young women and men. The ten-story building was around the corner from Washington Square Park in Greenwich Village. Unable to escape the intense heat of the fast-moving conflagration, the stitchers and machinists died on the shop floor, piled up against blocked exits, in the elevator, and some on the concrete below when they leapt from windows eight to ten stories above to avoid the flames. An investigation later revealed that the factory doors had been illegally locked to prevent people from coming in and going out (possibly to prevent union organizers from talking to workers). It was also found that the fire escapes were under-built, the New York City fire truck ladders were too short to service most of the city's buildings, and no one had bothered to train staff about fire safety.

The Triangle Shirtwaist fire was the *Titanic* of the labor movement. (That ill-fated luxury liner would sink almost exactly one year
later, another tragic example of corporate malfeasance and inadequate
safety standards.) While countless American workers had died over
the years—in the coal mines, while building railroads, or in other
industrial accidents, some slowly and imperceptibly while handling
toxic materials without protection—it was impossible to ignore the
charred bodies of the young female stitchers, many of whom perished
while clutching their scant weekly pay.

One person who witnessed the horror of the Triangle Shirtwaist
fire was Frances Perkins, at the time the head of the National Consumers League. Profoundly moved by what she saw that day, she
worked with the city to improve fire safety protocols. Just two years
later, she would investigate another clothing factory fire, this time
in Binghamton, New York, which would take the lives of thirty-one
young needleworkers. Perkins made powerful friends, including New
York's governor, Franklin Roosevelt. During the Great Depression,
she served for twelve years as his secretary of labor and would help
enact laws, including Social Security, to protect America's workers
from greed, neglect, and outright abuse.

Frances Perkins worked alongside another pioneer in worker
safety, the indefatigable Alice Hamilton, one of the first scientists to
investigate workplace hazards. At the time, making things in America
was seriously hazardous for your health. The Bureau of Labor Statistics reported about 23,000 industrial deaths in 1913 among a workforce of 38 million—a rate of 61 deaths per 100,000 workers. (In
the twenty-first century, the rate is closer to 3.3 deaths per 100,000
workers.) Throughout Hamilton's long career as a medical doctor
and investigator, she helped alert policymakers and industrialists to
the toxicity of lead, aniline dyes, carbon monoxide, mercury, tetra-
ethyl lead, radium, benzene, and the by-products of manufacturing
viscose rayon—carbon disulfide and hydrogen sulfide gases.

Thanks to Hamilton's work, supported by union leadership, the
U.S. created the Bureau of Labor Standards in 1922, the predecessor

of the Occupational Safety and Health Administration (OSHA), created by President Nixon in 1971, just as union membership peaked.

Unfortunately, the union's power and wealth would eventually
attract bad actors, especially following the repeal of Prohibition.
Bootlegging had been the lifeblood of organized crime. The major
syndicates (essentially, the Italian and Jewish mafias) grew strong
during Prohibition, protected by a nationwide network of sympathetic judges, politicians, and police officers. The professionalization
of the underground economy that supported rum-running included
infiltrating the International Brotherhood of Teamsters, which represented the truckers who warehoused and distributed alcohol.

Once alcohol was legal again, the underworld had to find other
revenue streams. Gangsters worked their way into the apparel industry via trucking—and eventually took over union leadership using
ill-gotten gains to buy off politicians, the police, and DAs. At one
point, some labor unions were completely run by organized crime.

The ILGWU, along with other major unions, continued to grow
in membership and influence. But as they expanded, union-busting
became a big, dirty business in which the mob was playing both sides.
To fend off organizing efforts, some apparel manufacturers paid the
mob for protection from union infiltration. Mob muscle was used to
rough up labor reps to keep them away from nonunion shops.

Union organizers cried foul but were forced to make unholy alliances with mobsters to protect themselves and their members when
they realized that the government and law enforcement were in the
pocket of the mob. Officials summarily dismissed workers' reports
of violence and coercion, leaving them without recourse. In the
1940s, fully 30 percent of all Americans carried union cards. The
Great Depression, Roosevelt's pro-worker agenda, and Prohibition
had combined to simultaneously buoy unions and the underworld.
In other words, these two forces in America grew up side by side—
brother and sister—problematic but close crib mates.

By the mid-1980s, the media and conservative-leaning politicians depicted unions as cesspools of bigotry and corruption and,

somehow, also communist. Union bosses seemed indistinguishable from the red-faced mobsters who appeared on the front pages of the *Inquirer,* the *Daily News,* and the *Bulletin.* Please forgive younger me for thinking that all labor leaders ended up in Meadowlands concrete (so went the Teamsters' former president Jimmy Hoffa, according to urban legend), or finished off by a shotgun to the face while sitting in a car (like crime boss Angelo Bruno, who died in South Philly in 1980, precipitating a bloody four-year battle over Atlantic City gambling profits and the heroin turf that left at least twenty guys dead).

Antiunion sentiment was further stoked by Ronald Reagan, ironically the first American president to have once served as a union official. (He'd been the president of the Screen Actors Guild during the Red Scare in the 1950s and willingly tattled on his colleagues to the FBI.) After a liberal youth, Reagan swerved heavily to the right in the 1960s, traveling the country espousing free trade and right-to-work laws for GE. He stumped for presidential candidate Barry Goldwater in 1964, rallying citizens to oppose abortion, food stamps, and Medicare, which, he warned, would signal the end of freedom. "We will awake to find that we have socialism," he cautioned television audiences in 1964. "One of these days, you and I are going to spend our sunset years telling our children, and our children's children, what it once was like in America when men were free."

Unions were depicted as a drag on the economy or outright criminal.

In stark contrast, the media fawned over corporate raiders, stockbrokers, and deregulators. These were the people my classmates aspired to be when I first arrived at Columbia University in 1987. Remarkable to think that just a generation earlier, Columbia students were holding sit-ins in support of civil rights and protesting the Vietnam War.

IT TAKES CHUTZPAH

On January 3, 2020, Maine was hunkering down for another winter. Ben Waxman backed his gray Dodge Ram 1500 out of his driveway, ice crunching under the tires. It was 7 a.m. according to the dash clock. In the backseat, plastic dinosaurs, sticky sippy cups, picture books, plus tot-size sports equipment were wedged under and around the kiddie car seats—two mini Barca Loungers that took up much of the backseat.

Alone at the factory, preparing for the workday ahead, Ben felt nothing but pride and hope for a successful year. They'd cleared over $1,000,000 in annual sales in 2019, a 20 percent uptick from the year before. They'd lifted dozens of families out of poverty. They'd accomplished all this in spite of the uncertainties of the Trump presidency.

Thinking about the future, Ben felt in his bones that 2020 would be their year.

They were hitting their marks and growing steadily.

There was only one reason why they couldn't double sales and production over the next twelve months: money. Ben and Whitney had had several small investors, but never had enough cash to grow from a big little Maine company into a national powerhouse.

They had a line of credit for $25,000, which would cover about one payroll. But they were leveraged to the hilt at a moment when an infusion of cash would help them scale up, which would make all the difference. The previous November, they'd petitioned their bank for a large commercial loan.

With more money, they could do their own custom embroidering instead of outsourcing the work, which would remove some uncertainty from their production cycle. They could hire a dedicated designer to introduce new products—Ben got requests from their union and commercial clients all the time for polos, windbreakers, and baseball jackets—and refine the ones they had. They could also refine their existing wares. The American Roots hoodie, for example, was designed for men, not women. As such, it was cut a bit long, square, and bulky. The future of unions was female; Ben and Whitney knew they needed to offer more products built from the ground up for women.

Most importantly, with a sizable loan, they could buffer their stitchers from the feast-or-famine union buying cycle and work toward building inventory.

With more money, Ben and Whitney could hire a marketing team to help them get the word out about their mission-driven company. They had a good story to tell. They were putting in twelve-hour days to build a tiny community of union employees in southern Maine. Their generous pay packages were putting upward pressure on area companies to do better. Word on the street was that companies like Portland-based Sea Bags, which produced totes made of used sailcloth, were raising their employees' rates to retain them.

A savvy marketer could write ad copy that would resonate more strongly with ethically motivated buyers. A graphic designer could help them replace their simple five-pointed star logo with a new one that felt truer to their company.

Once they had all those things in place, Ben hoped, they could go direct to consumers to support their inventory production model.

Ben often talked about his ideal consumer: a mythical tech bro in Brooklyn who'd pay $140 for an ethically made workingman's hoodie.

The Waxmans had faith that once the American Roots story got out, their market share would blow up, so they also wanted a social media guru to work their Instagram and Facebook accounts and connect with influencers who jibed with what they were up to and willingly pushed their products.

Ben and Whitney needed cash to strengthen their business. Once again, their bank dragged them through the commercial loan muck. And once again, the answer to their November application was no. Too much at risk. Not enough collateral.

They refused to give up. Instead, they resolved to raise capital some other way. Through parents, friends, and Ben's union contacts, they had an impressive network of informal business advisers. Now it was time for them to get a fully invested strategic team.

They decided to build a corporate board.

Ben and Whitney had to be tactical about who they pulled into their company. They were acutely aware that a partner who was fixated on growth or profit would force them to manufacture elsewhere or pay their employees less. They refused to compromise on these foundational values. If they did, they figured, what would be the point?

They were searching for the rare investor who understood the whole picture, their mission, their methods, and maybe understood something about manufacturing, as well.

One possibility was Alex Laskey, the cofounder of Opower Inc., a tech-based service marketed to utility companies. Opower produced detailed, user-friendly energy-usage reports designed for consumers without requiring the installation of additional monitoring equipment. Opower reports offered techniques and incentives to help homeowners reduce energy consumption. Opower went public in 2014 and was acquired by Oracle in 2016. Ben first met Alex through an AFL-CIO colleague in 2010. They couldn't have been more different. Alex had cooked up the Opower concept with a classmate while they were at Harvard Business School. He was a fleece-vest guy, a fast talker who wielded the start-up lingo like a native speaker, direct and focused. Ben's style was personal, anecdotal, expressive, and raw. Improbably, the two men hit it off.

In 2019, Ben was on his way to a union conference in D.C. when he reached out to Alex. They met at a pub that night and spent two hours catching up. Just before Alex drove away, he asked Ben to send him more information about American Roots. As soon as Ben got back to his hotel room, Ben texted Alex a link to a short video about the company. Ten minutes later, Alex texted: "I gotta see this." Within a couple weeks, he was touring the Westbrook factory.

Then Ben asked him to invest. Alex wasn't sure. A month later, Ben was back in D.C. and, over coffee, worked Alex once again. Finally, Alex agreed to become American Roots' first official board member.

Dory knew another person who might be interested in joining the board: Justin Alfond. She'd met Justin through her work in local politics. Justin was a little older than Ben, and a true believer in helping government and business work together to lift up his fellow Mainers. In 2008, he was elected to the state's Senate, representing much of Portland. Four years later, he became the youngest president of Maine's Senate.

Justin also had manufacturing in his blood.

Justin's grandfather Harold—son of Russian Jewish immigrants—founded Dexter Shoe Company in a former wool mill in 1958 in Dexter, Maine. Justin spent the first six years of his life bouncing between Maine and Puerto Rico, where Dexter had a few large shoe-making plants. He spent the next decade of his life in Dexter, a town of 4,500 people, attending public school alongside factory workers' children.

"Small towns are amazing," Justin reminisced. "You don't have to lock your doors. Everyone's kind of overseeing each other, so if you get out of line, word spreads fast. There's a lot of accountability. It was a remarkable experience growing up in a town that really valued community and the hard work ethic, sports, and the outdoors."

Justin started school in Dexter in the second grade and guesses that about 40 percent of his classmates were working for his father and grandfather. In those days, he says, people went right into the workforce after graduating high school. "At the factory, they could earn a great living and have a great career," he says.

He credits his family's connection to Dexter for building goodwill between workers and owners. "We were right there, going to the same school, playing on the same sports teams, so I think that established a relationship with everyone in the community and with my family."

Justin spent a lot of time with his dad in the factories. Among other things, Dexter made bowling shoes. "[My father] loved the shoe industry," Justin says. "There was never a vacation that I can remember that we didn't end up in some bowling alley. He loved talking to the owner, talking to the people at the pro shop."

At first, Justin's classmates treated him like everyone else, which he attributed to his grandfather's compassion for the people working in the factory. "I think that one of my grandfather's greatest strengths was that he was a natural-born people person, a salesperson, who cared about his employees. He had a very high standard for his company, but he understood that all of it depended on incredible communication and relationships with the employees."

By junior high, however, there was a growing awareness among Justin's peers that he wasn't just another kid. He was Justin Alfond, the grandson of the man who'd started the company on which the entire town relied, and unlike the factory workers, they were Jewish. Justin says his classmates sometimes repeated "hurtful things" about his family that he assumes they'd heard at home. "There were definitely some challenges," he says. When he hit sixteen, the tension became untenable.

At exactly that moment, the national discourse was taking an ugly turn. The Soviet Union had fallen; communism was no longer a threat to U.S. hegemony. In America, freedom began to take on new meaning: deregulation, of literally everything, including the media.

In 1987, when Justin turned twelve, the FCC abolished the Fairness Doctrine, a forty-year-old law that required news media to present opposing views and treat positions with a degree of neutrality. The purpose of the Fairness Doctrine was to ensure that the American voting public was well informed and exposed to diverse perspectives on issues in a truly fair and balanced way.

Opponents of the law argued that the Fairness Doctrine violated free speech, a challenge that had previously been debunked in upper courts. This time, the Republican-led FCC devoured itself.

As soon as the doctrine was repealed, a pill-popping right-wing conspiracy theorist named Rush Limbaugh hit the airwaves. Limbaugh began minting money by fomenting working-class rage at "entitlements"—Medicaid, welfare, food stamps, Section 8 housing—arguing that hardworking Americans financed all these luxurious offerings through their federal taxes but didn't directly benefit from them. Limbaugh was using coded language to churn up racial resentment, dropping gems like: "Let the unskilled jobs that take absolutely no knowledge whatsoever to do—let stupid and unskilled Mexicans do that work."

Limbaugh's success spawned a spate of copycats eager to build their own "conservative talk radio" market, and plenty of people in Maine were listening. Many Americans started saying the quiet parts out loud.

Mainers made especially good targets. As a group, they're radio listeners. Even in 2022, 93 percent of adults in Maine listen to the radio at some point throughout the day—while driving, working, or cooking. Radio remains an integral part of life in the state. That was certainly true for the factory workers at Dexter Shoe in 1987.

The new nasty rhetoric crept into everyday conversations and made junior high in Dexter unbearable for the Alfond kids. Justin's father was on the road thirty-plus weeks a year peddling Dexter's bowling and golf shoe lines; Justin made the case that life would be easier if the family was based near busy Logan Airport rather than sleepy Bangor International. Dexter had their sales office just outside of Boston and when the family relocated, Justin began attending private school there.

Three years later, the weaponization of words by the right became standard operating procedure when House minority whip Newt Gingrich released a widely distributed memo, "Language: A Key Mechanism of Control," so that his fellow Republicans could copy Gingrich's belligerent rhetorical style. The memo listed "words to memorize," calibrated to sanctify Republicans while dehumanizing Democrats. Make these words stick to your opponents—*decay, sick, unionized bureaucracy, greed, corruption, radical, permissive, bizarre*—the memo recommended, and watch them lose.

Studying each of those words, it's clear why NAFTA had such broad support at the time. Everything FDR's New Deal had represented was being demonized and dismantled, sometimes cheered on by the men and women who had the most to lose in the deal.

In 1993, Justin's grandfather sat down with billionaire Warren Buffett and wrote out details of the sale of Dexter Shoe on a napkin. In exchange for the company, the Alfonds got $433 million in Berkshire Class A stock. When he bought Dexter, Buffett thought American industries would be able to resist the forces of globalization. He'd grossly miscalculated the combined effects of NAFTA and the WTO on American manufacturing.

Justin says that Dexter faced the same obstacles that Ben and Whitney are facing today. "The decision that my grandfather and others had made to keep manufacturing in the U.S. and Puerto Rico started becoming more and more and more difficult," he says. "The writing was on the wall."

You can still buy Dexter-brand bowling shoes and sports shoes, but they have nothing to do with the little town where it all started. Buffett ceased Dexter's shoe production in the U.S. and Puerto Rico in 2001, leaving the eight hundred Dexter shoe workers high and dry. In 2008, Buffett wrote in his annual letter to shareholders: "To date,

Dexter is the worst deal that I've made. . . . What I had assessed as durable competitive advantage vanished within a few years."

Justin sympathizes with Buffett's decision to end domestic manufacturing: "I believe the only way the company could continue was to move. The pressure was just too great to keep manufacturing in the U.S."

In 2012, an entrepreneur with dreams of reviving the shoemaking business raised $200,000 and rented 10,000 square feet in an old wool mill in Dexter. He hired former Dexter employees and started producing beautiful hand-sewn moccasins and boat shoes for $200 a pair under the MaineSole brand. Much of his leather came from a nearby tannery where 115 people made their living. The thread he used was manufactured in Lewiston at the Maine Thread Company. But neither MaineSole nor the tannery survived the pandemic.

Justin graduated from Tulane and tried becoming a pro golfer; he eventually ended up in Portland, where he met Dory Waxman while working as a political activist. When she introduced him to Ben and Whitney, he was impressed. "They cared very much about how they treated people and the planet. They had the passion to do something very important that had a mission and purpose."

Justin invested in American Roots and joined the board, though he acknowledges that manufacturing in the U.S. continues to be "incredibly challenging." Sourcing, he adds, is more complex than ever. But he thinks that American Roots has a chance. "Ben has this way of turning obstacles into opportunities," he says. "If you build your business from that foundation, then you work every day trying to figure out all the barriers and knocking them down."

Ben pulled in another board member through his labor connections: Patti Devlin, the federation liaison to the general president of the Laborers' International Union of North America. Patti agreed to represent nine other labor investors. Patti wasn't rich. She wasn't an angel investor. She wasn't a gambler. She was just someone who'd stumbled into the labor movement as a young woman and became captivated by the power people could amass when they united for a cause.

Patti was born and raised in D.C., and when she graduated from high school in the mid-1980s, college wasn't an option. Her father had been a University of Virginia–trained economist with the federal government when Reagan cleared out everyone who was in the "wrong political camp," she says. Demoted to file clerk, her father fell on hard times; Patti's older sister and brother-in-law bought the family home so that Patti could finish high school in the same place, but she spent most of that time alone in an empty house. Her father had found work teaching at a college in southern Maryland, too far for a daily commute.

After graduating from high school, Patti worked at Urban Outfitters, where she says the "management was fucked-up," and when she quit, she realized she needed a real job, one that offered health insurance and a pension. No one else was going to take care of her.

At the time, Patti's sister was temping at the United Mine Workers of America, and encouraged Patti to apply for a typist position. It was a good union job, and the UMWA was a good place for a young woman to start a career. Patti would be working under the new president, Rich Trumka.

"I didn't know anything about the labor movement," Patti says. "To me, I just had references like Jimmy Hoffa being dead and murdered and just a bunch of goons." After landing her UMWA gig, she went to her first local union meeting and thought to herself, *What are you all complaining about?*

But then she read her first collective bargaining agreement. She also realized that the UMWA would pay for her to go to college, plus she'd earn overtime after a seven-and-three-quarter-hour workday. So she took advantage of the offer and got her degree.

A year later, she landed a job in the union communications department as a research assistant for their monthly magazine.

Patti spent her days scouring newspapers to make press-clip

packets for union leadership. She also had access to the union's photo archives. That's where she first saw Lewis Hine's haunting portraits of child mineworkers from the turn of the century, photos that brought union history to life.

Patti saw photographs of Mother Jones—a dressmaker who became an indomitable labor organizer after losing her husband and four children in the yellow fever epidemic in 1867. Mother Jones famously led the "Children's Crusade" of child workers, many of whom had been maimed while working in coal mines and mills. Chanting "We want to go to school and not the mines," the children marched from Philadelphia to the doorstep of President Theodore Roosevelt's estate in Oyster Bay, New York. Mother Jones's ceaseless activism caused one West Virginian DA to call her "the most dangerous woman in America."

(Ben keeps a framed poster of Mother Jones in his office, emblazoned with her battle cry: "Pray for the dead and fight like hell for the living.")

All this history shaped Patti's understanding of the link between the economy and labor. "We'd been fed a line of goods by neoliberals," she says. "You know, trickle-down doesn't work. It's taken me a long time to really understand how all of this is connected." She learned that when workers lacked bargaining power over their employers, companies were capable of committing unspeakable atrocities against their workers. Patti says, "Workers need to be able to engage in the decision-making process that defines their lives and communities. That's why unions capture my imagination."

Patti thought labor troubles were ancient history, but it got real during the Pittston Coal Strike of 1989. Under Trumka's leadership, tens of thousands of people engaged in mass protest against Pittston Coal Company, then the largest exporter of coal in the U.S., which, in February 1988, informed miners that their retirement and health benefits were being taken away. Given the hazardous nature of the work, loss of protection would have grave consequences for miners and their families. The union fought and won passage of the historic

Coal Industry Retiree Health Benefit Act of 1992, which extended benefits to union miners who had worked for defunct companies.

"Seeing the labor movement come together during that strike was huge," Patti says. "I had never, ever seen that kind of action before and I was captivated by it."

Patti met Ben while working on Senator Elizabeth Warren's campaign in Massachusetts. She learned more about his family's history when she started listening to a tape of his brother's band, Adam and the Waxmen, while she was on the campaign.

A few years ago, Patti inherited a large sum of money from a colleague of her father—a Jewish man who, in his youth, fell in love with a non-Jewish woman. Her family refused to allow them to marry, and he remained single for the rest of his life. When he died, he left Patti and her sister everything he had.

Patti believed in Ben and Whitney's mission with every fiber of her being, and she used the money to invest in American Roots. "I put money on the fucking table," Patti says. "The United States is a pull-yourself-up-by-the-bootstraps type of country. There's this idea that you'll succeed because of your own hard work and drive. But that's a myth."

Patti had high hopes that the business would grow because "more and more people—young people in particular, the next generation, the Z's—they very much care about what's happening and where their stuff is coming from, and that's a great opportunity. They're tired of the cheap-ass shit that ends up in landfills. How much suffering has gone into getting you a cheap shirt?"

When asked what would bring manufacturing back to the U.S., Patti didn't mention tariffs or trade deals. She didn't talk about policy at all. Instead, she argued that all Americans have real power—purchasing power. She said that all Americans could steer the fate of their country if they wanted to. They just needed to feel pride in things made in the USA. They needed to buy American.

"How old are you?" Patti asked me. "Do you remember 'Look for the union label'?"

In fact, when I was a kid, my maternal grandmother gave me an honest-to-God full-length record of union songs, featuring "Look for the Union Label." I can't swear I listened to it, but reading the simple, straightforward lyrics of that song in 2021, I realize exactly how much the world has fundamentally shifted:

Look for the union label
when you are buying that coat, dress, or blouse,

Remember somewhere, our union's sewing,
our wages going to feed the kids and run the house.

We work hard, but who's complaining?
Thanks to the I.L.G. we're making our way.

So always look for the union label,
it says we're able to make it in the U.S.A.!

When I was young, I dutifully did look for those red-white-and-blue ILGWU labels sewn into the seams of all my T-shirts and pants, but only to slice them off. The labels were as ubiquitous as they were scratchy. They featured the ILGWU logo, an instant classic when it was registered in 1963. The logo looked like a corporate seal, with a wavy piece of blue yarn encircling a bright red circle proudly announcing in bold letters, "ILGWU," "UNION MADE," "INT. LADIES GARMENT WORKERS UNION," and "AFL-CIO." The yarn was threaded through a needle that pierced the logo like Cupid's arrow.

None of those words and letters meant anything to me at the time.

And that was Patti's point: "How much of America's GDP is personal consumption? Pretty significant numbers. We're buying more that's shipped from afar and often made by women who are working in horrific conditions."

Every dollar we spend has consequences.

Like Patti, Justin didn't mention tariffs when asked how to restore domestic manufacturing. "I hope more consumers want to buy American made and union made and support companies that are on a journey to really treat people and the planet in an exceptional way."

It was clear to me that neither Patti nor Justin fully understood the economic policies of the past that had protected American industries for more than a century.

PANDEMIC PANIC ALONG ROUTE 66

Ben and Whitney met with their new corporate board for the first time in mid-January 2020. Thanks to their new investors, they finally had some cash to check some things off their wish list, as well as a group of smart advisers who were invested in their success. They were certain they were hitting their stride.

But the evening of March 9 found Ben pacing the living room again, this time rehashing what he knew so far about a new virus ravaging China. Whitney sat on the sofa nursing four-month-old Wyatt, his tiny hands grasping at her hair. Arlo was finally asleep in his toddler bed upstairs. They should have been in bed themselves.

Throughout Trump's presidency, Ben's phone buzzed with news from the world outside the factory. Whenever friends' texts about Trump's latest racist statements or outright fabrications started up, Ben would kick everyone out of his office, slam the door, dial a number, then let the f-bombs fly, venting his frustration over Trump's idiocy on whoever happened to be on the other end of the line. His blood pressure was going through the roof.

Trump knew his base—many of them were the former factory workers who Ben had met during his AFL-CIO days. He recognized the time-tested tropes Trump was using to galvanize them. Blame the

Chinese. Blame immigrants. Blame people of color. Trump espoused a simple but effective narrative that ignored the complex forces that had undercut America's middle and working class. He stoked the white grievance story line that had pitted workers against each other since the dawn of America's Industrial Revolution.

Everything Trump did flew in the face of what Rich Trumka was trying to build. Trump's rants against immigration, his capricious trade wars, but most importantly, the broad general uncertainty he created with reactionary policies were simply bad for business. Guessing right from wrong, fact from falsehood, real threats from imagined sucked tons of time and energy away from America's productivity.

Ben was the kind of guy to power through it all, but Covid was starting to feel like something real. A few days prior, he'd flown down to Florida to attend the AFL-CIO Executive Council meeting, and as soon as he landed, he found out that the event had been canceled due to fears of the virus. So he got right back on a plane and returned to Portland. Was everyone overreacting? Was this threat real?

Now, pacing his living room, Ben was trying to figure out whether he could take off a few precious days to honor an old friend. His plan was to fly to Phoenix to meet up with two buddies for a quick getaway to honor another—a Swedish exchange student they'd befriended when they were at Portland High who'd taken his life the previous fall. Between the demands of the factory and their newborn, Ben hadn't been able to give his family or friends the care and attention they deserved. American Roots, and by extension, his life, felt like it had been one long exercise in crisis management. He hadn't had a minute to mourn his friend. He needed this trip. He needed to recharge.

But now there was only uncertainty. If the virus hit America and it was as bad as it sounded, it would wipe out everything Ben and Whitney had built over the last five years. Labor conferences would be canceled. Hoodie orders would be pulled. They'd be forced to shut down their Westbrook factory, and if they did that they'd have no money to pay for rent. They'd be forced to sell the hundreds of industrial sewing machines they'd bought and lay off the workforce they'd patiently trained to become professional apparel workers.

Ben and Whitney had used their home as collateral for their loans. If they defaulted, they'd lose that, too.

"I can't leave you guys here like this," Ben said to Whitney.

She gently slung Wyatt over her shoulder and patted his tiny back. Whitney knew how much this trip meant to him. Ben's friends came second to family, but just barely. "I think you should go," she told him.

Ben knew that Whitney didn't make decisions lightly.

"You sure you'll be okay?" he asked, fully aware she'd made up her mind.

"We'll manage."

She carefully maneuvered herself off the sofa without waking Wyatt, cradled the little bundle in her arms, and headed upstairs. Ben stopped pacing to gaze at them, mother and child. His heart nearly burst in that moment, seeing Whitney holding their infant son. How did he get so goddamn lucky?

When she was gone, Ben turned out the lights and headed to the basement. As usual, he'd sleep on the sofa down there. His workdays started at 5 a.m. He needed those early morning hours to ride his exercise bike while listening to the news and collecting his thoughts. In the basement, his morning routine didn't disturb Whitney and the kids.

He barely slept. At 3 a.m. he was on his laptop, devouring the news.

The next morning, Ben drove to Manchester, New Hampshire, and boarded a plane to Phoenix to meet up with his childhood friend Derek Meader. Their ultimate destination: the "Mother Road," aka Route 66.

This would be Ben and Derek's sixth trip along the iconic route. They started back in 2005 after Derek stumbled on a Route 66 coffee table book in a Portland bookstore. To the New Englander with deep Maine roots (his great-great-great-grandfather, Captain Isaac Davis, was the first officer killed in the Revolutionary War), photos of deserts and ghost towns seemed exotic. When their mutual friend Kevin Kane, who'd studied architecture at Rensselaer Polytechnic Institute, invited them to visit him in Las Vegas, where he was living at the time, Ben and Derek hit the road from D.C. in a rented RV.

Three years later, they rented a bigger RV and brought along their Swedish friend Fillip, who would take his life eleven years later.

Being with his crew, traveling the open road, drinking beer, there weren't a lot of things that made Ben happier. He'd walk into any joint along the way and start gladhanding like a politician. His lack of pretension and big personality instantly put folks at ease. Wherever they went, Ben would make a slew of new friends. In those moments, it was tough to imagine the divided America all the pundits were complaining about.

The band of Mainers was drawn to the randomness of the road, the small towns and mom-and-pop diners, the weird attractions like the Museum of Barbed Wire in Texas, Meteor Crater, and Cadillac Ranch that made American travel so unique. Plenty of parts of Route 66 reminded them of their home state, Maine, where a sleepy economy (and sparse population) had sheltered quirky businesses with punny names along Route One—"Curl Up and Dye," "Seas the Day," "Brewed Awakenings," and "Snuggle Inn" from the big chain stores.

Route 66's teepee-shaped motels, the massive billboards that wildly overpromised and underdelivered, the Wild West "ghost towns" where actors performed drunken shootouts daily at 2 p.m. and 4 p.m., the Indian trading posts, the stuck-in-time diners with watery, bitter coffee, the rattlesnake museums—these wacky (and in many cases, culturally problematic) offerings sprang up during the heyday of American industrialization.

Until Route 66 was built, America's roadways were a jumble of unnumbered private "auto trails," mostly unpaved and poorly maintained. They'd start and stop at random. They were often unmarked, too. That made travel by car a challenging and expensive pastime.

Roadways west of the Mississippi were particularly underdeveloped because for a long time the Midwest had been contested territory. With the passage of the Dawes Act in 1887, more than 50,000 white Americans wagoned across the savannah, seizing 90 million acres from Native Americans. Waves of immigrants from congested East Coast cities settled on "free" land across the Great Plains— a vast, complex biome, second in size only to the 5,000-mile-long Eurasian Steppe, which stretches from Hungary to China.

White Americans homesteaded on the Kansas, Nebraska, and Oklahoma grasslands and started farming. They borrowed heavily from banks to buy seeds, machinery, and gasoline, plowed up the deep-rooted native grasses that held the thin topsoil in place, and began planting corn and wheat in its stead. The new farmers were serviced by a spidery railroad system designed to connect nodes, reinforcing the centralized movement of goods from remote locations to big cities like Chicago, St. Louis, and Memphis.

But traveling from small town to small town remained difficult, which kept communities isolated from one another, strengthening the "bootstrapping" myth that Americans succeeded by their wits alone, independent of larger political and economic forces.

Henry Ford's Model T would change all that. Once Ford mastered vertical integration and the assembly line, he put the automobile within reach for most Americans, albeit without the lush interiors of a Packard. Over a single decade, the number of cars on the road skyrocketed from 180,000 in 1908 to more than 17 million in 1920. Demand for a network of highways grew, and the U.S. government sent millions of dollars to the states to improve their roadways. But jurisdictional issues plagued state-run projects. Although the Office of Public Roads and Rural Engineering (OPRRE) approved 572 projects totaling 6,249 miles, by July 1918 only five projects—just 17.6 miles—had been built.

World War I laid bare the pitiful state of America's infrastructure. When war broke out in 1914, American farmers could grow enough food to supply the European nations that could no longer feed themselves, and eventually supply the millions of American troops who were sent to France. But efforts to move those crops across states and the Atlantic Ocean were stymied by the country's lack of a national road system. The railways weren't standardized enough to transport all that grain, corn, and material from the heartland. (Because the rail lines were privately owned, they weren't standardized; rail gauges and car size varied widely.) By November 1917, the U.S. was about 158,000 railcars short, unable to move high-priority war shipments from west to east. When supplies finally did arrive at ports, they piled up along the Eastern Seaboard for weeks because there were too few ships to carry them across the Atlantic.

The U.S. emerged from World War I as a bona fide world power, and the federal government was finally empowered to address the nation's weak, confused, privatized infrastructure. The Merchant Marine Act, passed in 1920, spawned a shipbuilding spree from which American manufacturing would benefit immensely. But it would take three administrations—Wilson, Harding, and Coolidge—to get something like a national highway system fully approved and funded. Echoes of the Civil War plagued such efforts. Decades after the U.S. withdrew troops from the former Confederacy, thereby ending Reconstruction, many southerners still viewed the federal government with suspicion. The former Confederate states didn't want U.S. government cash, thank you very much, even if it did lead to healthier interstate commerce. Others warned that a nationwide system would lead to dreaded socialism, which is funny to think about considering the incalculable economic impact of America's highway system once it finally got built.

Plans for Route 66—a highway stretching 2,500 miles from Chicago to Los Angeles—were drawn up in 1926. It would be the first major federal project executed after the Civil War. And while southern lawmakers were still wary about federally financed infrastructure, the logistical transformation required to deploy the U.S. Army to Europe during World War I changed many minds. The route roughly followed an 1857 wagon road across seven states, stitching together three private highways, including the Ozark Trail system, the Santa Fe

Trail, and the National Old Trails Road. Road markers went up, but the asphalt was slow in coming. By 1934, Texas, New Mexico, Arizona, and the California desert boasted a total of 64.1 miles of paved highway.

Although much of it was yet to be paved, Route 66 became a major thoroughfare during the Depression. Whether by foot or truck or horse, nearly all Dust Bowl refugees traveled along Route 66 to the promised land of California. The same Midwest farming families who had thrived throughout the 1920s became victims of their own success. Eager to hedge against bad times (fiscally conservative, small-government-minded Calvin Coolidge had vetoed farm subsidies), farmers were encouraged to shore up their income by expanding their acreage, borrowing heavily against future earnings. They plowed up millions of acres of the tall, thick-rooted grasses that covered the plains, leaving the land raw, exposed, and highly vulnerable to drought. At least one Native American observed that the freshly plowed fields looked like the land was "upside down."

When rain refused to fall in 1930, dry westerly winds from the Rockies swept heartland topsoil into massive clouds of dust, killing people and tens of thousands of heads of livestock. The drought continued for several years, wiping out some 750,000 farms between 1930 and 1935. With those farms went the businesses that supported communities, triggering a great migration westward. Like economic pilgrims, the faithful followed the sun west. Those who owned cars loaded everything they could into their Fords and hit the road. The Dust Bowl victims who didn't have cars walked. Once they arrived in California, the majority of them received an icy welcome. Most would be chased back into Arizona by vigilantes who patrolled the border to fight off the "hobos," "indigents," "Arkies," and "Okies."

At the height of the Depression, Franklin Roosevelt would get America back to work by commissioning major infrastructure projects, including Route 66, and the Mother Road was finally fully surfaced in 1938.

The high concentration of travelers along this single road created a unique opportunity for entrepreneurs. Even the poorest travelers needed food and provisions, lodging (or a safe campsite), and gasoline.

Once Route 66 was paved, the land promised economic opportunity for nearly anyone willing to take a risk. It was practically lawless, with little zoning or restrictions. A young couple could scrounge together some cash and start a motel, an all-night diner, or a curio shop, all of which evolved to grab drivers' attention, and serve the new automobile-centric America exactly what it needed. In 1940 in San Bernardino, California, for example, brothers Dick and Mac McDonald opened their first eponymous fast-food restaurant.

The American Southwest was sunny, dry, and vast—perfect for filmmaking, military maneuvers, top secret weapons projects, and testing atomic bombs. Demand for services along the highway exploded during World War II, when the U.S. government invested in military bases along the route and spent an astonishing $70 billion to build up defense contracting in Southern California. Some 10 million job-seekers migrated from points north and east to the Southwest and California.

To move goods and personnel, the military chose to invest in trucking—cheaper, quicker, and easier, with considerably lower overhead—over railroads. America would never be the same.

After the war, people continued migrating west along the newly paved highway. Between 1930 and 1960, California's population tripled from five million to 15 million. New Mexico's population doubled; Arizona's population increased 74 percent.

Throughout the 1950s and 1960s, America's (mostly white) post-agricultural, tech-and-manufacturing middle class road-tripped down the Mother Road in American cars burning American oil wearing American-made clothes, discovering and rediscovering the scenic, geologic, and historic wonders of the Southwest, cementing a uniquely American concept of freedom in capitalism, guns, cars, and kitsch—all proudly made in the US of A.

It's important to recognize that many American citizens were denied equal access to this booming economy, especially Black Americans, Native Americans, Mexicans, Puerto Ricans, and others from Latin America. At the height of Route 66's popularity, much of the United States was segregated; most of the businesses along Route 66 were closed to people of color. Half the counties along the route were "sundown towns," posted with signs warning Black citizens to leave before dark. Some businesses encoded white supremacy into their name—Kozy Kottage Kamp or the Klean Kountry Kottages—which left little to the imagination. Without *The Negro Motorist Green Book*, a road guide for Black travelers published by a Harlem postman starting in 1936, Black travelers would have great difficulty buying gasoline, a room for the night, or a meal.

But Route 66's days were numbered. Eisenhower's Interstate Highway System—inspired by the German Autobahn and developed to support the needs of a modern military—put an end to the free-for-all. Its multilane design rendered highways like Route 66 obsolete. The road was officially decommissioned as a federal highway in 1985.

Derek and Ben loved traveling Route 66 because the quirky roadside attractions were homegrown. The businesses that survived into the twenty-first century were relics of the moment when Americans nearly reached economic equality. Union membership hit 33 percent in the 1950s. The majority of American households were middle-class. More people were attending college, thanks to the G.I. Bill, than at any other time in history. American companies were making things, and new roads were moving people and manufactured goods around the country to nurture an expanding economy.

Ben landed in Phoenix on Wednesday, March 11, and met up with his friends Derek and Jeff Morris, a former classmate who lived in Philadelphia. They overheard talk of Covid, which they did their best to ignore. They piled into their rental car and hit the road.

When they reached Winslow, Arizona, Derek had a surprise—he'd bought a memorial stone for Fillip and planned to place it on a corner, which was only natural if you were an Eagles fan. They held an impromptu ceremony for their friend by humming "Take It Easy": "Lighten up while you still can, don't even try to understand, just find a place to make your stand, and take it easy." Who can say how many people have cued that song during a Route 66 road trip, but Ben is the kind of guy who can look a cliché square in the eye and say, *Yeah, that's me.*

Fillip's suicide was a reminder that it was easy to overlook mental health issues, even when they were your own. Ben knew about that firsthand.

That night, the three friends were in Jerome, Arizona—once a copper mining city of 15,000, now the biggest ghost town in America. They got dinner at the Haunted Hamburger, where they watched the increasingly alarming Covid news with a handful of other patrons while a thick fog rolled into the mountain town.

The next morning, March 12, they got on the phone with their wives and "realized they had to get the fuck home," Ben says. They climbed into their rental car and drove 450 miles to Santa Fe.

Ben says, "It was crazy, no one knew what was going on. No one was wearing masks. And I remember sitting down for dinner that night and the town was eerily quiet."

Ben called Whitney when he got back to the hotel. "How you doing?" he asked.

She said she wasn't feeling great. The next morning, Friday, March 13, Ben and his friends drove to Albuquerque. In the airport, Ben saw that people were starting to wear masks.

Just before they took off, Ben checked in with Whitney again.

"I don't want you to panic," she said. "I'm lying on the floor, and I've got a fever of 102."

WE'LL COME BACK

Ben's heart rate went through the roof. "Nobody knew what this virus was," Ben reminds me. "We didn't know if it was airborne, we didn't know about masks, nothing. Nothing." But he did know that if Whitney had the virus, twenty-seven people at the factory might have been exposed. Whitney had gone to work every day that week, pushing through her illness, as one did before the pandemic. It wasn't just the stitchers, inspectors, cutters, and packers at American Roots who were vulnerable, it was also their families. If they had been exposed to Covid, American Roots would be the epicenter of the first outbreak in Maine.

Ben did some back-of-the-envelope math in the airport with CNN running in the background. American Roots had about two payrolls cash in the bank. Their monthly overhead was $100,000—including rent, salaries, health care, and debt service. If they had to shut down for a few months, they wouldn't make it. They'd have to sell dozens of industrial sewing machines and lay off the workforce they'd patiently trained to become professional apparel workers. If they closed down indefinitely, Ben says, "there would be no more American Roots." They'd spent nothing on marketing, had no online presence, and relied solely on face-to-face relationship building. "I'm a sales guy, that's what I am. I like selling our story, mission, and product," Ben says. "And at that point, I didn't know what we were gonna do."

Ben called their CFO that morning and asked him to gather all twenty-seven employees around the speakerphone, in hindsight not a good idea. "Listen," he told them, "Whitney's not feeling well and we want everyone to go home and stay home. We'll pay you. Just go home and take care of your families."

Then he asked his parents to help with the kids. When he and his friends landed for a connecting flight in Chicago, Jeff rerouted his flight from Maine to his home in Philly. They hugged and got him onto the plane. "Little did we know, we weren't going to see him for two years," Ben says.

Ben called Whitney again to find out how she was doing. "I'm not good," she told him. Her doctor had advised her to go to the clinic immediately.

Ben started working through his contacts, calling every local Maine official he knew, finally reaching Portland's city manager. Look, he told him, Whitney's sick and we're shutting down. But if she's positive, we're going to have a problem. That's twenty-seven people possibly exposed, multiplied by five because people have families. If it was Covid, American Roots would be the epicenter of the first outbreak in Maine.

Ben's plane landed in Manchester at 3:30 in the afternoon. He scored one of the last rental cars and tore through New Hampshire to southern Maine, praying not to get another ticket. At 5:30, he pulled into their Westbrook driveway, threw the car into park, and leapt up the side steps two at a time. As soon as he was in the kitchen, he dropped to his knees to catch Arlo in a big bear hug.

Holding his little boy tight, Ben could feel the rush of his own heartbeat.

Scooping the toddler up with one arm, he asked, "Where's Mom?"

Arlo pointed to the living room. Whitney looked wiped out but very much alive. Wyatt reached for Ben from Whitney's lap and she hoisted the baby to his father, relieved to have her husband back in the house. Ben got the kids fed and put them to bed while Whitney waited for her Covid test results. They barely slept.

At 8:30 the next morning, March 14, they got the call: negative.

The last few days had been hellish—being apart at the beginning of the pandemic, Whitney down with possible Covid. The mix of relief and trepidation was exhausting. They couldn't go through that again. They called up their brand-new board members—Alex, Justin, and Patti—and scheduled an emergency meeting. They told them they were shutting down for a week to "figure out what the hell this all meant."

That Saturday night, March 14, Whitney and Ben, like millions of people around the world, sat in their living room watching horrific scenes coming out of New York City. It looked like the entire city had fallen ill with the mysterious, perplexing virus. ICUs were filling up with sedated and intubated Covid victims. It was apocalyptic.

Some people were already sounding the medical supply chain alarm. With China shutting down and the ports closing, in just six weeks all hospitals in the U.S. would run out of personal protective equipment (PPE)—gloves, face shields, masks, booties. Nurses were going on the news warning they would have to wear garbage bags when they ran out of surgical gowns.

The hospitals found themselves in this situation because long ago, most hospital administrators had decided to pool their purchasing decisions, handing over billions of dollars' worth of medical supply orders to a handful of buying groups. The middlemen weren't running a charity. Following standard business practices, they minimized their costs and maximized profit by building a just-in-time supply chain completely dependent on Asian manufacturers. They gave little thought to the chain's vulnerabilities because building a backup plan didn't seem worth the expense and time. They seemed too big to fail.

The buying groups' choke hold on purchasing gutted domestic manufacturing of protective gear. American makers of gowns and masks simply couldn't compete with their Asian counterparts on price. It wasn't just a matter of cheaper labor. Asian manufacturers could keep their prices low because their logistics—shipping of raw goods in and finished products out—was heavily subsidized by their governments; they operated under looser environmental and labor regulations; and with such huge contracts, they could support a large workforce, which made the work of manufacturing more dependable. They also had a tendency to monkey around with their currencies to create even more trade-favorable conditions.

Many Americans first learned about those mega hospital buying groups when a Texas-based medical supply company filed an antitrust lawsuit against the two biggest buyers in 2003. The story goes something like this: During the AIDS crisis, inventor Thomas Shaw read about the shocking number of times health care professionals accidentally stuck themselves with hypodermic needles while administering care, exposing themselves to all manner of infection. Shaw founded Retractable Technologies to develop and manufacture a needle that worked like a ballpoint pen—with one click, the sharp end retracted safely back into its holder—and spent years patenting his device and refining the manufacturing process. But when he began trying to sell, he struggled to find a market. Calling hospitals across America, he kept getting referred to the same two buyers. He eventually sued the two biggest medical supply middlemen for the harm they caused by refusing to consider his product. He settled for an undisclosed sum. (Shaw took his company public in 2020 and began to experience significant growth shortly after, thanks to government orders for syringes during the pandemic vaccination efforts. In the first nine months of 2021, Retractable Technologies did business worth $129 million.)

When Covid hit, foreign suppliers shut down their factories and hoarded PPE, abruptly ending the flow of medical masks and gowns from Asia to the U.S. on which all hospitals depended. Shady PPE brokers emerged from the darkness to connect buyers (desperate hospitals) to sellers (randos on the internet) "on a black market fueled by desperation and opportunism, a Wild West occupied by oddballs, ganjapreneurs and a shadowy network of investors," wrote investigative reporter David McSwane in *ProPublica.* Some of those deals involved no-bid multimillion-dollar contracts with brand-new corporate entities that had no track record of delivering a single N95 mask, let alone a hospital's worth.

Whitney and Ben didn't know any of this. But watching the chaos unfolding in New York, they knew that America's first responders would need domestic manufacturers to step up. Whitney turned to Ben and said, "We have to go in. We've got to turn the lights on. We have to make stuff."

Would they be able to open again? If so, how? What would keep them and their employees safe? Masks? Distancing? Regular disinfecting?

That same night, Ben's friend James Moran, who ran Flowfold, a small manufacturing company nearby that made bags and wallets out of recycled sailcloth, called Ben to tell him that he'd collaborated with MaineHealth to design a protective face shield, but didn't have the workers to mass-produce it. Could American Roots help? Flowfold was racing against the clock. Hospital administrators knew they'd be out of protective gear within weeks. It was kind of like going to war.

The next morning, Sunday, Ben joined his fellow Mainers and raided the grocery store. He panic-shopped, grabbing anything and everything he could. Big bags of rice, cans of beans, what was left in the butcher aisle, a week's worth of milk. And then, well, he went to Cabela's. Before the pandemic, he sometimes took Arlo to the sporting goods emporium to look at the taxidermy animals. The moose, the deer, the game fowl. This time, he was going to protect his family. From what? He didn't really know. Ben owned a 12-gauge shotgun and one case of shells. He wasn't sure that would be enough. "I didn't know if we'd be hunting birds or shooting right-wing nut jobs," he says, but by the time Ben got to Cabela's, he says, "there wasn't an ounce of ammo on the shelf."

From his truck, Ben called his friend Kevin in California and said, "This is getting real."

The CDC's messaging was disturbingly inconsistent. Americans were already hoarding toilet paper, stripping grocery aisles bare. The profiteers were coming out, too: some kid bought up a huge supply of hand sanitizer and started selling it out of his garage for $70 per bottle on eBay. Trying to prevent people from hoarding masks, the official message was that you didn't need them. But anyone who took a minute to think about what we knew so far about Covid knew that that was a cynical untruth. Based on reports coming out of Italy and China, it was clear that the virus was airborne.

During their emergency board meeting later that day, Ben and Whitney shared that they'd bought five hundred surgical masks, had kept more than two dozen people on payroll, and hoped to work with prototypes from MaineHealth to make face shields. Before Ben could finish describing their reopening plan, Alex said, "You two have to do this and we have to support you. You're risking everything. We've got your back."

Manufacturers of every size joined the effort. Within a week, home-crafting e-marketplace Etsy sent out a plea to its millions of members: please consider adding homemade masks to your offerings. Across America, crafters dug into closets, hauling out their sewing machines and thread, dragged bolts of fabrics from their attics, and began stitching and selling masks. Many Etsy members pledged to donate masks to first responders for every one purchased. Craft stores quickly ran out of elastic, which people were using to make ear loops. Etsy later reported that 110,000 Etsy sellers sold a total of 29 million face masks worth $346 million in the second quarter of 2020.

That Monday, Ben and Whitney called all their employees into the office. They wore masks and sat six feet apart. Social distancing had entered the lexicon. The Waxmans told their staff that they planned to shut down for a week to figure out if they could make protective clothing and face shields for first responders and hospitals. Ben then said, "If we reopened in a week and operated safely, how many of you would be willing to come back in?"

"And I'll never forget the moment as long as I live," he continues. "I want you to think about this: On March 16, when the entire world was shutting down, twenty-seven people were sitting in our factory—82 percent of them had emigrated to this country in the last few years, in some cases, six months. They were New Americans at a time when the president of the United States was denouncing immigrants and immigration across the board. It was immigrants, New Americans, whose twenty-seven hands went up. They all said, 'We'll come back.' Every single fucking hand."

Khalid Al Kinani was one of those New Americans. Like Anaam, he had fled Iraq with his children. Growing up in Baghdad, he had been obsessed with American culture and taught himself English by reading a dictionary. During the Iraq war, he aided the U.S. military as a translator, proud to serve the Americans. When the Americans withdrew, he had a big target on his back. Someone in the State Department took mercy on him and helped him escape to the U.S. with his wife and three children. Other translators weren't so lucky.

Khalid tried living in D.C., but it was too expensive. In North Carolina, his family found that the schools weren't great, which came as a surprise to Khalid. From afar, he couldn't appreciate how different the states were from one another in terms of basic services and culture. A friend told him to go to Maine; it was less expensive, he said, the schools were good, and there were jobs for recent immigrants.

Exhausted but hopeful, Khalid moved his family to Portland. Back in Iraq, he'd been an amateur boxer. His son, Mohammed, took up boxing in Portland at age thirteen. In 2021, he was the number one amateur lightweight fighter in New England. To Khalid, his son's success was further proof that the U.S. was a land of opportunity.

At the end of the meeting, Khalid stood up and said to the group, "Of course we're coming back. It's our duty as Americans."

Ben says, "People want to know why I get emotionally charged when I talk about the Trump era? Because it was those people whose lives he was making a living hell. They were the ones who were willing to walk into a factory, making seventeen, eighteen, nineteen dollars an hour, and make face shields and face masks for people they never met. That's the America that we should all be proud of. Not an America of division.

"When those hands went up, Whitney and I looked at each other and said, 'We're doing this.'"

Ben and Whitney sent most of their crew home to care for their families. They worked alongside the few people who stayed and gave the factory a deep clean. They quickly fitted out a huge adjacent room to create "Factory 2," which would allow for more space between sewing tables. Following state guidelines, they decided to hang 7,000 square feet of heavy plastic sheeting from the ceilings to isolate workstations.

Ben called around to see if anyone was willing to help. Doug Born, secretary-treasurer of AFL-CIO Maine, called and said, "Ben, we got you." He was in the film business, but all the sets had shut down and no one was working. He asked a few members from Portland's International Alliance of Theatrical Stage Employees Local 114 to help out American Roots.

At seven the next morning, Ben pulled into the loading dock at the factory. "The country was completely locked down," he says. "But there were seven people sitting there—all had been laid off—waiting to get to work. I fought back tears." Whitney arrived fourteen hours later to see the factory being rebuilt to follow state guidelines. When she saw what they'd accomplished, tears streamed down her cheeks. A volunteer team had worked since dawn to prepare American Roots for pandemic manufacturing.

A small group of factory employees collaborated with Whitney for a few days doing time trials to see how many workers they'd need to fulfill the face shield order. As soon as they sent out their first batch, other orders came flooding in: fire departments, nursing homes, hospitals. Then came a 50,000-unit contract from the New Jersey State Police. Within seven days of shutting down, American Roots hired back everyone they'd laid off and added a dozen more.

As face shield production was getting off the ground, Whitney collaborated with their production team and physicist Jason Hancock of the University of Connecticut's Institute of Materials Science to design a washable knit cotton jersey mask. It was a clever design—two layers of material formed a pocket for a disposable filter. The mask was comfortable, too. In early April, after the factory build-out was complete and stitchers were trained, they put the masks into production. The fabric was cut by their cutter in Fall River, Massachusetts, then driven up in neat bundles to the Westbrook factory. Buyers of the American Roots masks included the State of Maine, which in April announced a contract to buy 27,500 of them, enough to provide two for every state employee.

Later that month, Rich Trumka got on a national labor call and said, *American Roots has pivoted to PPE. If you need it, call them.* That announcement was the key to their survival. To make their face shields and masks, American Roots needed aluminum, elastic, cotton, and plastic—materials suddenly in short supply across the nation. Ben was pulling every string he had to secure the supplies.

Following Trumka's call to suppliers on behalf of American Roots, multiple unions stepped up to build a supply chain so that the factory could continue producing protective gear for American workers. Sheetmetal Workers Local 17 provided the aluminum nose strips; Painters District Council 35 coordinated delivering the cut mask fabric from Fall River to Westbrook. They also screen printed two million masks.

Thomas Conway, the president of United Steelworkers, called Ben and told him that whatever he needed, they were there for him. Ben said he was having trouble finding material for mask filters. Jason, the UConn physicist, had told Ben and Whitney that they needed a very dense paperlike material for filters, but they were having a hard time tracking down a suitable material. On Monday, April 6, Roxanne Brown of United Steelworkers connected Ben with Brian McAlary, the VP of development at Twin Rivers Paper Company in Madawaska, Maine, who called Ben and told him that whatever he needed, they were there for him. Ben told him what they were looking for.

That same day, McAlary emailed Ben to let him know that he had the samples and was sending them out ASAP. He closed his missive this way: "We appreciate the efforts that you and your teams are making to help out during this unbelievable crisis."

American Roots had their filters. And bonus, they were made in Maine.

By mid-April, frustrated by the lack of coordination at the federal level, the Waxmans submitted an op-ed to *The Washington Post* that was widely shared on social media. Their story described their wild pivot from manufacturing garments to PPE; it rallied small businesses like theirs to rise to pandemic-era challenges while calling for national coordination to get PPE produced and delivered where it was needed.

From the moment the op-ed hit, Ben says, "the phone rang nonstop, all day, seven days a week, from 6:30 in the morning to 11 at night." American Roots filled orders from unions, public works departments, Reporters Without Borders, schools, and more. But running a million miles an hour, staffing up to more than a hundred employees while following protocols—distancing, mask-wearing, and hand-sanitizing—was exceedingly stressful.

Ben keeps a photo of Whitney, taken in March before they reopened, on his phone. She's standing on the factory floor—empty, cleared of furniture and machines—just before the plastic went up. She's got toddler Arlo on her hip, but barely. He's in his PJs, half asleep, kind of draped over her, kind of sliding down. Both of them look exhausted. "We hadn't slept in days," Ben says. "That was the beginning of us barely seeing our sons for several weeks. If we failed, more people would get sick. We could get sick, our team could get sick, our kids could get sick. This photo sums up the rawness of those early days."

In just ninety days, American Roots grew from twenty-seven people to 150 and took on an additional 15,000 square feet of space inside the Dana Mill Building.

WE GOTTA SHUT
UP AND LISTEN

Ben and Whitney's *Washington Post* op-ed ran around the same time that Whitney learned she was pregnant again. She would turn forty-two at the end of July, which meant the window for having their third child was closing. But she couldn't afford to take time off. Every day was a crapshoot. Schools were open, then they were closed, then they reopened. Their workers risked everything every time they took the bus to the factory or shared rides. Life was especially hard on the women stitchers who also had to coordinate child care, shopping, and cooking for their families between their shifts.

Then the video of New York cop Derek Chauvin kneeling on the neck of George Floyd for an excruciating nine minutes, twenty-nine seconds went viral. The video was irrefutable proof of the white-cop-kills-Black-citizen narrative, right there on everyone's phone, in everyone's social media feed.

Anger spread through the country like wildfire and people took to the streets.

Ben got a text from Paul Lemon at 4:55 a.m. on Monday, June 1, that the lobby of the AFL-CIO headquarters in D.C. was on fire.

A few hours later, Ben and Whitney held a staff meeting in Ben's office with American Roots' upper management—nine people, including Makenga and Anaam, who ran the shop floor; Amy McGowen, their new production manager (whose father was a retired cop); their CFO, a navy veteran; and Dave Butler, who'd grown up with children of law officers. Some of Ben's closest friends were cops, too.

They met to figure out the best way to come together as a community and support their workforce. Ben told the team that he and Whitney wanted to be thoughtful in their response to what was happening across the country and were mulling over putting out a statement. Maybe they could do a photo shoot with a Black Lives Matter banner above them to show the diversity of their workforce, pointing out that of the hundred-plus of people making face shields and masks, dozens were New Americans who had come from Africa.

What followed, Ben says, was "profound."

The room got quiet. No one said a thing.

Finally, Gina Alibrio, American Roots' thirtysomething customer service manager, looked around the room and said, "I'm sorry, but I think we gotta shut the fuck up and listen."

Ben and Whitney could count on Gina to call it like she saw it. Before the pandemic, she'd been a successful musician, fronting a big band with her rich alto and outsize personality, but since Covid killed Portland's club scene, her career was on hold. She planned to get back into the recording studio as soon as the country opened up. She was working at American Roots to survive until then.

After Gina spoke, everyone agreed that it would be better to hold listening tours in the factory.

Ben and Whitney knew they couldn't share people's pain, but they wanted to make it clear that they knew that what had happened was wrong. "I said right out of the gate: *It was murder,*" Ben said. "And the face shield team, the young people, I'll never forget their faces. They breathed a sigh of relief that the white boss was with them."

One of those young people was Fuad Umer, whose family had emigrated from Ethiopia. Both of his parents had worked for American Roots since the company's founding. Ben says, "Fuad's gonna work for NASA, brilliant kid, soccer player, straight A's." Fuad approached Ben after the meeting. Ben tried to read the young man's face. "We good?" Ben asked.

Fuad answered, "We good. I didn't know if we were gonna be good. It had been a week [since Floyd's death] and I hadn't heard from you, and we didn't know where you stood."

Ben recalls, "That drives home the fact that if you are silent, you are complicit."

The stress of managing unprecedented volume while keeping their workers safe took its toll on Whitney. She miscarried in late June and Ben tried not to succumb to the pain of loss or fatalistic thinking. They couldn't afford to.

The morning after her miscarriage, Whitney got up like any other day. Ben asked her if she felt strong enough to go in. She told him, in no uncertain terms, that she did. She didn't have a choice. She had to keep going.

"People gotta remember that 2020 was one of the most divisive years in history—with BLM, the pandemic, and a sociopathic, narcissistic dictator igniting fires every single day," Ben told me a year later. "It was exhausting for our company, for our families. You don't even realize how tense it was, life or death, outbreaks, because of unsafe, nonunion facilities where other family members were bringing home Covid to our employees."

A couple of weeks later, Ben and Whitney were able to stake out a few days to join Ben's parents and brothers and their families for the annual Waxman Family Week at a rented run-down cottage with a huge porch overlooking the ocean. It was the Fourth of July weekend; they assumed things at the factory would be quiet.

Whitney and Ben were exhausted. They'd lost a pregnancy but saved the company. Ben shares a photo taken on July Fourth, a warm, misty Saturday afternoon, snapped by his sister-in-law. Ben is sound asleep on the floor of the porch, cuddling baby Wyatt. Ben still had color in his hair back then. Two years later, it's pretty much white.

They got just a few days of peace. On the morning of July 7,

Whitney's phone buzzed on the bedside table. She rolled over to silence it, let it go to voice mail. Ben pulled her in close, but who were they kidding? An early morning call couldn't be anything but bad news. They enjoyed their last few moments of blissful ignorance, then Whitney got up, made coffee, and listened to the message. It was from their production manager, Amy. Contact tracing revealed that an employee had been in close proximity with someone who'd tested positive for Covid. Amy assured Whitney that the employee in question had stayed home, but half of the individual's family had worked in the factory that day.

Maybe they'd dodged a bullet. But Ben and Whitney's vacation was over.

The following day, contact tracers identified two more employees who had spent time with the individual. The Waxmans kept the factory running while they awaited test results. Two stressful days later, Whitney got a text: the first American Roots employee had tested positive. "My heart just stopped," Whitney says. "This was the real deal." They met with the entire staff, announced they had a positive case, and shut down for a deep clean and reassessment. There was fear, Whitney says, but it was contained. By Sunday, two more employees tested positive.

American Roots was officially experiencing an outbreak. Maine CDC officials recommended the company implement staff-wide testing, which they did on July 14. The next evening, the Waxmans learned they had eight additional cases, all mild. Contact tracing identified several more employees who might have had contact with those infected, and American Roots kept them home with pay. Eighty-six people returned to work; twenty-one stayed in quarantine.

"Here we were doing everything we could to keep staff safe," Whitney says, "and we realized that, as much as you do, the threat is still there. We'd put up plastic sheeting, we had Xs on floors marking out six feet, we were doing daily temperature checks, we'd implemented touchless time clocks and a full-time janitorial staff. It's like you're running toward a fire. No one is immune."

Eventually, everyone diagnosed with Covid recovered and returned to work. The Waxmans did company-wide testing four more times, with no additional cases as of mid-September. "Every time we got that 100 percent negative result," Whitney says, "it was another hurdle we'd jumped over. It confirmed that we were here for a reason."

A visitor to the factory in September would have seen that reason still very much in evidence: rows of masked employees on the floor stitching navy-blue masks, separated by reams of plastic sheeting. In a sense, it was a bittersweet scene. In spite of months of nationwide shutdowns, demand for protection had only grown. Kids were back in school and workers returning to jobsites. The masks were saving lives while allowing the country to function, sort of.

That fall, Ben and Whitney still had 130 people on payroll and were up $3.6 million in annual revenue. They'd had a few health scares and one Covid outbreak, but somehow they'd managed to contain the virus and keep going.

Then the WTO ruled that Trump's embargo of Chinese goods violated international law. Cheap masks from China began flowing back into the United States. And that was that.

"The Chinese weren't allowed to export shit," Ben said. "Nothing was coming out of China until July, and we didn't see the effect until late August." By September, he says, "cheap masks were everywhere." He said that Alibaba owned one of the largest mask manufacturers in the world, and at one point they were making 10 million masks a day. But he says that the masks they made weren't any good. "My neighbor, a working-class steelworker, came over to me in late April and said, 'Ben, I need a mask from you guys.' Then he pulled out a Chinese-made mask he'd bought online. It looked like a thong for a groundhog."

Mask orders were slowing down, and Ben and Whitney felt relief mixed with dread. They'd been running nonstop for eight months. Their lives had been consumed by Covid, masks, testing, masks, Covid.

In November, they dared to imagine a post-Covid future. Along the long wall of the factory overlooking the Presumpscot, piles of cut hoodie pieces were stacked on shelves, untouched since March. A few weeks back, a silk-screen artist had come in to customize a few finished hoodies with a mermaid motif for a customer. Anyone exhausted with mask wearing and social distancing could look at those army-green sweatshirts and remember that there was a time before Covid. And that there would be a time after.

Those brand-new, American-made, union-made, hand-screened hoodies seemed like a promise that American Roots would get back to doing what it was built to do.

Ben and Whitney's mask orders dried up, and Ben began to pivot from selling masks to finding new markets for their hoodies. Without new mask orders, they were forced to scale back their workforce, an awful thing to do. All those people had risked their lives to come to the factory every day throughout the first year of the pandemic. They could have stayed home. But they didn't.

Ben and Whitney waited until after Thanksgiving to let half of their employees go, out of consideration for those who had sustained the company over that crazy year.

Now that they were bigger, Ben had to sell harder. But the world wasn't ready to open. In December, Ben told me, "We're already $295,000 behind for orders for the first quarter of 2021, and there are nine days left to sell."

AN OMEN

When American Roots shut down in March 2020, less than 10 percent of the N95 masks used in the U.S. were manufactured in the States. Ben and Whitney retooled the factory floor, designed a cotton knit mask with a filter from scratch, and put it in production. They sold $3.6 million of them to first responders, unions, state workers, and private companies, which gave Ben and Whitney a taste of the big time.

At the peak of production in 2020, they had 150 employees.

With the new year, and soon a new U.S. president, it was time to launch American Roots 3.0.

In a way, Ben thought as he pulled into the Dana Mill lot on the morning of January 6, the pandemic, as horrific as it had been, had given them a taste of their potential. Wasn't that part of the reason they'd worked so hard to restart manufacturing? A nation that made its own goods could weather most storms. The pandemic proved the point.

Whitney and Ben had spent their first six years at American Roots learning the business, scaling up, building their reputation as the kind of company that stood by its work. During the year of the pandemic, they'd run a million miles an hour under extreme conditions. They'd earned goodwill from new customers across the country.

This year—2021—would be the year they got it right. They planned a capital raise of $2 million and had a long wish list for that cash, including a $75,000 Japanese embroidery machine, which would help them bring more operations in-house to establish more predictability in production.

Within the first ten minutes of the first American Roots board meeting of the new year, Patti Devlin announced that she was sending Ben and Whitney another $50,000 check. It was a very emotional moment. To avoid embarrassing her, Ben tried to play it cool while feeling immense gratitude to her.

But Covid wasn't over; another wave was hitting Maine. So they started 2021 with a whisper, not a roar. They kept a skeleton crew on the payroll and tasked them with making hoodies for a union client.

January 6 started out for Ben like all the other days. Lights on, a quick glance at the newspaper, black coffee. Just another day at the factory where half of American Roots' stitchers would soon be working in Factory 2 down the hall.

He often gazed out the window while contemplating the things they'd be able to accomplish with a little more time, a little more money. That morning, he witnessed a bald eagle pluck a songbird from midair with its talons and fly off, trailed by a team of tiny, furious birds. Dory would call that an omen.

Ben spent the rest of the morning on the phone. He'd been working for weeks to close a big WeatherTech deal that involved thousands of customized T-shirts, a product they'd developed just before the pandemic struck. He thought American Roots and WeatherTech's values aligned, and he cut his price multiple times to get their business, which would be a big win for Ben, Whitney, and their seventy-eight employees.

An order that size would keep the factory going through spring.

WeatherTech made car and truck mats in Illinois. The company had spent millions of dollars on a Super Bowl ad that ran the previous February. "Strength comes from an industrial infrastructure that can ramp up instantly," said David MacNeil, the company's founder

and CEO. "If you're a society with no industry, you have a problem."
MacNeil spent his time extolling the virtues of building up American
industry. "First and foremost," he told a journalist, "if my neighbor
doesn't have a job, sooner or later, I won't have a job. I think of my
neighbors as the 300-plus million people here in America—that's
our family. You have to have an industrial infrastructure. It's part of
our national defense to have steel mills and machine shops. Peace is
through strength."

In the afternoon, Ben was on a call with Texas Dems, who were
in the process of ordering custom-printed masks for a fundraising
campaign. The design, screen-printed in white on navy-blue fabric, pictured JFK with the quote: "MASK what you can do for your
country." The customer thought the design was problematic because
it took a while to see the "M" in the word "mask." He wanted the
design changed and gave Ben a series of fixes to relay to his graphic
designer.

During the call, Ben's phone began buzzing like crazy, and he
glanced down at the texts pouring in. Instantly, he saw that something was going on in D.C. While the meeting continued, Ben took
a moment to read what people were saying.

A mob of white supremacists and radicalized libertarians had gathered en masse at the Capitol to protest the result of the election and
was now in the process of breaching police barricades. In a few minutes, they were inside the Capitol building. Once they were there,
they began hunting for Speaker of the House Nancy Pelosi and Vice
President Mike Pence. One guy showed up with duct tape and zip
ties. They wandered around, defacing the building, a bit stunned that
they'd gotten that far without being arrested. They took selfies and sat
in seats reserved for congresspeople.

They stood at the dais and fist-pumped.

That's all Ben knew.

For the thousandth time during the Trump administration, Ben
couldn't focus on growing American Roots. His phone was blowing up. Ben wanted to cut the Zoom call short but the Texas Dems

were unfazed. Maybe they didn't quite get the seriousness of what was going on. Maybe they were ready to move on. Maybe they were exhausted. Anyone paying attention had expected at least one more Trump stunt.

In Factory 2, the stitchers and inspectors were cranking out hoodies for an order due at the end of the week.

When the call ended, Ben finally caught up on the news. "We should make an announcement," he told Whitney.

"Wait until 3:40," she responded. No reason to disrupt work before the end of the day and lose twenty minutes of production.

Ben paced, checked his phone, looked at the footage online.

When it was time, he and Whitney went to Factory 2 together. They stood in front of the few dozen workers, mostly women, some in hijabs, some wearing headwraps, all wearing face masks. Over the past four years, they'd gathered their staff like this several times. It was almost always to tell them bad news—George Floyd's murder, Trump's election. Speaking to people who might not understand every word, Ben tried his best to explain American behavior, which was sometimes inexplicable. He had to reassure his staff that they were safe, even if he wasn't so sure himself. The past year had been particularly hard—pandemic, furloughs, hiring, layoffs, fear. Once again, there was more chaos coming out of D.C.

Ben spoke slowly so that Anaam could later translate his message into Arabic. Because everyone was wearing masks, they could only see each other's eyes. The needleworkers looked at Ben and tried to read the threat level, trying to parse what he was saying. Some stared blankly, uncomprehendingly.

Ben delivered news of the attack on the Capitol with shame and disgust, emphasizing that it was the act of a few people gone rogue, not an expression of American will. He finished his short speech with "We'll be okay." Stitchers huddled in their language groups to confer. There was confusion, concern, disbelief. What did it all mean? Would they have to move again? If so, where would they go?

When Ben and Whitney left the room, people immediately fished out their phones for news from the outside world, then headed home to their families.

The next day, Anaam described how the immigrant community at American Roots had processed what they'd seen and heard. "Yesterday, they were scared. There was fear," she said. Everyone knew there were Trump supporters in Maine. They'd seen the signs on lawns and barns; they'd seen the jacked-up trucks flying obscenely large Trump flags, a few modified to "roll coal"—spew black diesel exhaust, unmitigated by the vehicle's catalytic converter, to deliberately pollute the environment and piss off the libs. They knew the sinister meaning of the Thin Blue Line flag. They worried that a mob would ignite an attack in Maine. They wondered whether they were safe in their homes or in their cars. They worried about their children.

Anaam's husband stopped delivering food from their restaurant early that evening, just to be safe.

But today, the mood was lighter. She found it reassuring that this particular wound—the January 6 attack—was self-inflicted, small, and nonsensical. She said things are different in Iraq, where three neighboring countries are trying to destabilize the government. "We have seen entire regimes overthrown," she said. "We never felt this could happen here because there are good rules, good people."

Khalid added, "When the Capitol was attacked yesterday, we knew the United States would get it together because this is America, where people love their country and believe in the law."

CORNERING THE COTTON MARKET

By March, the January 6 wound still felt raw, but there was good news, too: Covid vaccines were coming. The states were meting out the first available doses to those most vulnerable, including the elderly and health care workers, and American Roots was scheduled to host a vaccination clinic for workers in early April. There was a sense that things could return to normal by the summer.

But the supply chain was breaking down.

On March 19, Ben got a panicked call from Ned Pilchman, their fabric supplier, about another huge wrench in the works. Ned told him that China was—at that very moment—cornering the global cotton market. The price of fabric could potentially triple over the next year. Ned and Ben conferenced with Ned's partner Gary, who worked directly with the mills that produced the fabric.

The fabric guys had seen this kind of thing before and said it wasn't pretty. China may be the world's top cotton grower and top cotton consumer, but a major share of those Chinese-made goods ends up on U.S. soil, not in Chinese closets. About 97 percent of the apparel sold in the U.S. is imported, the bulk of it from China.

Gary said that whenever Chinese producers got a sense that the global cotton supply wouldn't meet demand, they'd buy up American cotton contracts. The same thing happened in 2009, causing the cost of cotton to surge 300 percent over two years. "Nine years ago, China went in and bought all of that year's future cotton contracts. They owned them all at 40 cents," Gary said. "That forced the price up. Cotton went in the field from 40 cents per pound to over a $1.20 and yarn prices tripled. It was a total disaster, but everybody had to do business."

The last time cotton prices skyrocketed like that was just after the Civil War.

By the time Gary and Ned got Ben on the phone, the pandemic had cast the pall of uncertainty over every market. Raw goods looked particularly vulnerable to shortages due to labor issues, shipping problems, and drought. Awash in cash with easy access to government loans, Chinese producers could easily buy up 75 percent of the world's cotton futures as a hedge against their domestic supply.

Ned later explained the situation in more detail. "If you wanted to start a manufacturing business today, you couldn't do it because you can't get yarn. Not just because of China. It's just that it's sold out." He said part of the problem was that there were very few independent yarn mills left in the U.S. Canada-based T-shirt giant Gildan, which bought American Apparel* in 2017, needed so much yarn for their T-shirts (made in Central America) that they simply bought one of Ned's main yarn suppliers.

Supply for independent manufacturers like American Roots was as scarce as a union-made hoodie.

"What's the long-term outlook? Is this a temporary thing as mills reopen?" Ned asked Gary.

"Right now the demand for the yarn is so great that I suspect this is going to continue through the year."

"You mentioned a number of mills shut down because of the pandemic," Ben said. "Are those plants coming on line?"

---

* A Berry Amendment supplier of apparel to the Department of Defense.

"Only if there's business to run them. They're not gonna come on line to produce extra capacity. People who can are planning out further ahead to lock in a price and make sure they're gonna get their goods. Short-term orders are almost impossible, no one is stocking up," Gary said.

No one on the call mentioned that the buy-up might have been spurred by darker forces as well. A few weeks prior, the U.S., the EU, and Britain had sanctioned Chinese officials for their treatment of the country's 12.8 million Uyghurs, an ethnic Muslim minority. Reports of concentration-camp-like conditions had been trickling out of the cotton-producing region, Xinjiang, in northwest China, where the Uyghurs have lived for more than 1,200 years. Those who managed to escape spoke of forced labor, child-separation practices, lifetime internment, and forced sterilization. The Chinese government repeatedly blocked auditors and U.N. inspectors from confirming reports. And still, horror stories leaked out.

Dependency on Chinese cotton goods kept some international brands from crying foul or working too hard to uncover what was happening in Xinjiang. Instead, they hired independent auditors to confirm that their supply chain was "clean," but those auditors knew where their bread was buttered and tended to look the other way—giving the thumbs-up even when they suspected tainted cotton was somewhere in the supply chain.

Human rights groups, on the other hand, continued issuing reports that were becoming too damning to ignore. Mainstream media finally began reporting on the Uyghurs' plight, which made brands nervous.

Chinese retaliation was a real concern. When fashion giant H&M announced that it was severing ties with some Xinjiang cotton suppliers due to concerns that it might be associated with Uyghur slave labor, the Chinese government quickly unleashed a youth army to attack the company on social media. Chinese influencers went to work smearing the Swedish multinational brand for hypocrisy. Their thorniest campaigns focused on America's history of slavery in an effort to highlight Westerners' apparent hypocrisy. One user posted an animated video of white-hooded men pointing guns at Black cotton pickers; it ended with a lynching.

"Today's China is not one that just anyone can bully," a television star wrote to his nearly seven million followers. "We do not ask for trouble, but we are not afraid of trouble either."

Zhao Lijian, a spokesman for China's Foreign Ministry, announced, "These foreign companies refuse to use Xinjiang cotton purely on the basis of lies. Of course this will trigger the Chinese people's dislike and anger."

Whether China's 2021 cotton buying spree was motivated by supply concerns or rigging the market in retaliation for embarrassing Western sanctions was above Ned's and Gary's pay grade. All they knew, as Gary said, was that "the ground game has changed. People who can are planning out further ahead to lock in a price and make sure they're gonna get their goods."

American apparel companies that depended on the global supply chain began to scramble back to domestic suppliers, in an effort to stabilize production and stay out of headlines.

Consumers' preferences were also shifting. Before Covid, Gary said, "Everybody was into high-tech stretchy fabrics, so demand for cotton started to slide and they planted less." Now, with so many people working from home, "they don't wanna be in that stretchy exercise stuff. They wanna be in a nice cotton garment. They wanna be comfortable. So demand has increased but the supply isn't there."

Take Fruit of the Loom, he said. "Those guys historically spin their own or outsource it all over the world, a lot in Central America. They're now finding that they've gotta source here in the States because they can't get everything they need. They're going to domestic mills and saying 'Hey, I wanna lock up 50 percent of your production.' Who's gonna say no to that?"

Ben hunched over his speakerphone, listening to what his suppliers were telling him, trying not to have a heart attack. This was their world, not his. He knew how to sell hoodies and T-shirts to unions, but the intricacy of the supply chain was something he had to leave to them.

Privately, Ben would let loose about middlemen in America, how everyone seems to get a piece of the action, jacking up the price of everything we buy. But in this instance, a lot of what they were telling him sounded right, confirmed by things he'd read in *The Wall Street Journal* or heard from his colleagues in the unions. He took their warning to heart.

At that very moment, the Biden administration was crafting its trade agenda to support a $3 trillion spending bill that read like a new New Deal—worker-centric trade policy, sustainability, racial equity, much of it geared to address China's "coercive and unfair economic trade practices." American policymakers' romance with free trade was over, but now that China was such a powerful economic presence around the globe, they had to work gingerly.

Wasn't everything aligning for domestic manufacturing? Wasn't Biden speaking the same language as the aggrieved Americans who had elected Trump?

Ben and Whitney didn't have the bandwidth to manage the news about the Chinese hedge on cotton futures, and Ned and Gary weren't there to coach American Roots. Whitney was in the first trimester of another pregnancy, and some days, like this one in early March, she just couldn't make it to the factory. Pandemic stress also continued taking its toll on their family. Ben's parents were taking care of Arlo and Wyatt—a classmate had tested positive for Covid, so school was closed for the next ten days. Before they could leave the kids with Dan and Dory, they had to get them tested. In the middle of the Zoom call, an exasperated Ben told Ned and Gary, "If you haven't witnessed a four-year-old and an eighteen-month-old get that swab up their noses, well, it's horrible." Ned had only so much compassion for them. Experience told him that manufacturing was a cutthroat business—supply, labor, sales, machines—so many steps along the way to a finished garment could bust the business. Every single part of it was complex and vulnerable to global forces out of a producer's control. That's why most major American companies got out of the business altogether.

You just gotta take the lumps and keep fighting. That's how Ned's business stayed alive.

Ned and Gary told Ben and Whitney to get in their orders early, like right now, to lock in a price. They stressed that moving fast wouldn't just save them money. If American Roots didn't place their orders for the entire year, they might not be able to get cotton fleece when they needed it. Without fleece, there'd be nothing for their workers to do. There'd be nothing to make and nothing to sell.

Ben hated putting more pressure on his wife, but he was convinced that they didn't have a choice. Over Zoom, he asked Whitney if she and Evan Sullivan, her right-hand man, could spend the next week figuring out how much fabric they'd need for 2021.

Whitney knew this was coming but couldn't conceal her exasperation. From the beginning, American Roots was a made-to-order company. When orders landed on her desk, Whitney and her production team made it work, but that business model stressed everyone, from Whitney to the floor manager to the stitchers racing against deadlines. The background on her computer was a fireman putting out a fire.

At the end of a typical busy week, thousands of hoodies might pile up on tables, waiting to be inspected, tagged, bagged, and packed. Stitchers would get up from their machines, stretch, and leave, while upper management stayed behind to help the packers finish the job.

Whitney could ballpark how much fleece she'd need based on previous years, but this being 2021, who really knew?

"Should we go through the calendar and literally write up production orders for the entire year and send them to you?" Ben asked.

"Yes," said Ned and Gary. "Yes!"

"But here's the caveat," said Ben. "I can't move a half a million dollars next week, guys."

"We only need money for the order when it's delivered. If you order the fabric, I can place a contract to buy the yarn at a certain price. When we get close to the point we need to manufacture it, then we'll need money."

"In that scenario, what if business conditions change and our sales tank. Are we locked in to buy that fabric?" Ben asked.

"That's the whole other point," Gary said. "Once I buy a contract, I'm bound to take the yarn, unless through the goodness of my supplier's heart, they'll let me out of it, but that's not gonna happen."

"If you want the price locked in now," Ned said, "I've gotta place the order for yarn. This is a whole new ball game."

"We'll do a conservative schedule for the year," Ben said.

"Good. Otherwise, you can't count on a stable price," Gary said, "and you can't count on the idea that the yarn will be there when you want it."

Six days later, *Ever Given,* a 1,312-foot container ship—sixty-two feet longer than the Empire State Building—got broadsided by high winds while she was creeping through the Suez Canal. The ship began to yaw. Lacking a tugboat assist, the pilot couldn't correct course quickly enough, and over several painful minutes, he stood helplessly by as the bow and stern of the massive ship dug into the soft, sandy banks.

About 30 percent of the world's shipping container volume travels through the Suez Canal daily, accounting for about 12 percent of total global trade of all goods.

Ever Given would block shipping traffic both ways for six days, at an estimated cost of $400 million per hour. The ship was Japanese-owned, chartered by a Taiwanese shipping company, registered in Panama, en route from China to Rotterdam. It was capable of carrying 200,000 tons—equivalent to about one hundred Statues of Liberty.

Globally, shipping costs were spiking. At the ports of Los Angeles and Long Beach—where 40 percent of apparel and footwear imports cross into the U.S.—the shortage of shipping containers was wreaking havoc and causing extensive delays.

For the first time in forever, American businesspeople and analysts were seriously starting to talk about onshoring manufacturing.

LABOR PAINS

On April 7, 2021, Ben wrote in his notebook: "Today we get vaccinated. Lot of emotion. Things are tough right now—uncertainty has
riddled the economy and caused significant problems in our ability
to pivot back to our clothing line. We will get through it. American
Roots is at $329K [revenue] needs to be at $500K by next Friday.
Morale is getting better with the vaccine. Cash is tight."

With the $700,000 they'd raised from their board and a handful
of investors, Ben and Whitney hired a marketing firm and began
intense weekly hour-long sessions with Cam Burns and Mike Daitch
of Versed Creative. They hoped that getting their message out to a
broader audience would bring in more consumers willing to use their
spending power to build a better world.

These were soul-searching discussions, designed to help Cam and
Mike refine American Roots' mission statement and create a new
logo. Whitney's goal was to communicate how difficult their path
had been. "There's nothing about what we do that's comfortable,"
she told Cam and Mike. "This is fucking hard work. Hardest thing
I've ever done. Any of us have ever done. Manufacturing in the U.S.,
it's not comfortable."

Ben thought about the word *comfortable*. He wanted to be sure that Cam and Mike understood what they'd been through to make American Roots work. "This is gonna come across really arrogant," Ben said. "You can open a restaurant, you can open a marketing firm, but there's no roadmap for what we're doing. It doesn't exist. People who do it, they won't give it to you. They don't want the competition.

"That's why I want a mission statement that punches people in the face and inspires them in the heart. I want to get a little bit rawer. We've literally bled and sweated. I think the consumer wants to know that. They won't even give a shit about the price [of the hoodies] because they'll be so moved by this company.

"We do believe in keeping our workers safe and retiring with dignity, and we're never gonna apologize about who we are. This is our way, this is who we are. You got a problem with it? Don't come in."

Evan Sullivan, American Roots' designer and production assistant, added, "To boil this down, we're selling a value system, and what we're making is clothing."

How much *did* ethics drive buying decisions? Ben knew that many Americans couldn't afford to make choices. Another swatch of Americans couldn't give a damn where their clothes were made or by whom under what conditions. Research however suggested that nearly 80 percent of Americans were willing to spend more for domestically made goods. But how much more? Who knew? Ben and Whitney hoped that a big marketing campaign would, at the very least, get their hoodies in front of consumers who maybe, possibly, perhaps might choose an American Roots hoodie when given a chance.

Mike and Cam proposed the mission statement: "Everything American Roots makes is 100 percent American-made, by hand with union labor. When you put on one of our sweatshirts you'll never have to worry about where your clothing came from, what the conditions were in the factory, or who made it. Because at American Roots we know nothing is as comfortable as wearing your values." Mike told Ben and Whitney to "mull it over."

Meanwhile, the ruthlessness of American business leaders like Jeff

Bezos continued to have a pervasive effect on all Americans, whether they knew it or not.

In March 2021, mainstream media focused on the unionization effort at an Amazon warehouse in Bessemer, Alabama. The trial of the Derek Chauvin, the murderer of George Floyd, was running in the background.

Leading up to the unionization effort, multiple exposés had been published on the inhumane working conditions forced on Amazon employees—people passing out from heat in un-air-conditioned warehouses, or wearing diapers while working because they didn't want to take bathroom breaks for fear of losing their bonuses. A few Amazon delivery drivers claimed they peed in bottles to meet their demanding schedules. Amazon managers revealed that they were expected to fire a certain percentage of their workers every year. In aggregate, a picture was emerging that Bezos, one of the world's richest people, had created an uncertain and unstable work environment to control his workforce, a tactic forged in the 1980s by GE chairman and CEO "Neutron Jack" Welch.

Labor advocates hoped that organizing would not only make life better for Amazon's workers but also ignite unionization efforts across the country. Or, at the very least, encourage business leaders to behave better.

But during the voting period, Amazon workers alleged, the company used classic intimidation and coercion tactics to keep the union out. A month before the voting began, Amazon hired Labor Information Services, a well-known union-busting consulting firm, which instituted mandatory antiunion meetings where employees were told that they would lose benefits or their jobs if unionization succeeded. Workers who dared to ask questions had their badges scanned—a form of intimidation. The company also installed tamper-prone USPS boxes in the warehouse parking lot to collect votes. (Workers were supposed to mail their votes directly to the National Labor Relations Board.) Subsequently, two large shipments of ballots arrived at the NRLB full of "no" votes, comprising 20 percent of the total Bessemer count.

The initial Amazon union effort failed in mid-April. "They got beat up by Amazon last week," Ben said. "We need labor law reform laws now." He knew something was amiss: "I'm pissed about the reporting on that."

Following an investigation, the NRLB determined that Amazon had "essentially hijacked" the election and ordered a second Bessemer election.

In the struggle to organize Amazon workers, Ben saw the bigger story of American business. He knew that the American economy wouldn't be rescued by cryptocurrencies, altruistic billionaires, or rockets aimed at Mars. Not at all. He didn't even have much faith in policy. He believed that rebuilding the economy would require an army of ordinary heroes just like Whitney and him who believed that domestic industries could support each other, thereby becoming self-sustaining.

"American Roots isn't just American Roots," Ben would say. "It's the cotton facility in North Carolina. It's the binding facility in South Carolina. It's the thread facility in South Carolina. It's the label company in Auburn, Maine. It's the stamp company in Massachusetts. It's the cutter who cuts in Massachusetts. It's all those things, right? If you invest in that, you're investing in the economy of the country. That's how you can actually rebuild the middle class."

But domestic manufacturing would only succeed if a majority of business leaders shifted their goals from profit to sustainability, from growth to equilibrium: "If you can't figure out a way to keep your shareholders happy and your workers employed with living wages, retirement, and benefits, then you're not doing your job," Ben says. "Eventually you hit a breaking point when you have so much wealth at the top, it's no longer feeding the ecosystem."

That's precisely what he and Whitney were fighting against, one sweatshirt at a time.

Covid kept many American workers home for a second year;

conventions were canceled. Ben and the sales team cleared only $382,000 in the first quarter; 2021 was starting to look a lot like 2019, but now they had nearly three times the workforce. How could American Roots afford to keep them?

During their branding brainstorms, Ben and Whitney contemplated using the American flag in their new logo. They were worried that the symbol had become too politicized, with the subtle Thin Blue Line flag popping up everywhere. There was a lot of discussion about how the image of the American flag had been wielded during the riot on January 6. At the moment, the image of the flag seemed angry, divisive, dangerous. In contrast, American Roots was wide open and inclusive. They wanted to appeal to all working people. Could any version of the flag a designer came up with be misinterpreted?

"Maybe we don't need an American flag in the logo," Ben said, thinking about the fraught political climate.

Later in the conversation, Whitney summed up their thinking: "So, no fists, no eagles, no flags."

In May, Ben and Whitney faced another crisis. There were so few textile professionals left in New England that they relied on a single pattern-cutter based in Fall River, Massachusetts, to do all their fabric cutting. It was a cumbersome process. They had their fleece shipped to him, then waited for him to cut and ship the garment pieces back. Because they didn't have an in-house cutter, their production schedule was bound to the vagaries of local shipping and their fabric-cutter's occasional personal issues. They had to trust that he was cutting well to maximize their yield. They also had to trust that he was taking care of himself.

American Roots' cutter worked in a blocks-long cut-granite former cotton mill, built in the late nineteenth century, near the Taunton River, upriver from Buzzards Bay. The building sat in a sea of open parking lots dotted by fast-food joints. Much of the historic manufacturing city had been bulldozed during the urban renewal era, then cleaved by the construction of I-95.

The pattern-cutter worked on the dusty top floor under the

timber-framed roof. In the summer, it was like a sauna; in the winter, he could see his breath while he worked.

To cut American Roots hoodie backs, fronts, sleeves, and hoods, he rolled out 100-foot lengths of cotton fleece on his table, creating a neat pile of fabric, maybe twenty layers thick. Then he laid Ann's pattern pieces on top, using his expertise to determine the best way to fit the pieces together so that they nested well without leaving much fabric waste. Cutting was done with a rotary saw equipped with a ten-inch exposed vertical blade that ran on a small wheeled stand. Their cutter wore a metal-mesh glove on his left hand to avoid accidentally slicing off a finger.

Bigger fabric-cutting outfits had tables hundreds of feet long and used computer-aided robotic cutters to slice through pieces with more speed and precision. High-tech cutters could get through fifty layers of fabric at a time, compressed into a solid, easy-to-cut block by tables outfitted with an air compression system. At L.A.'s Bella + Canvas, the country's largest cutting and dyeing operation, mechanized fabric spreaders rolled out fabric on the company's eighty-one tables, built so long that the person manning the spreader rode on a mechanized platform alongside the bolt as it unfurled—back and forth, dozens of times a day.

Ben knew that the man who did their pattern-cutting had issues, but he'd managed to keep it together. As someone who'd grappled with drug dependency, Ben was sympathetic. In May 2021, though, the cutter experienced a personal crisis and was unable to deliver work he'd promised weeks earlier.

That was it—Ben and Whitney couldn't keep outsourcing such a critical part of their operation. It was a lesson all American companies were learning during the pandemic.

Ben and Whitney wanted to bring the cutting operation in-house but didn't have anyone trained in that line of work. The temporary fix was to have Merrow, another five-plus-generation family-owned Fall River company, take over their cutting operation until they could train their own cutter. That decision meant that Ben and two of his employees would lose yet another few days of work driving down to Fall River to transfer half a million dollars' worth of American Roots fabric from their cutter's studio to Merrow.

On a steamy Monday in late May, Ben picked up a twenty-six-foot U-Haul in Portland and drove three hours down to southern Massachusetts with Khalid and Ludovic Ndengabeka Bobe. Both men had landed in Maine with their families after fleeing their own countries. Both of them were victims of postcolonial politics.

When Ludovic was a small boy in the early 1960s, he lived in Paris, where his father served as a diplomat for the Congo Republic—"the other Congo"—from which the French had withdrawn in 1958. The entire region was in flux. France and Belgium had subjugated the Congolese in the nineteenth century and forced native populations, sometimes at gunpoint, to sacrifice their rich, multilingual systems of making and trading for the sake of a monoculture devoted to extracting natural resources and building a dependency on European goods, services, and support. Complex social structures on which economic and labor relationships had once been based were deliberately decimated.

When Congo gained its independence shortly before Ludovic was born, its citizens had to conjure much more than a government from whole cloth. They had to rebuild markets and create new manufacturing infrastructure from thin air, while fighting off tasty cash offers from all-powerful mining and oil interests. Any manufacturing and trading structures that did exist needed to be reconsidered within the new global landscape. Where would the financing come from? Who would make what to drive the local economies?

Unlike Britain's former slave-owning and slave-trading families—who shockingly, until 2015, received reparations from the U.K. government for loss of income when the slave trade was banned—there would be no reparations to the people who had suffered under colonialism.

Reentry as a developing country into a fully globalized world must have been rough going. Government officials had to wean people off costly imports while nurturing the reboot of myriad necessary industries and supply chains. Every part of society would need to be reinvented.

The first elected officials of tiny Congo-Brazzaville explored various ways to bolster industry, repair the social fabric, and redistribute wealth after nearly a century of occupation. Like most postcolonial governments at the time, the first leaders of the Congo Republic believed the fastest route to recovery should have strong socialist underpinnings. The country became one of the few Marxist countries in Africa, fully aligned with the Soviet Union. This situation caught the attention of the CIA, which had a robust presence in the neighboring Democratic Republic of the Congo.

As in Chile, CIA operatives worked to destabilize the region and undermine the Marxist Congo Republic government. The country's president was assassinated in 1977. After the fall of the Soviet Union, the oil-rich country fell under the spell of the IMF and the World Bank—two organizations that extended massive cash loans backed by global banks. As mentioned previously, lending is another form of subjugation. The Congo Republic could take the money only if its leaders swore to give up any communist leanings. They accepted IMF loans and agreed to reprivatize industry, abandon expensive social programs, and let the market work its magic.

After the IMF forced debt restructuring in 1997, civil war broke out and dictator Sassou Nguesso assumed power. Decades later, he remains the leader of one of the most corrupt and repressive governments in Africa, infamous for embezzling astounding wealth from his country's petroleum production, leaving its citizens impoverished.

Nguesso's greed knows no bounds. In 2015, under the guise of rousting rebel factions, his military forces went berserk on unsuspecting agrarian villages. Nguesso's goal was to terrorize citizens into submission so that he could alter the constitution and install himself for a fourth term as president. An untold number of people were killed in the attacks (the destruction was documented by humanitarian groups through satellite imagery), and some 83,000 people fled their homes, causing a major crisis.

Ludovic was one of the few Congolese to gain asylum in the United States before Trump effectively shut down immigration. He arrived in the U.S. a few years ago with his wife and three young boys. He was fluent in French and Bantu, but even with his limited English he communicated a thoughtfulness and kindness that drew people to him. In 2021, his wife was pregnant with their fourth child.

In the old mill building in Fall River, Ben, Ludovic, and Khalid found American Roots' bolts of fabric in shoulder-high piles scattered around the shop floor. The men loaded the heavy rolls onto carts under the sun-scorched roof and pushed them to the ancient freight elevator. It was hot, sweaty work.

Their biggest concern was whether someone would end up getting stuck in that ancient lift.

Merrow charged American Roots a lot more for the service than their original cutter. Too much for them to afford, given the $80 they were charging for their hoodies.

Once again, any financial lead Ben and Whitney gained in the second quarter evaporated overnight due to this unexpected increase in production costs.

But really, American Roots had a production problem. Ben could pick up the phone and turn strangers into allies, then into loyal customers, but a lot of his time was spent justifying their price.

While most union leaders recognized that strong values and good quality cost money, the pandemic had hit the economy hard. Ben knew that $20 foreign-made hoodies were everywhere, tempting their customers. He needed more pricing wiggle room, which they could get from speeding up the line.

The profit in manufacturing depends on how quickly you can bang out your product. You can keep squeezing your fixed costs—labor, rent, insurance—but as you raise the rate of production, those fixed costs matter less and less.

To stabilize, to get enough market share to keep the workforce busy, to earn more money to reinvest in the company, Ben and Whitney needed to make hoodies faster. It was that simple.

But the usual methods managers used to speed up the line felt inhumane and contrary to the Waxmans' values. Whenever they talked about their company, Ben and Whitney never framed it in terms of production. They talked about their mission. They talked about the fact that they were paying their employees top dollar plus benefits. They talked about the seventy Maine families American Roots had pulled out of poverty. Ben and Whitney knew their stories; they knew their children and spouses. They knew what they'd been through.

The Waxmans didn't want to come down hard on the people making their product. Life was hard enough. "When we have big celebrations," Ben pointed out, "there's no food left. It goes in bags. It goes in boxes. Because the people that make American Roots work are survivors. When you're a survivor, you don't leave a crumb anywhere, even if you're making a living."

But day after day, they could feel their empathy banging up against the realities of manufacturing. Occasionally, Ben would have a fit when things were going too slow or there were too many screwups. One time he wrote in his notebook: "Today was a tough day. It was an ugly day in the factory. I had to drop a hammer. People are just not doing what they should be doing. I haven't done it in a long time."

Immediately, he felt regret and added: "But with that said, there's this underbelly of perseverance and grit, and just toughness in this company."

Ben's instinct was to throw money at problems. In 2020, their biggest year to date, they invested $366,000 in training.

Evan Sullivan, twenty-nine, thought he might have another answer. He was a clever, clear-eyed millennial who'd arrived at American Roots in 2020 with idealism in his heart and a knack for creating systems in his soul. Evan was a different kind of refugee—a victim of the fast fashion industry. The Maine native had graduated in 2013 from

Massachusetts College of Art and Design, the only publicly funded art school left in the country, founded by Massachusetts's textile and mercantile titans in the 1860s along with MIT and the Museum of Fine Arts. When he saw a help wanted ad in 2015 for a designer for American Roots, he applied.

Ben and Whitney didn't know what to make of the young designer's portfolio of leather catsuits and gothic black-lace lingerie ensembles, and hired someone else to oversee the initial design of their products.

Evan moved to Australia, where he eventually landed a job at an apparel-manufacturing company.

While Down Under, Evan says that he watched the demands of the cutthroat industry turn his boss into a tyrant. Evan says that he got increasingly uncomfortable working at the company but didn't have the perspective or knowledge to understand the systemic issues of fast fashion.

Eventually, burned out and disillusioned, Evan left his job in Australia and returned to Maine to wait tables in Kennebunkport. One night, he found a documentary series on YouTube about the fashion industry called *True Cost.* He says that while watching it, he got "super triggered." The documentary covered everything about fashion that he says he "didn't know about, or turned a blind eye to, or just was ignorant about." He realized that he'd personally witnessed the lengths to which managers would go—"always cutting safety corners and polluting the environment because fast fashion is all about the bottom line."

Evan thought he was done with fashion. "This is a horrible industry," he said. "It's always the garment workers getting squeezed. People say, *We need this polo to cost $1.25 to make a profit,* and the injustices just spin out from there." But when the pandemic forced the restaurant where he worked to close in April 2020, he found himself with nothing to do, and answered an American Roots ad for stitchers.

Ben and Whitney still weren't ready to hire a full-time designer, but Evan had sewing experience. Whitney admired his persistence, too. They offered him a sewing job and he took it.

For four months, Evan sat at a sewing table alongside the other women and men of American Roots and cranked out thousands of masks.

Evan didn't care that he wasn't designing. Working at American Roots, he felt he'd finally found his place in the fashion industry. "[Ben and Whitney] are doing it the right way," he told me. "If somebody asked me, 'What's the true cost of an American Roots piece?' I can say, 'This is where this comes from and this is the process.' It's very transparent here."

But Evan couldn't help himself; he saw dozens of ways that he could improve American Roots' production line. There were a few managers between him and Whitney, and he didn't want to step on any toes. But her door was always open, and they bonded while swapping stories of life in Australia.

One day, he walked into Whitney's office and proposed that American Roots initiate a stitcher program to better align skills with pay while developing a professional workforce.

At the time, stitchers' pay was commensurate with time employed. Evan proposed a different pay scale. With regular training sessions, he argued, stitchers could gain mastery on all the sewing machines and grow their arsenal of skills in return for higher compensation. His idea was to build flexibility into the American Roots workforce so that they could quickly switch from garment to garment—from hoodies to T-shirts to track jackets (their newest offering)—without having to spend a lot of time retraining.

When Evan told me about his plan in the early days of January 2021, I pointed out that most manufacturers wanted the opposite. Typically in mass production, each worker is encouraged to master a single task and do it endlessly but quickly and skillfully, rather than expand his or her skill set. They gained efficiency through specialization. I also mentioned that the more a worker knows, the more money the worker can theoretically demand, which would increase fixed costs.

I could sense Evan cringing behind his face mask. The classic production model sounded inhumane and antithetical to American Roots' mission, as well as his own.

By spring 2021, however, there was a growing sense that production needed to be overhauled, but no one inside American Roots had the bandwidth or training to make a change.

The production line is like a machine that needs constant feeding, but sometimes it wasn't easy to find things people needed when they needed them. Boxes were piled up everywhere. Stitchers sometimes sat idle waiting for thread, a replacement needle, or a new pile of garments to work on.

Evan thought there was a better way to lay out the space to reduce all that wait time. At the very least, maybe there was a way to reduce handling time—the seconds between picking up a piece, moving a piece under the needle, and actually stitching it. He also thought there were ways to incentivize working smarter. Poking around the internet, he stumbled on a manufacturing strategy called *kaizen,* Japanese for "continuous improvement." The strategy was based on the idea that you could vastly improve a system by making tiny, empirical tweaks.

Toyota was the first major company to fully apply the philosophy to every facet of its organization (which is why it's often called the Toyota Method), but it was originally an American concept. Kaizen was first developed by the U.S. War Department during World War II to help conscripted American companies produce materiel better and faster. After the war, the strategy was exported by the State Department to occupied Japan, where it was perfected, then reintroduced when Japanese auto manufacturers began setting up factories in the U.S. in the 1980s.

Evan found a book about kaizen in the library, but he didn't have much time to absorb it. The book landed on Ben's desk, where it sat untouched. Still, at American Roots, the word *kaizen* wended its way into everyday conversations among upper management, like a talisman. No one really had a handle on what it meant, but it seemed to suggest "the way."

Soon, Ben and Whitney were forced to rethink everything when their production manager, Amy McGowen, a thirtysomething single mom, felt she needed to leave her position to care for her young family.

To replace Amy, Ben and Whitney posted an online ad that generated few quality responses. With so little manufacturing in the region, it was tough to find anyone qualified to do the work. Finally, a job candidate in Detroit applied. When Ben mentioned that they were having production issues, she told him that he should talk to a guy named Marty Bailey.

The following day, Ben found himself deep in conversation with the man *Fast Company* once called the "Forrest Gump of manufacturing." The sobriquet fit; Marty had been everywhere and seen everything in the apparel industry. He had four decades of manufacturing experience—first for Fruit of the Loom in the 1980s and 1990s, then for L.A.'s American Apparel until the company went bankrupt in 2015, when its quirky founder and CEO Dov Charney was, depending on whom you ask, ousted by a board in a perfectly executed coup, or forced out Harvey Weinstein–style after multiple sexual harassment settlements cut too deep into profits. (More on Charney later; no book about modern apparel manufacturing would be complete without him.)

Because the bar for entry in the apparel industry was so perilously low—you just need a sewing machine and a pattern—inside knowledge usually was locked up, in part because everyone in the supply chain was ripping off everyone else just a little bit. Opacity keeps competitors guessing how the other guy can put out a $3 T-shirt or a $17 hoodie and still make a buck.

But here was a guy who'd been in a factory for decades and was willing to talk shop. Ben wasn't accustomed to anyone in the industry being so generous with their expertise without getting a check first.

As Marty spoke, Ben grabbed one of the multiple yellow legal pads on his desk and began scribbling the words and names Marty was throwing at him.

Ben hoped a few hours with Marty could save American Roots years of trial and error. They could skip up a few rungs toward global domination. Marty explained that he was currently working as a consultant for major manufacturers around the world. Ben asked him if he'd consider spending a couple days at the Westbrook factory on the Waxmans' dime to see whether there was a future American Roots with him in it. Marty said yes.

Why was this manufacturing master willing to fly from Long Beach, California, to an obscure apparel factory in Maine? Maybe Ben's idealism was infectious. Then again, maybe Marty wanted a reason to get out of L.A. Or maybe he'd heard that Maine real estate was hot and was looking for an excuse to check it out.

Whatever got Marty on the red-eye, American Roots needed help. There was no doubt about that.

The day he was expected to arrive, a heap of seconds was growing in the middle of the shop floor. They planned to donate the seconds that were usable, but no one had the time to pack them up. Some of the flaws were obvious, like a sleeve sewn onto itself. But most of the flaws, marked here and there with pieces of masking tape, were invisible to me. I never would have noticed that a zipper was positioned one-eighth inch too high. Hours and hours of work had been wasted making this pile of rejects. I wondered how the stitchers felt when they passed that mounting monument to error.

Even though it was only June, the outdoor temperature was hitting 90. The window air conditioner in Ben's office was set on stun; ceiling fans spun in a frenzy. Ben spent the morning making sales calls.

At 11 a.m., Marty quietly appeared in Ben's doorway. Marty was in his early sixties and Midwest-big—hands wide enough to sling bales of hay (which he'd done as a kid), long legs slightly truncated by middle-age paunch. What was really disarming about him, though, was his Kentucky accent, which seemed more out of place in the Maine factory than Arabic or Swahili. In that context, his inexplicable trouble keeping his face mask over his nose during those pandemic days could be mistaken as a form of protest. My first impression was that he was a good old boy.

Marty slid into a chair in Ben's office and sipped black coffee from a paper cup while Ben told him the American Roots story. Whitney was seated beside Ben, hands resting on her swelling belly. Their third child was due in October.

"We bootstrapped this, Marty, with all the money Whitney and I had," Ben began. He talked about their commitment to values and their supportive board. So many people had an emotional or ideo-logical stake in Ben and Whitney's success. He talked about Evan's new additional role as the efficiency expert.

Then he talked candidly about management burnout at the com-pany. "I tend to cause chaos," Ben admitted. He sold and sold. He never stopped. That left Whitney and the rest of the production team constantly scrambling to figure out how to get orders out the door.

It was when Ben began talking about the future of the company that his big, well-oiled sales pitch kicked into high gear. "Marty, we've only scratched the surface," he said. "There are 33,000 local unions in America that spend $250 million a year on clothing. We've been in touch with less than one percent of them. We'll hit the $10 million mark in sales on December 15th of this year. Our goal by 2031 is to own 10 percent of the labor apparel market, and get into direct-to-consumer. We believe our story and the quality of our clothes appeal to a large part of the population of this country. Whether it's a hipster in Brooklyn or a working-class guy in Ohio, everybody loves an all-American-made sweatshirt. We've just got to convince them to buy. Until then, we've got to figure out how to make these things faster. And it sounds like you know how to do that."

All eyes turned to Marty, who, up to that point, had sat quietly listening.

Then, in a slow, low, drawl, he said, "The word I would use is *sooner*, not *faster*."

Everyone in the room paused to ponder the significance of what he'd said.

"Sooner," repeated Ben tentatively, trying it out.

"It's not how fast you sew," Marty clarified, "it's how sooner you sew. So much of our time in this business is lost in the transition, in the handling, much more than under the needle. I take away the trash—the wasted movement and wasted motion that cost you time. That's it."

"Wasted movement," Ben repeated, wrapping his head around the concept.

"Wasted time. Anything that a professional apparel-worker does is absolutely vital to your operation. We work to eliminate the things that are happening every day that just don't have to happen. Because that's what gets in the way of success."

For the first time, maybe ever, an honest-to-god professional man-ufacturer was in the American Roots factory, but his big innovation was a century-old concept called Taylorism.

Taylorism was first proposed by Frederick Winslow Taylor, an upper-middle-class, well-connected Philadelphian who was one of the first nineteenth-century industrialists to analyze how actual humans were working from an efficiency standpoint. He's probably best remembered for hovering over workers with a stopwatch, timing their movements to the hundredth of a minute to determine the ideal time for any operation. His first paper, presented in June 1895, was titled "A Piece Rate System."

Taylor's "scientific management" system codified how workers should do their jobs. He reduced complex tasks to a series of simple operations that could be assigned to individuals on an assembly line. One person, one task. Taylor wasn't concerned about the dehuman-ization of factory workers; he regarded people who worked with their hands—laborers—as machines. He maintained that to get human machines working faster, you simply had to incentivize them with money. Take away their base pay, and make them work for every penny.

Taylor's observations became the foundation of a first-year course at Harvard Business School in 1906. His system influenced Henry Ford, and was admired by Lenin and Stalin—who both strove to transform Russia from an agrarian economy to an industrial one. Taylorism and its ilk also spawned a body of futuristic dystopian literature in the twentieth century, including *Brave New World* and *1984*—books in which workers are closely surveilled by faceless managers in an authoritarian hellscape designed to maximize efficiency.

Taylor was antiunion to the core, and hoped that by demystifying and codifying the manufacturing process, he could defang organized labor. Once that was accomplished, productivity could be uncoupled from the messiness of humanity.

In that final point, Taylor proved prophetic. Since 1950, U.S. productivity has increased 254 percent, but workers' actual wages decoupled from profits in the mid-1970s and have pretty much flatlined ever since. Economists will tell you all sorts of poppycock to justify the trend. None other than Larry Summers, who served as Clinton's secretary of the treasury and Obama's National Economic Counsel director, when looking at the now-ubiquitous graph showing productivity peeling up and away from average workers' wages over time, declared that actually, growth slowed over the past few decades, so why wouldn't wage increases slow as well? "If productivity growth had been as fast over 1973 to 2016 as it was over 1949 to 1973," he wrote, "median and mean compensation would have been around 41 percent higher in 2015, holding other factors constant."

Perhaps not so coincidentally, top CEO pay increased 1,322 percent during this same period, outpacing the stock market by 60 percent and crushing the paltry 18 percent increase in workers' annual compensation. Today's CEOs are no more effective at increasing productivity or innovation than their mid-century counterparts, but they're experts at setting their compensation, inflating the value of companies short-term, and reaping huge profits through stock options and stock awards. Summers's bonkers analysis of self-evident data reveals that he's a fantasist, not a scientist.

Talk of excessive executive compensation always got Ben fuming. One of the promises that he and Whitney made when they founded American Roots was that they would never earn more than four times their lowest-paid worker. It was obvious to anyone earning less than $24 million a year that no manager was worth that much. The AFL-CIO even has a webpage dedicated to tracking the most egregious offenders. Topping the CEO-to-worker pay ratio list in 2021 was Fran Horowitz, CEO of made-everywhere-else-but-America clothing line Abercrombie & Fitch. Fitch sells sweaters and jeans indistinguishable from other sweaters and jeans, manufactured in more than a hundred factories located in Bangladesh, Cambodia, China, and Vietnam. Fitch offers a "Soft AF" (short for "soft as fuck") zip-up hoodie for $59.* Horowitz earned 6,565 times her employees' median pay in 2021.

Marty wasn't interested in discussions about executive compensation, and he hadn't heard of Taylorism. He cared solely about production.

Ben finally handed Marty the floor, and the efficiency expert slowly unreeled his tale.

"I grew up in Campbellsville, Kentucky," Marty began. "I know you've never heard of Campbellsville, Kentucky. It's a town of about 8,000 people. After graduating from high school, I walked down to Campbellsville College and got a basketball scholarship, which paid for four years of school.

"Didn't pay to support my wife and my daughter, though.

"So when the NBA didn't call me, Fruit of the Loom did. Back then, in 1984, Campbellsville, Kentucky, was home to the largest

* Based on the Zara hoodie analysis, that Soft AF hoodie might earn the company as much as a 59 percent profit, or about $35.

apparel facility in the world. Forty-one hundred people in the facility, 3,100 sewing operators on one shift, producing 365,000 dozens of pieces a week." Marty's lenses magnified his pouchy eyes, which made it that much more startling when he opened them wide. "Dozens," he repeated.

"I took my last three final exams and went to the factory. I hadn't slept in three days. The president of Fruit of the Loom asked me what I wanted, and I said, 'I want your job' and he hired me.

"Fruit was doing $500 million in sales at that point and looking to expand. The trade wars hadn't started yet. The only war Fruit was in the middle of was between Walmart and Kmart. Pricing wars. They were trying to put each other out of business. I heard stories of the chairman saying, 'We're just going to go to Walmart and buy our stuff back because we can buy it back cheaper than we can make it.' It was that crazy.

"My job was to learn. I was hired as a sewing supervisor of six units, about six hundred people. Of course, the only thing I knew about underwear was how to put it on, and I didn't always get that right. But I spent two years with them, the best in the industrial apparel-manufacturing business, and within two years, I was opening a facility for Fruit of the Loom in Montreal, then North Carolina, then Mississippi. Over the next several years, I was opening facilities all over the country. We went from half a billion to $2.4 billion in seven years."

A year after Marty took the job at Fruit, the company was taken over in a leveraged buyout by serial corporate raider William Farley, a Dale Carnegie–esque figure—handsome, fit, charming—who was itching to try his hand at creating a 1980s-style monopoly through mergers and acquisitions. He began expanding Fruit.

The Federal Trade Commission had just stopped enforcing antitrust laws, launching a thirty-five-year mergers and acquisitions frenzy.

The new monopolists like Farley used easy access to cash to consolidate companies at a terrifying rate, from a couple of thousand mergers and acquisitions in 1985 to 15,465 in 1998. Since 1985, more than one million mergers and acquisition deals have been completed globally, which explains why homespun ice cream brand Ben & Jerry's is now owned by multinational British conglomerate Unilever.

Fruit of the Loom's main competitor, Hanes, itself was a family business until 1979, when it was the target of a hostile takeover by the Sara Lee Corporation.

The new monopolists' goal wasn't to control prices by creating value, rather it was to "pit supplier against supplier, and worker against worker, and community against community," writes Barry C. Lynn in *Cornered: The New Monopoly of Capitalism and the Economics of Destruction.* "Unlike a generation ago," he writes, "the purpose of these first is no longer mainly to make things, nor to plan how to keep making things, nor even to understand how things are made. The purpose is to engineer rivalry among the actual people who make things in a way that results in a more rapid generation of cash in the accounts of the rich."

In his first five years, Farley borrowed heavily against Fruit and went on a shopping spree, "buying labels and whatnot, buying every kind of operation out there," Marty said. "Building, building, building capacity throughout the Southeast United States—North Carolina, growth in Kentucky, growth in Mississippi, a lot of growth in Texas, in Arkansas, in Louisiana."

Marty spent those first five years opening new factories and training new workers. "When Fruit of the Loom built production," he said, "it wasn't just in the sewing room. It was the knitting mill, the dyehouse, and the cut, sew, and distribution."

He told us about a huge pickle factory on the banks of the Mississippi River that he was charged with converting into a mill. He arrived on a hot Delta afternoon. Walking the factory with his engineer, Marty wondered how they'd dispose of the enormous vats of pickle juice that had been left behind—concrete bins stinking of vinegar and whatever other things happened to crawl in—without violating EPA rules. Suddenly—boom!—one exploded right in front of them, sending the huge steel lid straight up to the ceiling. Apparently, the microbes in the vats produced gas that rapidly expanded in the heat of the midday sun, and sometimes detonated the vats like bombs.

"Well, I guess that solves that problem," his engineer said.

While Marty was helping Fruit expand operations, Farley borrowed heavily to buy up resource-rich companies similar to Fruit of the Loom. Then he allegedly used the company's assets as his personal checkbook to enrich himself, buying fine art, luxury properties in Chicago and Maine, and courting at least one Miss America. Marty told me that Farley kept a Czech MiG fighter jet in the company hangar.

The offshoring began right on schedule, in 1995, Marty said, just as NAFTA was kicking in. "I think Fruit was one of the last holdouts," he added.

Price competition from Hanes had been fierce, and within a few years, Fruit lost the "Underwear Wars." But there was another major bad actor working to undo domestic manufacturing.

By the mid-1990s, there were only a few major underwear buyers left in America, and the biggest was Walmart, which had just about finished off Kmart. Once Kmart was vanquished (the company shuttered 110 stores in 1994), Walmart set out to shut down every other lower-market retailer in America. How? By using the same tactics it had employed to crush Kmart: sell impossibly cheap goods. Offer staple merchandise at prices so low, consumers can't resist and other retailers can't compete. In one of the most vicious maneuvers in American history, Walmart spread like a fungus across America, draining every dollar out of Main Street.

The new monopolists had argued that America's antitrust laws should focus on consumer pricing instead of company size to determine whether or not to break up a monopoly or block an acquisition. But the price of a good is just one economic metric. Monopolists can pledge to keep prices low to avert an antitrust case. But who pays the collateral? In the case of Walmart, the manufacturers. Who, by the way, employed millions of Americans.

Consumers were saving money, so according to an extremely narrow reading of antitrust law, Walmart was left alone to do its thing. By 2010, Walmart had a de facto "complete monopoly" over retail in smaller cities, and delivered at least 30 percent, and sometimes more than 50 percent, of the entire U.S. consumption of products. As of 2022, Walmart is the largest company on earth, with nearly 20 percent more revenue than Amazon. Its revenue is higher than every state-owned Chinese oil, gas, and electricity conglomerate.

A monopoly concentrates buying power into a single entity. Walmart uses its power not to gouge customers, but rather to dominate its supply chain. Approximately 40 percent of products sold in Walmart are proprietary labels, produced for the company through contract manufacturers. The retailing behemoth dominates so much of the American market that it can squeeze its suppliers to the point of bankruptcy. In sum, Walmart dictates how much it will pay manufacturers for their goods, instead of the other way around. Even the biggest makers, nay, especially the biggest makers, need Walmart contracts to survive. And that approach, repeated through countless mergers and acquisitions, eventually put out of work hundreds of thousands of the same Americans who lost good jobs in exchange for cheap socks while enriching stockholders and executives.

I'm not saying that Walmart was the only force at work pushing Fruit to offshore operations after NAFTA opened Central America to American manufacturing, but a pattern was emerging. Barry Lynn points out that monopolists increasingly don't make anything because manufacturing involves too much risk. "Instead, they use banks to run trading companies, built to retail products that are manufactured abroad, built to arbitrage among suppliers, communities and workers."

American companies, led by monopolists, purged manufacturing from their books—the most expensive and difficult part of their operation. Thus, all the wealth from a bought entity was in the additional market share, and the buyer, and any assets that could be sold, like real estate or machinery. Walmart dominated the American market and set pricing, forcing manufacturers to offshore. Brands became mere middlemen between a monopolistic retailer and countless Asian and Central American plants churning out millions of dozens of panties and tighty-whities.

America's biggest apparel company, Nike, for example, entirely abandoned manufacturing in the 1990s, opting to contract all its manufacturing in Asia instead of tying up capital in machines and skilled laborers. Less than a decade later, Boeing, once the pride of America, went the same way. Under CEO James McNerney, Boeing offshored most of the production of its 737 MAX to hundreds of small companies around the globe. The results were disastrous. Parts and pieces didn't quite work together as planned, costing the company inordinate time and money to fix issues. The plane also had a fatal flaw in its design—a flight control system that would override pilots' commands, plunging the plane's nose down during takeoff. After two commercial flights crashed in 2018 and 2019, killing 346 passengers and crew, Boeing finally grounded the 737 MAX. The company paid $2.5 billion to settle the Department of Justice's conspiracy and fraud case, but McNerney's wealth was safe. After collecting nearly $100 million in salary and bonuses from the company, he retired from Boeing in 2015.

Marty didn't just witness offshoring. He was the guy who had to give workers the bad news. "The hard thing was that with Fruit," Marty said, "you're working in small towns. You don't just work with folks, but you go to church with folks, your kids go to school together, you play ball together. That's what happens when one company employs thousands of people in a small community."

Ben interjected, "When I was a kid there were 1,800 guys at S.D. Warren [the Westbrook paper mill].* Today, there's about 150. It was the beginning of the exodus."

* Now owned by South African Pulp and Paper Industries (SAPPI).

Marty nodded. "The hard part was having to tell people that we're closing."

Once he shut down the domestic plants, Marty, as director of manufacturing services, was immediately sent to open facilities in Mexico and Central America "to cover for the jobs we just took away." At first, he says, he went in with a chip on his shoulder about training foreign workers. But it didn't take him long to get over it. "Folks all over the world do this work. And folks all over the world, whether it's Central America, or Mexico, or the United States, or Canada, or more recently, I've been in Pakistan and Sri Lanka and India, for the most part people are just doing their best to be their best and to, in some cases, survive."

Marty was a small-town guy who wouldn't waste his energy parsing cultural differences or language barriers. He had specific expertise, and he spread it around the world. "I make a T-shirt in Morocco the same way I do in L.A. When folks are doing their best to survive, you can't help but be compassionate. I had twenty-six facilities in seven countries around the world—8,000 employees in Mexico, 8,000 in El Salvador, 7,000 in Honduras and Morocco. And that's what I did for the next part of my career. I was out of the country forty-eight weeks a year for three years."

Unfortunately, even with all that offshoring, Fruit struggled to pay off the debt Farley racked up while building an empire. It was about to come crashing down. Just before Fruit declared bankruptcy in 1998, Farley presided over a major stock buyback, a practice legalized in 1982.* The company bought back a huge quantity of its own

---

* So much profit in American companies is now going to shareholders that it's a wonder any industries can function. According to Emily Stewart in Vox: "From 2007 through 2016, S&P 500 companies distributed $4.2 trillion to shareholders through stock buybacks and an additional $2.8 trillion through dividends, totaling $7 trillion in shareholder payouts. From 2003 through 2012, S&P companies used 54 percent of their total earnings—$2.4 trillion—to buy back stock."

shares from the marketplace, jacking up the price long enough for Farley and other executives to cash out their stock. Then he was gone.

And so was Marty. Longtime employees lost their nest egg when their stock options lost all value in the bankruptcy. For many older employees who were hoping to retire, Fruit's collapse meant they'd have to work decades longer than they'd planned. Was that why Marty had boarded the plane from L.A. to Maine in June 2021? Because he'd worked his whole life for a retirement that evaporated in a matter of minutes?

After the bankruptcy, Marty got a job working for another American manufacturer that was opening and managing factories in Mexico and Honduras. He was traveling more than ever. "And one Sunday I was kissing my five-year-old good night when she grabbed my cheek and said, 'Dad, when are you going to get a job here so I can see you?'"

That was it. He finally realized his demanding schedule was hurting his family. Around that time, Dov Charney of American Apparel called. "I flew out to L.A. and thought we were going to talk," Marty says, "and he kind of handed me the keys."

Dov had started his apparel company in the 1990s out of the trunk of his car. Ben identified with that part: "We like to tell the story of when our first son was born, we had $147 in our checking account," he said. "We needed ten grand to make payroll that week. And I got in that Ford Explorer with a coat hanger holding up the tailpipe, and I drove to Boston and sold some sweatshirts."

"Let me guess," Marty said. "You've never missed a payroll."

"Never missed a payroll."

"That's the important part of that story," Marty replied.

Dov wanted Marty to change his company's culture to increase production rates. American Apparel was making 30,000 garments a day, and Dov needed 50,000. American Apparel's Los Angeles plant would become the forty-first that Marty converted to the kaizen model, which he'd learned at Fruit.

Evan, American Roots' designer, had been sitting quietly while Marty and Ben talked, but perked up when he heard the word *kaizen*.

He was considering getting certification in it, but here was Marty, already an expert. Evan asked, "Was it difficult to change the culture on the factory floor?"

"Converting factories always went the same way," Marty said. "People protested, and then people watched, and then people understood, and then people started begging, 'I want to do that too.'"

Marty said he started at American Apparel in mid-March 2002, and by July he'd converted the entire company to kaizen principles. They went from producing 30,000 to 90,000 pieces a day with the same workforce.

What did that look like? Marty cracked open his laptop and began searching for a video he wanted to show us. "The best T-shirt team I ever put together was in Morocco," he said, pressing play. The video was made with someone's phone, amateur and shaky, but the information was clear. Ben, Whitney, and Evan watched in fascination as the humans produced like machines.

The Moroccan T-shirt team on his screen was on fire. Every seven and a half seconds, a garment moved from one operation to the next, which meant in seven and a half seconds, a completed garment rolled off the line.

"That's possible because you have people who are experts at one thing," Marty said dreamily. "If you have volume to be able to support that, then that's as good as it gets."

Pointing at one of the stitchers, Marty said, "He's got two responsibilities. His first responsibility is to sew as good a quality as possible. And that's all he does. Secondly, his responsibility is to give the piece to the next operator when, where, and how she needs it. That's kaizen. Kaizen is the act of service to the next operation."

Marty explained that all the machine operators were fast, but it was the transition from one point to the next that made them superfast. He had one person for every operation, and each worker got paid by the total number of pieces they produced as a team.

When he said that, Ben and Whitney shot each other a look. Piece-rate payment was anathema in the garment industry because it's where workers often got screwed. Production managers could lie about the number of pieces completed in a day or lowball the amount of time it took to make a garment and set the piece rate too low, or simply change the rate midstream. If stitchers lack a decent base wage, as is the case in many parts of the world, they've been known to literally work themselves to death trying to earn enough money to support their families. Forget Bangladesh. This was happening in America. In L.A., where more than 45,000 professional garment workers make clothes for major fast fashion brands, piece workers earned an average of $6 per hour.

In short, Marty was recommending a compensation/incentive system that was notoriously easy for companies to use to exploit workers.

But Marty was a pro; he deftly spun piece-rate incentivizing as a triumph for both workers and employers. "If you give them an opportunity, to earn, they will." By way of example, he talked about the worker earning a $10 base wage. For the company to break even, that worker would have to produce 1,600 pieces a day. "But they're not here to make 1,600 pieces. They're not here to make $10. They're here to earn all that they can. If I give them 45 cents for every piece they produce above the 1,600, and they produce 2,400 pieces, now they're earning $120 a day against a guarantee of $80."*

Ben wasn't completely comfortable with what Marty was suggesting; incentivizing production didn't fit with the model he and Whitney had set up at American Roots. "Whitney and I fundamentally believe that people need health care. So you got to factor that in—for a family of four, it's a $672 biweekly deduction—as well as retirement, all that shit."

Marty took a breath. He said he'd seen plenty of people who wanted to be good employers launch businesses and offer their workers everything straight out of the gate. By doing that, he said flatly,

---

* A few months later, California would ban piece-rate pay for garment workers, effective January 1, 2022.

they lose their leverage over production. In six months, they're forced to either claw that back or go out of business.

Was he talking about Ben and Whitney?

Marty explained that he had a set system that he knew worked around the world, and he wanted Ben and Whitney to succeed. If they wanted his services, they had to buy the whole package.

"The one thing that doesn't change is my overhead," Marty said, "what it costs me to open the doors every day." That's the number that sets all this in motion. So, he asked, what are you paying for fabric? Whitney said they paid $3.75 to $4.25 per yard for T-shirt fabric.

Marty's eyebrows shot up. "Well, you're spending more on fabric than I was spending on an entire constructed garment in Los Angeles."

Certainly, Dov was a bigger buyer and could negotiate better prices. Regardless, Ben suddenly realized that they may be getting ripped off. He knew that other competitors were selling U.S.-made T-shirts for as little as $6.25 apiece; now he knew how they were able to do it. Marty asked who they bought from and nodded when they told him but kept his cards close. He didn't say whether he'd been buying from the same company.

Ben was fuming. He popped out of his seat and started pacing the room. "See, something's fucked-up. You just said basically we're getting fucked on fabric. This is what's driving me insane."

He leaned his palms on the table and looked across the table at Marty. It was important that Marty understand he wasn't a sucker.

"There's somebody who's getting rich on American Roots, and it ain't Whitney and I, and it ain't the workers in this company and it's got to stop. I don't care what it takes. I don't care if it's you, Marty, telling us who to call or us getting on a plane. This is the last year we're going to be making other people rich, because we've all worked too hard."

The conversation continued, but Ben was distracted thinking about the time three years ago when he and Whitney went down to

North Carolina to negotiate price and product with his team of fabric manufacturers and finishers. He'd always thought of that meeting as a benchmark moment for American Roots.

Previously, he'd told me about that day wistfully—the awe he and Whitney had felt seeing large-scale textile manufacturing in real life; the thrill they experienced making meaningful connections in the industry they were hoping to help repair. He told me how Whitney dazzled the southerners with her intelligence and beauty; he thought they'd really impressed the Carolinians with their mission.

Now he had a completely different take. "Our first meeting in North Carolina was like walking into an old union boss meeting," he told the group, revisiting the memory with eyes wide open. "I think those guys had met before we got there," he told Whitney. "They all got on the same page on price, and they said, *We're going to tell this young northern couple how this works for us.*"

Ben and Whitney decided to bring Marty on as a consultant to implement his methods but hoped that they could find a way to incentivize working faster without changing how they paid their stitchers. They had compassion for their employees and wanted their paychecks to be consistent and predictable. Marty agreed to return to Maine in a few weeks to reconfigure the factory for high-production manufacturing.

There's a little more to the Fruit of the Loom saga that's worth telling. Immediately after Fruit shut down, Campbellsville unemployment hit 28 percent. Later that year, a little-known tech start-up took over a vacant Fruit warehouse and rehired textile workers at a fraction of their Fruit wages. Stitchers who made $15 in 1970 were earning a little over $7 in 1998.

The name of that start-up: Amazon.

To woo the company to the state, Kentucky offered a crazy tax break. Amazon would receive 5 percent of its workers' paychecks—money which would have gone to the county and the state to finance schools, roads, and other support services. Amazon netted millions of dollars from this incentive over a decade, money that Jeff Bezos used to shoot himself into space.

Amazon is now the town's largest private employer and the town's biggest problem. In a 2019 story published in the *New York Times,* one man who had worked for Fruit for twenty-four years and then for Amazon said he took pride in being part of the e-commerce start-up, but eventually ran headlong into the churn culture. "My manager called me into the office one day and said, 'Dave, your performance is not what it needs to be.' I said, 'How can I improve?' He said, 'You don't fire enough people.'" Several months later, Dave was out the door.

By 2021, Amazon may have reduced Walmart's power, but the mega-retailer had already done irreparable damage to America's workers and manufacturers. Unlike Walmart, Amazon was using its might not necessarily to drive down prices but to lock up the labor market, which promises to further undermine America's remaining small businesses.

Companies like American Roots can't compete with the $18-per-hour wage (plus signing bonuses) Amazon offers drivers and warehouse workers, though American Roots can offer more job security and flexibility.

And once they're hired by Amazon, workers don't last long. A 2021 *New York Times* investigation revealed that the annual turnover rate at fulfillment centers averaged 150 percent. In other words, Amazon replaces its entire workforce about every eight months.

Bezos once said that an entrenched workforce created a "march to mediocrity," claims David Niekerk, a former long-serving vice president for the company. Certainly churn prevents workers from organizing each other into a union and demanding better working conditions.

Amazon's business model—make nothing, sell everything—landed at the perfect time to inject Chinese-made goods, many of which violate intellectual property and copyright laws, directly into American homes.

Even big American brands—once domestic manufacturers, now a company of designers, marketers, and contractors—are getting cut out of the Amazon market. You can buy half a dozen different "pop-up" food storage systems on Amazon from brands you've never heard of, all manufactured and shipped from China. They bear a striking resemblance to products designed by OXO, an American company.

Amazon has access to vast consumer and product data that it has used to replicate goods under its own mark and push in front of consumers. In 2021, the company got busted selling its own knock-offs of popular products in India while manipulating the Amazon search function to boost its wares. According to the lawsuit, Amazon employees even planned to contract production with the same companies making the original product to ensure perfect replication.

YOUR JOB IS TO PRODUCE

Over a hot week in July 2021, Marty stayed at a Portland hotel surviving on a family-size pack of Oscar Mayer bologna, a supermarket rotisserie chicken, and a liter a day of Mountain Dew.

He spent his waking hours at American Roots.

Whitney was getting ready for maternity leave and hoped to shift production responsibility to Evan in her absence, so she advised him to work closely with Marty and learn all he could.

From dawn to closing bell on the first day, Marty studied the sewing machine operators. They sat at machine tables arranged like a classroom—in rows and columns—with space all around them where half-finished work sometimes piled up.

Making a hoodie involved fifty-four separate operations. Marty considered time between each operation waste; as he'd said on the first day, it was his job to take out the garbage.

On day two, he walked the shop floor, counting his steps to estimate the size of the factory. Then he began to lay out a floor plan on an Excel spreadsheet. His goal was to organize stitchers into teams so that a hoodie-in-process could glide along the line seamlessly.

On his computer, Marty created three pods: one for waist-and-cuff makers, one for hood makers, and one for pocket makers. The first pod featured four workstations equipped with single-needle lock-stitch machines in a pinwheel configuration so that the waistband-and-cuff team could spend all day prepping those parts, independent of other teams. The second five-person-team pod, which Marty organized into a serpentine pattern, would be tasked with making hoods. At the third pod sat four people who would set the pockets and label onto the front and left panels of the hoodie.

All these components would pile up, waiting to be sewed into the garment itself.

Marty then arranged fourteen tables into an elongated serpentine configuration to complete the garment. Each step along the line that used a manufactured component (hood, waistband, panel with pocket) was positioned as close as possible to the corresponding pod.

That night, after all the workers went home, Marty began laying out his factory configuration. He soon realized that the sewing tables at American Roots were too small to arrange into a continuous work surface, so he bought a few rolls of duct tape at Home Depot and taped pieces of cardboard to the tabletops to fill in the gaps, making one giant jigsaw puzzle of a surface into which the operators and machines could be slotted.

It was midnight when Marty's setup was ready. He stood back to admire his work. It wasn't pretty, but he figured it would do the trick.

The next morning, Marty and Evan moved a dozen chairs into the break area and assembled the crew of American Roots stitchers. Marty explained the new plan to them, but as usual, it wasn't easy to determine how much they understood, due to language issues. He showed his Moroccan T-shirt video and told them that today they should focus on working as a team, meaning they needed to think not only about their own task, but about how they could set up the next person on the line so that they could do their job quickly.

Then he walked them over to the newly arranged tables.

The team of mostly female workers—nearly all immigrants from Africa—stood looking doubtfully at the makeshift setup. Makenga, Anaam, and Evan assigned each stitcher a seat and task.

They shrugged, tucked their handbags under their chairs, and sat at their machines. Some popped in earbuds.

Soon the needles at the pods were moving. Evan distributed piles of cut fabric pieces where they were needed along the line. By midday, the whole line was up and running as Marty had designed it, filling the room with the familiar ratatat of twentysome machines going at once.

Ludovic sat at the long table at the end of the line with Makenga's son Jared, cheerfully snipping off loose threads from hoodies and looking for missed or misplaced stitches.

To the untrained eye, it looked like this was the fix American Roots needed.

Marty spent the next two days tweaking his work. He'd watch the shoulder seam stitcher for several minutes, then hunt for a piece of unused cardboard that he would duct-tape to further extend her work surface, showing her how to reorient the garment when she passed it on so that the next machine operator could just grab and go. Occasionally, he'd offer someone a lumbar pillow, trying to break ergonomically bad habits.

The women tried to focus on their work as the large Kentuckian maneuvered around them. They'd seen Marty working a sewing machine himself, so they knew he wasn't completely full of shit. On Friday night, he got on a plane and headed back to L.A., entrusting the entire system—cardboard, duct tape, and all—to Evan.

At the end of July, Cam and Mike—the marketing duo—called a meeting to present the final version of the new American Roots logo over Zoom. Mike shared his screen and everyone leaned in. The logo was shaped like a shield. In bold relief, it depicted a stylized tree growing up from the stripes of a sideways American flag.

American. Roots. Pine Tree State. The logo had clarity, even if it didn't capture their entire story. Whitney got her wish, too. She'd always hated the capitalized "AMERICAN ROOTS" of their original logo. In this one, the company name was lowercase.

They discussed launching the new logo on Labor Day.

But Ben didn't get much time to plan an event. On Thursday, August 5, he woke up to the news that Rich Trumka had died. From President Joe Biden to Senator Sherrod Brown, from *Time* to the opinion pages of *The Wall Street Journal,* tributes to the storied labor leader poured out.

Ben was heartbroken. "It wasn't supposed to end like that," Ben later told me, once he could talk about Trumka's death. "It was supposed to end in Philadelphia, where Rich was planning to retire at the AFL-CIO convention. But it didn't happen. And my friend [American Roots board member] Patti Devlin said, 'Rich wanted to lead and he died a leader.' He was it, you know? Leaders have to be able to do things that people don't want to do."

Ben flew to western Pennsylvania for the wake, then to D.C. for the service. The night after the ceremony, Ben's flight back to Boston was delayed. As soon as he settled in at the gate, Labor Secretary Marty Walsh showed up for the flight with two aides. He'd been to the Trumka service, too.

Ben and Walsh spent the evening reminiscing over microwaved pizza, watching passengers come and go. It felt good for Ben to reconnect with his people and talk Boston politics.

Secretary Walsh is a big fan of Ben's. He says that when Ben started working on his mayoral campaign in 2013, the two men "just clicked." When he learned about Ben's struggle with addiction, "that bond got even closer and tighter."

Walsh cites American Roots' pivot to masks during the pandemic as an example of the critical role the apparel industry plays in the nation's infrastructure. But to bring apparel-making back to the U.S., he put the responsibility on consumers. "There has to be a sense of pride," he told me. "American people really need to focus and support American-made products, particularly when it comes to clothes, because these industries are not easy to bring back."

Walsh adds, "I'm one of those people who buys clothes because of where they're made. The brand for me is America."

As for American Roots, Walsh says, "You can say it's the American dream. Ben struggled, he's fallen down a couple times, he's picked himself back up, and I hope he makes it because I know Ben Waxman pretty well. If American Roots continues to grow, he'll expand that into other opportunities." And that energy, Walsh says, would have a positive effect on domestic manufacturing in general—another little nudge in the right direction.

At 2 a.m. on October 1, 2021, while the container ship pileup outside L.A. was making headlines and U.S. trade rep Katherine Tai and Secretary of Treasury Janet Yellen wrestled with China over trade deals and tariffs, Owen Daniel Waxman was born in Portland.

Ben was permitted to visit Whitney and Owen in the hospital but, due to Covid concerns, couldn't bring Arlo and Wyatt. Fortunately, Whitney felt well enough to go home the next day. She wanted to be with her boys.

"All just coming up for air," Dory texted me a few days later. "Love is everywhere."

Around 2:30 a.m. the following day, a mega container ship full of imported goods waiting to dock at L.A. dropped its multiton anchor on an undersea oil pipeline. The seventeen-mile artery, which carried crude oil from three offshore rigs to a pumping station at the Port of Long Beach, had been encased in concrete that probably had been cracked by another ship's anchor earlier that year. The second ship's anchor hooked the pipe, and as the huge vessel attached to it drifted downwind, it dragged the pipe until it was as taut as a bowstring. At some point, the pipeline ruptured, dumping up to 132,000 gallons of heavy crude into the ocean. It took a few hours for an operator at Amplify Energy to notice the dip in oil pressure in the pipeline. An oil slick quickly spread over thirteen miles.

Along the Southern California coast, fisheries, marinas, and beaches were closed as dozens of seabirds engaged in a lethal battle with the toxic mess. More casualties of Americans' love for imported things.

—

But even with a newborn at home, Ben was eager to press the flesh, get himself in front of local unions, brothers and sisters, sell, sell, sell. The first three quarters for American Roots in 2021 were much better than 2019's numbers. Ben and Whitney had retained forty-five employees and closed about $1.5 million in revenue. But after a summer relatively free of Covid, the Delta variant was threatening to shut down the country again. Ben couldn't sit out the busy convention season. He had to hit the road.

Ben and Whitney began strategizing which conventions he should attend, even with a newborn at home. October was always the busiest month. Half a dozen events across the country were penciled into his schedule.

Once again, they debated the threat level of Covid and decided they had to take chances. "We were vaccinated and planes were supposedly the safest place to be," Whitney said. "So I told Ben, 'I think you need to go. We've got to do this.'"

Two weeks after Owen was born, Whitney's parents came to help with the kids. Ben kissed his family goodbye and boarded a plane for Denver, but he wasn't feeling well. He could come up with a thousand reasons why he might be tired, so he powered through.

When he got back to Portland on Tuesday afternoon, he still felt under the weather, so he tested himself for Covid in the airport parking lot with the two rapid tests he kept in his truck. Both came out negative.

That night, Covid took him down.

On October 23, I got a text from Dory: "Rachel, Just letting you know Ben has been very sick with Covid since Tuesday. He was taken by ambulance to hospital yesterday for about 6 hrs. Sent him home better than before he went in but still really sick. Light a candle. Say a prayer. We have all been exposed unwittingly and getting tested tomorrow. ♥"

Ben had been admitted to Maine Medical in Portland, the state's biggest hospital—637 beds. The place was overrun with Covid patients. The medical staff stabilized Ben and told him, *You're forty-two years old, you're vaccinated, your oxygen is at 74 percent. We're full. You've got to ride this out at home.*

Ben returned to the basement sofa of their 1,600-square-foot house, ill with nausea, fatigue, and shortness of breath, while Whitney quarantined upstairs with the boys, managing all three by herself for six days. Ben felt the company would collapse if he didn't get in those orders and was still closing deals via email and text to make sure they had the cash to stay afloat.

Whitney's parents stayed at a nearby Airbnb and came over a few times to sit on the patio by the fire pit, but fear of infection kept them from being as helpful as they'd planned. Mary Ann held Owen outside while Whitney cared for Arlo and Wyatt, running back and forth and downstairs to tend to Ben. "It was insane," Whitney recalls.

Four days later, Dory texted me again:

"Ben's been really sick. The past 10 days. In and out of hospital 2xs. They could not keep him because there are no beds. Whit Arlo and Wyatt tested positive today. She's got the cough and backache but not too debilitating. Just keep those candles lit and love light prayers. Thanks for all.♥"

Whitney had just given birth, and was trying to manage everything and everyone on her own. Now she was sick, too. Luckily, the boys were doing okay and baby Owen never tested positive. Ben couldn't hold anything down. An ambulance took him to the hospital a third time. "That morning when I went into the hospital," Ben says, "I didn't know if I was leaving my wife for two weeks, three weeks, four weeks, or whatever. I didn't know."

After nearly two years of weaving and bobbing, Covid finally found them. It was the closest either of them had come to their mortality.

Grappling with Covid forced them to confront the way they'd structured the company over the past six years. Because Ben was the principal salesman and Whitney oversaw the day-to-day operations at the factory, they left too many people—folks they cared deeply about—dangerously dependent on them. If American Roots was going to survive, the company structure needed to become more resilient.

They realized that for American Roots to flourish, they had to lean into their strengths and leave other tasks to someone better suited for them. To become more strategic, in other words, they needed to hire a CEO. They needed someone who could manage the business side of things and plan the next phase. Hiring a CEO would free up Ben to get out there and sell and free up Whitney to focus on managing production. But, very simply, they couldn't afford to.

In the meantime, Evan was losing his marbles trying to implement Marty's system. Their production numbers inched up, but by December they'd plateaued and remained stubbornly below goals, much to Evan's frustration.

Marty flew out to Portland the second week of December and stayed at Dan and Dory's house—they'd turned their sons' second-floor bedrooms into an Airbnb to earn extra income. I drove up to Westbrook one last time and rented a room in The Elms, the rambling Queen Anne–style house across from the paper mill.

I dropped off my bags in the giant master bedroom on the second-floor. The big, drafty bay windows overlooked a bend in the Presumpscot River, narrow and tame, nothing like the rushing falls a mile upriver at Dana Warp. I could see the abandoned railroad bridge and a ragged baseball field across the water. Nine identical turn-of-the-century millworker houses lined the northwest bank. Remarkable to think there was a time when owners, workers, and staff lived together like this along the river, sending their kids to the same schools, going to the same churches, shopping in the same stores.

A light snow began to fall as I drove down Brown Street following the river, past the old millworker homes, buttoned up against the cold. The Dana Mill parking lot was full under the sky, heavy and gray. I could hear the rush of the rapids down the steep bank beyond the asphalt's edge, and I thought about the thousands of mill girls and boys, and the men and the women, who had come before me, huffing up the wooden Dana Mill stairs for work or hustling down when the shift bell rang. The scuffle of thousands of shoes had worn a soft depression into each wooden stair.

I looked through the old mill windows onto Frenchtown and studied the spire of St. Hyacinth Church, built in 1894 by the French-Canadian immigrants who spent their days making warp at Dana Mill.

Inside the American Roots factory, a new fifty-four-foot cutting table took up one corner. Under a halo of dyed-pink curls, Adam Cleaves was manually rolling out cotton fleece, layer by layer, smoothing the fabric as he went. Adam had spent a couple of decades in high-end restaurants, but when the kitchen worker's chaotic lifestyle caught up with him, he had to tap out. Working at American Roots was lower-stress, more predictable. He had regular hours, a steady paycheck, benefits, and could spend quality time with his young daughter (who lived with her mother) on weekends.

Adam had been doing quality control at American Roots when the Fall River cutter quit. Nine months later, Adam was learning the craft. He used an electric cutter equipped with a ten-inch reciprocating blade to carve out pattern pieces from the sixty-inch-wide stack of fabric. To cut the pieces in the middle, Adam had to hop up on the table. It wasn't ideal, but he was chipper. He found the work meditative.

Evan buzzed around, looking stressed. They were trying to get out a big order, but things weren't moving fast enough.

Midmorning, he got a chance to conference with Marty. I could tell from his demeanor he'd been waiting for months to get his advice. Whitney had been on maternity leave since late September. There wasn't anyone else he could turn to.

Marty leaned back in a swivel chair in the small office area separated from the factory by a five-foot-high systems furniture wall. He was wearing jeans and white sneakers, nursing his first Mountain Dew of the morning. Evan sat at the edge of his chair opposite Marty, phone in hand. He made it clear that their plan was failing.

Financial incentives hadn't resonated with the stitchers. They weren't motivated by the promise of more money. He'd tried all kinds of tricks, including positioning himself at the end of the assembly line to pressure people to move more quickly. While he was there, he said, they did speed up, but as soon as he left, they went right back to their old pace.

Evan tried to reason with the stitchers. He sat down with each person individually and went over the numbers to impress upon them how important their work was to the company's survival. Look, he tried to show them, if we all work a little harder, American Roots will get stronger. "Some people couldn't be bothered that we were losing so much money," he said.

Frustrated and not a little worried, he told Marty that he was running out of ideas.

Evan didn't like what the gig was doing to him. "I know this job will eat me alive if I let it," he said. "My former boss showed me the person I never wanted to be. And now I get why he was like that." During the previous two weeks, he found himself ordering people to do things instead of asking them. "I was literally yelling at someone who was sitting with eyes closed at the machine. I never thought I'd get to that point."

He was desperate for a solution.

Marty had zero sympathy. "If you're in a manufacturing company," he said, "your job is to produce. That's the whole thing. Success depends on production." He told Evan to stay the course. Then he offered some coping tricks. He advised Evan to focus hour by hour instead of day by day. Every hour on the shop floor offered a fresh opportunity to make back time and improve, he said. "I've been in your position for decades. If you focus on the negative, you're going to have a lot of bad days."

Marty tried sharing his own experiences. He'd built plants from scratch, so he knew how difficult it was to establish a manufacturing culture. In North Carolina, he told Evan, he'd had to set up a

750,000-square-foot former Clark forklift transmission plant for garment-making. When he first arrived at the factory, there was nothing in there but oil and graphite dust. "Getting the building in position to start making apparel was defeating in itself, but we also had to find 3,000 people to work in the factory once it was ready. You hire thirty on Monday to replace the thirty you lost on Wednesday," he told Evan.

Marty said it took him three years to get 3,000 people working like a team, but even then, every day was a challenge because, frankly, human beings are complicated creatures. "That's why I do this work, but that's also why I'd never do it again."

After half an hour, Evan was itching to check in on his teams. As he walked away, he looked unsettled. I wondered whether he might be heading for the door. Marty asked me how I thought their conversation went, and I told him I thought Evan was looking for concrete advice, not a pep talk. Marty took a minute to consider that, and in that moment I realized that he'd given Evan everything he had. Money had always made people work faster.

Now we were entering uncharted territory.

If American Roots employees didn't want more money, what *did* they want? Evan and Whitney were determined to find out. In December, they asked their human resources expert, Bryony Roux, to meet with each employee to learn what was most important to them, what motivated them. Because so many languages were spoken in the factory, Bryony made sure she had a translator with her. Polling the workforce took weeks, but she got valuable feedback.

Some people appreciated a bump in pay, but for most American Roots employees, family came first. They wanted more time to care for their loved ones. They wanted scheduling flexibility and a four-day workweek so that they could take a full day to get other things done, such as taking kids to doctors' appointments, going food shopping, seeing immigration lawyers and checking on their visa status, maybe even taking some time for themselves.

Family came first. It was simple. Hadn't we all realized during the pandemic that time was our most valuable gift? Why would the workers at American Roots be any different?

But Ben and Whitney couldn't offer a more relaxed work schedule if they couldn't hire more people. Ben had closed more than $800,000 worth of orders in the last quarter; the stitchers they had were already booked through the end of April. If they had more capacity, they would have been able to finish that work in February.

All employers across America were facing the same labor crisis. At a November 2021 Southern Maine job fair, thirty-eight motivated employers waited at tables, eager to hire. Over four hours, just four job-seekers showed up. "There's certainly not a workforce in America that wants to come to American Roots and start at $17 an hour with benefits and work their way up to $20 or $21 an hour and be a part of this right now," Ben said. "We don't have that. There's no desire."

The media called it the Great Resignation. Ben called it apocalyptic. "It has nothing to do with people staying home collecting unemployment," he said. "Something else happened. I think Americans are tired. I think they're tired of the cost of groceries. I think they're tired of the cost of child care. I think they're tired of shitty expensive health care. I think they're saying, 'Fuck you.' So the whole idea that Americans are staying home just to stay home is absurd."

Native Mainers weren't interested in sewing jobs, and new Mainers weren't applying at the rate they once did because the U.S. Citizenship and Immigration Services was backed up for months. Obtaining asylum and working papers in the U.S. requires that refugees undergo a labyrinthine process in a foreign language. People fleeing genocide and oppressive regimes are expected to fill out complex forms, attend hearings, keep their information up to date—all while caring for their families, locating housing, finding food in a new country in a new language. "There are five hundred immigrants, new Americans, in hotels and apartments in Portland right now," Ben told me. "Many of them know how to sew. None of them have worker papers. Visa delays, Green Card delays."

But the American Roots model was working for the tiny percentage of immigrants who found their way to the Westbrook factory. While in Portland that December, I learned that Makenga and her family had moved into a new home, bought for no money down thanks to the federally insured USDA loan program. I asked her if I could visit, and she graciously said yes. I picked up a few pizzas and drove twenty minutes down I-95 from American Roots to a small development of modest homes in Saco. Makenga's 1,600-square-foot house, the same size as the Waxmans', sat a few miles from the ocean.

Winter nights in Maine fall hard and deep. I drove slowly trying to make out house numbers in the dark. Makenga's was at the end of a short driveway, sheltered by a grove of mature trees.

Inside, Makenga and her husband, as well as a friend from Angola, sat on two sofas, arranged in an L. Three of their children descended on the pizza left for them in the kitchen, then quietly vanished upstairs. Jared arrived a few minutes later. He was a senior at Portland High School and the starting center for the basketball team. He stood six-foot-eight and had to duck under the beam between the kitchen and living room to avoid hitting his head when he went upstairs to join his siblings.

Makenga had worked at American Roots for four years and said she enjoyed manufacturing. "The way we work at American Roots, we are working as one, as a family. We understand each other very well. We support each other. When new people come to American Roots, sometimes they're scared about what they hear outside—things like they lay off people when there are no jobs, or the salary is too small. People are afraid. But once they're there, I say, 'Guys, this is the right place to be.' If you know what you're doing, you're going to be happy. If you are a hard worker, you will get paid according to what you do. If you are not a hard worker, you cannot expect somebody to pay you more. You have to earn it. You have to work hard to get it."

She said it's not easy finding a job where the owner gives you time, listens to you. But Ben and Whitney, she said, "are very good people. That's why I want to be there. I need a place where when I have a problem—even personal, family problems—I have somebody who I can explain my problem to and get a solution. When you need support or you are concerned about something, they're there to listen to you and to help you."

To illustrate the difference between their lives in Johannesburg and Maine, Makenga told me that they were currently having trouble with one of their cars, which meant she had to drop off Robert, a machinist, at work at four in the morning. "It was very dark, but we drove. After I dropped him off, I drove back myself, which is not going to happen in South Africa. I cannot drive alone when it is dark like that. So I drove. And then when I got inside, you see the way it's dark outside? I came out from the car, I opened my house easily, I got inside. Nobody disturbed me. In South Africa, you cannot open the house door like that."

"We know as humans, there will always be problems, even in the United States," Robert said. "But compared to Africa, United States is a better country. Here, people are living well, there are job opportunities. They're living like they're in paradise. Yes, people get sick, people die. But where we come from, there aren't even jobs. Where we came from, we could not talk freely. People don't know if they'll be alive tomorrow. So if you get opportunity, you flee. If you don't get opportunity, you die. Now we have peace of mind. That's why if someone comes and says, 'Let us go somewhere else,' we feel no. What we were expecting, we are getting. We cannot go and start again."

"We are happy," Makenga added. "We now feel we are home."

THE NEVER-ENDING QUEST
FOR SMART MONEY

When the Omicron variant swept through Maine in December 2021 and into January, American Roots would be forced to operate with only half of the staff on any given day. The rest were out sick or tending to ill family members.

Ben and Whitney needed to train and hire more people.

Ever-resourceful Evan read somewhere that if you were looking for potential employees, these days you had to meet them where they were, which was, at that moment, in the smartphone-verse, scrolling through TikTok and dating apps. The great thing about the latter was that it was geo-specific, which gave Evan the ability to target potential job-seekers within a twenty-mile radius of the factory. He set up a Tinder account and posted a "sexy" job ad, along with photos of the factory captioned with cheeky, come-hither copy encouraging job-seekers to swipe right. He had to sort through the come-ons, but he did find a few prospects that way.

Ben and Whitney also encouraged their employees to tap into their networks. Word went out that the company was hiring and that it was a good place to work. In the end, it was the Iraqi, Congolese, Latinx, and Angolan communities that showed up to rescue American Roots.

To retain workers and attract more employees, Ben and Whitney raised everyone's pay 18 percent in March; the average annual salary at the company increased to $47,000, plus benefits, three weeks paid vacation, holidays, and sick days. To cover this additional cost, in April 2022, they raised the retail price of their heavyweight hoodie to $109.

In 2022, American Roots was riding a pro-union, pro-made-in-USA wave. Two years into the pandemic, organized labor was expanding its reach—baristas, grad student researchers, and hospitality workers were adding their names to union rolls, even as union strongholds, like state government workers, were reeling from the 2018 Supreme Court decision that workers didn't have to pay union dues if they didn't want to, even when the union negotiated on their behalf (a major conservative triumph).

The Biden administration was also making clear proclamations that the government was now pro-union by allocating more resources to the NRLB to investigate and prosecute labor violators. There was also lot of talk about bringing back manufacturing, which echoed Trump's winningest positions, though the general focus was on the high-tech sector, like microchips and electric vehicles. The Biden administration was also rethinking trade deals in the wake of Covid, the replacement of NAFTA with USMCA,* and concern over China.

In alignment with the president's pro-labor stance, the office of the U.S. Trade Representative (USTR) was paying special attention to the concerns of union leaders as it negotiated foreign trade policy,

---

* The differences between USMCA and NAFTA may seem minute, but from union and intellectual property perspectives, they're significant. USMCA increased the percentage of North American components in automobiles to qualify for zero tariffs from 62.5 percent to 75 percent. USMCA also included language to get Mexico to pass new labor laws to protect all workers and allow them to unionize, plus the establishment of a "rapid-response mechanism" to ensure Mexico follows union rules. (Trumka supported the deal.) U.S. farmers got more access to the Canadian dairy market while writers and internet companies got stronger copyright protections. The deal is subject to review every six years.

a never-ending, always thorny thicket of contradictory policy measures that would never fully please everyone—neither China, nor Central and South American countries, nor American companies and politicians.

At the same time, institutional investors—primarily those who ran pension funds—were beginning to deeply interrogate their investment choices. Unions were supposed to support each other, as well as all workers. The companies which benefited from that pension money should focus on sustainability, corporate culture, and governance, not just the bottom line. Pensions account for roughly $5.6 trillion of holdings, equivalent to about 77 percent of U.S. assets. Seeking to tap into that financial power, forward-thinking union leaders requested that their fund managers consider how the companies they invested in affected working people.

Some progressive labor leaders also wanted to get more creative with their investment power. Some began to ask the question: Could unions put their prodigious capital behind private unionized companies and help build them up, similar to how private equity operated?

Maybe Ben and Whitney were hitting their stride. They'd kept their factory running through good times and lean. They had an impressive customer base and a trained workforce. They'd weathered astronomical growth and moments when it looked like they'd lose the factory. Plus a global pandemic.

Other powerbrokers were watching American Roots with great interest. The former president of Amalgamated Bank, Keith Mestrich, a dedicated union man, had just moved to Maine and was looking for ways to support local manufacturers. That he'd come from Amalgamated Bank was significant. The bank was founded by the Amalgamated Clothing Workers of America in New York City in 1923 to provide men's clothing workers (many of them immigrants), as well as unions, a trustworthy place to deposit their money. During the twentieth century, the bank used its assets to build the Amalgamated Housing Cooperative in the Bronx, the first union-built housing in the U.S., and finance affordable housing projects while supporting striking workers at various moments by paying their bail. It went public in 2018 under Mestrich's leadership.

Mestrich had spent much of his career thinking about how to use money to support progressive causes. He'd coauthored *Organized Money* in 2019, a book intended to serve as a blueprint for how institutional investors could wield their vast financial power to nudge the world in a positive direction. Could American Roots benefit from his expertise?

Meanwhile, another high-profile union leader who knew Ben well was considering ways to grow the American manufacturing sector while creating more mid-skill union jobs.

We tend to forget some of America's highest-paid organized workers: professional athletes. And among them, no group needs more representation than football players, the 2 percent of college athletes who, against all odds, survived the physical toll of high school and college football long enough to get on an NFL team. On the field, they might play two seasons if they're lucky.* Then the NFL, which generated $15 billion in revenue in 2019, spits them out—their bodies wrecked, possibly suffering from chronic traumatic encephalopathy (CTE) from one too many blows to the head.

The majority of professional football players come from low-income families; the NFL is their one-in-a-million shot at big money. When guys get drafted and the dollars come in—the median salary of a professional running back was $630,000 in 2021—they want to share their windfall with their parents, siblings, and cousins. Few have a sense of how short their careers might be. A couple of years later, when the NFL's done with them, many of them end up broke.

That's where the NFL Players Association (NFLPA) came in. The union provides a lot more than collective bargaining, though that's a key part of what it does. Under Executive Director DeMaurice Smith, the NFLPA has negotiated for a bigger chunk of the total team profits,

---

* Careers of NFL running backs, cornerbacks, and wide receivers last, on average, under three years.

long-term health insurance (football injuries are considered preexisting conditions), and more than a billion dollars in research money to understand trauma-induced brain injuries. The NFLPA also offers financial consulting to the young, suddenly wealthy players, ensuring that they squirrel away some of their money for the future.

Ben knew Smith from his AFL-CIO days and had great admiration for the attorney and labor leader. Smith considered the possibility of buying union-branded swag for his members. He started watching American Roots, waiting for the right time to shine a spotlight on them.

Ben and Whitney had a good story to tell. More people needed to hear it. They were hopeful that a branding alliance with a high-profile organization like a professional players union would elevate American Roots. They suspected they were only one influencer away from breaking through, just one viral TikTok or Instagram post away from becoming a household name. With the right endorsement coupled with the right story, Americans might finally care about where their sweatshirts were made, and flock to the American Roots website.

There were other major operators thinking about using their resources to strengthen domestic apparel manufacturing. It was known that Michael Rubin, the young CEO of Fanatics—the largest seller of licensed sports fan merchandise in the world, valued at $12.5 billion—was a strong social justice advocate. Because some of his product was made on-demand but manufactured abroad, he'd run into supply chain issues during the pandemic. Finding local factories would help future-proof his company. Rubin was rumored to be quietly considering contracting with more domestic companies to manufacture his products.

Or could American Roots attract a private equity firm that aligned with their values? If a deal did go through, Ben and Whitney would finally have the cash and guidance they needed.

With access to more money, Ben and Whitney could focus on their strengths and let others strategize the growth of the company. Once on sturdier financial footing, American Roots could offer regular shifts built around four-day workweeks and build inventory to shelter workers from the feast-or-famine nature of the sales cycle.

A deep-pocketed investor dedicated to their mission would be a blessing for everyone.

With a deeper reservoir of cash and professional guidance, Ben and Whitney could turn their big-little company into a big-big company. These were the thoughts that fueled their days.

On the first Monday of 2023, Ben rose before dawn, as usual. He showered and trimmed his mustache and beard, slicked back his hair, zipped up his hoodie, and crept quietly through the house preparing for the day. The boys slept in their rooms; Whitney nestled under the comforter, trying to squeeze in a few more precious moments of rest.

Ben grabbed his wallet and keys, donned a jacket—too light for the frigid wind, but he was a goddamn Mainer—and scraped the ice off his windshield.

When he got to the factory, it was dark and quiet. No one had been there since Christmas Eve.

In the stillness, Ben gathered his thoughts. They'd closed out 2022 with $3.5 million in sales. They'd been up, they'd been down, and they'd crushed it, all things considered. The production line was finally running at a decent clip. They had real, tangible momentum; solid potential.

Ben leaned back and studied his sons' construction paper artworks, which he'd tacked to the wall. Nearly buried under all that was a motivational sign he'd printed out: "THE COMEBACK IS ALWAYS STRONGER THAN THE SETBACK."

Above hung the old poster-size 2022 calendar with long black lines drawn through the weeks he'd spent on the road away from his family, time he couldn't get back. He took a swig of black coffee from a paper cup.

The caffeine boost fueled his optimism. He felt in his bones that across America, pro-union voices were getting louder. Made in USA was more than a slogan. Onshoring wasn't a passing fad. And every American Roots hoodie reinforced that story right there on the tag: "By providing high-quality, durable clothing made from 100% American-sourced materials by Union labor in America, we are proving that success does not have to come at the expense of workers or the quality of the products they make."

History was on his side. His gaze drifted to the far wall to the framed print of Mother Jones, which featured her famous quote: "Pray for the dead and fight like hell for the living." Next to that was a framed photo of the Memphis Sanitation Workers Strike of 1968 showing a sea of Black workers holding signs that read, "I AM A MAN."

Ben glanced at the large whiteboard where he'd scrawled the names of past and future investors, mostly friends and family, people who'd given so much to them already. He and Whitney would never fail them.

Tucked in the corner sat an old oak barrister's cabinet where Ben kept some sports memorabilia, plus a tiny bust of JFK and a few hardcover books, including one by Nike's Phil Knight. Atop the cabinet were some small, framed photos, collecting dust. His eyes rested there. One showed Ben with his best friends, arms thrown over shoulders, the sun setting behind them, a moment caught one summer long ago. There was Whitney looking ravishing in a black dress, and Ben beaming next to her—his hair and beard still red—standing next to Marty Walsh during his mayoral inauguration nearly a decade ago. And another of Whitney, looking radiant under a white umbrella, seated beside Ben wearing a crisp white Oxford—a shot snapped half a dozen summers earlier. Then there was Whitney as a joyful new mom, leaning over giggling infant Arlo as he reached for his bottle.

This would be their year. They'd raise more money, make their website more consumer-friendly, and finally reach the countless people out there who believed in wearing their values. Someday soon, they'd move into a bigger factory and hire enough stitchers to run four-day workweeks. And in a few more years, Ben was sure they'd hit $10 million in annual revenue.

As he pondered the life he and Whitney were building, he could hear the voices of the men and women of Maine arriving at the factory to start the day's work. Through his office's interior window, he caught glimpses of them greeting each other as they hung up their coats and headed to the kitchen to stash their homecooked lunches in the fridge. By 7:30, the place was buzzing with vacation stories and news from extended families around the world. Someone turned on the radio. A group of women sat on the sofa sharing photos on their phones.

Seeing all these resilient people energized Ben. He and Whitney depended on them to show up day after day. They depended on Ben and Whitney to keep the factory going.

Ben pushed aside *The Wall Street Journal* and pulled a yellow legal pad out from under the pile of papers on his desk. He flipped through pages searching for the number of a potential customer. Then he picked up the phone and dialed. As he waited for someone to pick up, he heard the familiar voice inside his head, the one that kept him going all his days. It said, simply, *Game on.*

EPILOGUE

The American Roots story shows one way that manufacturing in the USA could work in the twenty-first century. But there are significant caveats to Ben and Whitney's success.

In the three years I reported this story, I watched Ben's hair go from auburn to white. In May 2023, he nearly died from a chronic infection that quickly spread to his skull. Maybe it was the stress that landed him in a hospital bed at the University of Pennsylvania.

Whitney was clearly exhausted, too.

Eight years in, American Roots was beginning to strain under the startup culture that had carried the company. That same scrappy determination, ego, and perseverance that made American Roots an initial success threatened to hold back the company's ability to evolve and retain people. In the end, they knew they needed to cede some control and ownership to others who could carry the company to the next level.

Evan left American Roots and returned to restaurant work.

Gina Alibrio, the musician who joined American Roots as their customer service manager during the pandemic, left to care for her mother in New Hampshire, then returned to Portland, recorded a solo album, and got her band back together.

Holland Corson, American Roots' operation manager, learned to make face shields and use industrial equipment. When American Roots' CFO needed an assistant, Holland learned how to use QuickBooks and studied business accounting in her spare time. But in the fall of 2022, she left for another manufacturing job that gave her a four-day workweek.

Reflecting on the exodus of his mid-level managers, Ben admitted that he was an imperfect manager. And I think that's one reason why manufacturing is so difficult in America. To hold on to, and motivate, the complex American workforce, managers must be nimble, creative, and responsive. That's not something you learn in school or in a book. Great managers are the product of years of on-the-job training and excellent mentors—an investment in individuals that most American companies stopped making decades ago.*

But then consider the impact of American Roots.

Every American Roots hoodie supports one-hundred-plus Maine workers who pay federal, state, and local taxes; buy or rent housing in the state; get their food and goods locally; and hire other local professionals—tradespeople, accountants, lawyers, health care providers—to do all kinds of things for them. American Roots family members might also launch local businesses, like Anaam's son, Qutaiba, a University of Southern Maine graduate who opened a restaurant in Portland called Falafel Time with his father in 2021.

Every hoodie stimulates demand for a more diverse range of jobs

---

* Over the past two decades, lack of investment in management training has led to the proliferation of comical perks. Instead of focusing on what workers really need—better work-life balance, growth opportunities, time to take care of sick kids or shop for groceries or go to medical appointments or develop skills—managers gave us Keurig machines, Slack, mandatory team-building workshops, foosball tables, mandatory company-wide full-day retreats, Taco Tuesdays, and meditation pods. At the end of the day, though, these perks didn't make workers any happier. No doubt, the Great Resignation was fueled by anger and resentment against poorly managed companies where Americans felt exploited—underpaid, overworked, and dog-tired.

and products and encourages recirculation of local dollars through taxes and government spending. And when you factor in the fact that the hoodie is made entirely from domestically sourced components, the positive effect is geometric. A terrific percentage of the cost of made-in-USA goods like the hoodie remains in the country.

Every foreign-made hoodie bought online injects almost nothing into the economy, save the tiny fraction of the purchase price that goes to local shipping. American consumers spend billions of dollars every year on overseas shipping, packaging, and importation fees. That's billions of American dollars in taxes lost to foreign workers and middlemen—money that could go to improving domestic infrastructure, schools, health care, and the environment.

Complexity and diversity are key to a nation's economic resilience. The export profiles of the most robust nations are a crazy quilt of offerings in a wide variety of sectors. At the bottom of the economic complexity list are countries that depend solely on a few exports, like the Democratic Republic of the Congo, which runs on copper and cobalt—mined ores that account for an astounding 73 percent of the country's exports, 80 percent of which goes to China.

Of course, the U.S. exports all kinds of things. It's strong in the machines, vehicles, and chemical products categories. But since the turn of the century, the nation's export profile has turned dramatically away from a diversity of industries, and toward the export of raw goods instead. It might come as a surprise to readers that the U.S. is now the third largest oil exporter, next to Saudi Arabia and Russia. This is a brand-new, twenty-first-century trend. Back in 2000, petroleum exports accounted for only about 1 percent of the U.S.'s export economy. The bulk of American refined and crude petroleum oil and gas is sent to Canada, Mexico, and China. These products now comprise a whopping 11 percent of America's total exports.

The U.S.'s trend toward economic simplification (and exporter of raw materials) should be concerning to Americans; each step down the complexity ladder signals more dependency on imports and less ability to produce necessary goods domestically, which ultimately determines the nation's economic health, as well as its power in international affairs.

The truth is that people can only innovate when they fully understand, fundamentally and completely, how things are made. In other words, it's easy to dream, but execution is impossible without the makers. I can't think of a single innovation that was plucked out of thin air. You need to know what works to imagine what is possible.

That's ultimately why I firmly believe that Americans' future depends on a manufacturing revival. The only way we can effectively address the pressing problems our planet faces is through technologically sophisticated manufacturing. Solutions are out there. We just need to build them.

Therefore, the primary focus of the U.S. government in the next decade should be supporting its workers and producers. We need to devote more resources to supporting people who want to make things, all kinds of things, right here, and we need to work to raise a new generation of inventors, creators, and innovators who know how to build.

The U.S. government could help manufacturers by enshrining a robust industrial policy, much as Alexander Hamilton did in the eighteenth century. That's already in the works. The $79 billion CHIPS-Plus Act (passed in 2022) includes $50 billion in direct subsidies for domestic semiconductor companies and a tax credit for chip makers. The state of California goes further, offering an array of incentives to support small manufacturers, including discounted electricity; funding for employee training; issuance of tax-exempt securities to help finance private manufacturers' growth; and sales tax exemptions on industrial equipment that manufacturers need to remain competitive.

When Americans finally commit to making more things here (and buying domestic goods—a necessary part of this equation), the tools available to support folks like Ben and Whitney will expand. At the very minimum, the government should mitigate the health insurance burden on employers by expanding Medicare to every American, young and old.* It seems everyone in the world knows this has to happen except Congress. In a 2021 Kaiser Family poll of business leaders, 87 percent of respondents said they felt that within the next decade, the cost of providing health benefits would be "unsustainable." Fully 85 percent responded that a "greater government role in coverage and costs" was needed.

Government also needs to rededicate significant resources to technical training. We've seen how Ben and Whitney spend much of their time and profit preparing their workers and staff for the job, and this remains true for every sector. As other industries consider on-shoring, the quality of the current workforce will continue to be a serious impediment. Quite simply, the question of whether Americans are equipped to do manufacturing work has dogged decision-making.

Frankly, the government is the only entity with the resources and reach to stimulate workforce training on a grand scale. "Congress can support and enhance strategies ensuring that all stakeholders, including students, workers, employers, and educational institutions, have the right incentives to improve the quality of technical education and training, and develop new models of governance to encourage fruitful experimentation and collaboration," writes Sujai Shivakumar of The Center for Strategic and International Studies (CSIS), a bipartisan, nonprofit D.C.-based policy center. "Universities, like other institutions, need to adapt to new challenges—and they need the right incentives to do so."

Growing domestic manufacturing across every industry might even begin to address some of the country's most pressing cultural problems. As we've seen, unions do much more than negotiate for better working conditions and decent pay. Unions lobby hard for worker-centric policies. But perhaps even more critically, they can be an invaluable source of critical information. Unions evaluate

---

* Health care is so expensive in the U.S. that it now accounts for nearly 20 percent of the country's GDP, and low-income workers bear a larger percentage of that cost due to rising employee premium contributions, high-deductible plans, and large co-pays.

candidates and legislation through the lens of working people. Then they try to get their members to vote in their best interests. Perhaps that's the element of organized labor that most threatens powerbrokers. When one-third of Americans received political information from their unions, policymakers had to take workers' demands seriously. When that voice was effectively silenced, much of the nation's agenda-setting power shifted to billionaires.

If we could transform our thinking, recognize the value of these jobs, and bring innovation into the manufacturing sector, we might just offer more fulfilling opportunities to the next generation as well. In that way, bringing back manufacturing could even boost happiness. Some researchers posit that the rise in stress and depression among Americans is related to their lack of engagement with the physical environment. Since 1980, desk jobs have increased 94 percent. Neuroscientist Kelly Lambert argues that that kind of work is unnatural, as well as physically and mentally unhealthy. Her research has shown that our brains are wired with an "effort-driven rewards circuit," which gives us a sense of deep satisfaction when we make things with our hands. She stresses that triggering this rewards circuit requires doing activities that "produce a result you can see, feel, and touch." Handwork, she writes, and the "thoughts, plans, and ultimate results" of handwork, "change the physiology and chemical makeup" of the brain, energizing cognition. That's why some of us enjoy taking a break from our computer-driven world to knit, vacuum, do the dishes, or rake leaves. Those kinds of physical, repetitive, completable activities tickle an essential part of the human brain—the one that we needed to survive all those millennia in the natural environment. In other words, nourishing the maker frees the thinker.

And more about that happiness: in 2018, anthropologist David Graeber published the bestselling *Bullshit Jobs: A Theory*, in which he argued that half of the jobs modern people hold today are "pointless" because they produce nothing but busywork. America's service economy depends on layer upon layer of middlemen and administrators who only increase the complexity and cost of basic systems, like health care, at the expense of true wealth- and stability-generating industries, like manufacturing. In his book, Graeber explores the psychological despair that comes with being marginally aware that one is contributing nothing to society and trying to justify that existence. It was a brutal analysis of the service sector, but it made a big splash.

Bringing back domestic manufacturing could offer an antidote to bullshit. It would help Americans appreciate the things they buy and wear and create more meaningful connections to the physical world. With more people involved in the process of making, innovation in every sector will surely follow.

The American Roots factory is stronger for the mix of skills, education levels, cultures, and ages of its employees. I can't think of a more twenty-first-century work environment than the Westbrook factory. While the U.S. Supreme Court has abolished affirmative action in higher education, factories provide an environment where nearly all Americans could find satisfying work—from designers to marketers to machinists to accountants to logistics managers.

By reviving manufacturing, Americans will also have more control over the quality of the things they wear, use, and put in their bodies, a decision that will have life-or-death consequences. Consider the fact that most of our generic drugs are made in India and China. Because Americans don't manufacture their own generic drugs, they've suffered from chronic shortages of basic meds, primarily due to supply chain interruptions, a fact that became alarmingly clear during the pandemic.* The American Society of Health-System Pharmacists (ASHP) keeps a running list of these drug shortages online and as of

---

* Located far away from regulators, many of these pharmaceutical factories lack proper oversight, writes Katherine Eban in *Bottle of Lies: The Inside Story of the Generic Drug Boom.* Eban's investigation revealed multiple examples of forged paperwork that concealed manufacturing shortcuts and sanitary violations, resulting in contaminated or ineffective drugs.

February 2023, 234 medications were on that list, including basic compounds like lidocaine, a topical anesthetic.*

When we appreciate the work that went into creating something, we value it more. Crafted with care in a regulated environment by well-paid workers who are treated with dignity, quality goods would last longer, reducing waste, which is another growing problem. Widespread mindful purchasing would weaken fast fashion's draw and reduce its destructive effects on our riverways, forests, and oceans, local economies, and people's lives.†

Politically, if Americans can disentangle themselves from problematic foreign suppliers, they will be in a stronger position to advocate for human rights, labor, and environmental protections on the international stage. An additional bonus to a prosperous domestic network: American companies will have more strength to lift each other up, creating a more resilient and reliable manufacturing environment. This isn't tautological. By providing well-paid work for people with high school diplomas, manufacturers will help more Americans afford the things they need to live a fulfilling life, opening up new markets right here at home.

I've put off the question of whether automation will eventually destroy all jobs anyway, partly because in the apparel industry, humans

---

* After tracking shortages for more than two decades, the ASHP concluded that drug shortages are "not resolving and new shortages are increasing." The lack of "local anesthetics and basic hospital drugs, albuterol solution, common oral and ophthalmic products, and ADHD treatments" affects a vast array of organizations and individuals. The ASHP also notes that shortages make health care in America more expensive: The "workload required to manage shortages, including work to change pharmacy automation and electronic health records is difficult in the face of staffing shortages."

† For evidence of the respect for American-made, look no further than New Balance's "Made in USA Collection" running shoes, built in Maine and Massachusetts, no doubt to attract government purchasers. In a poignant twist, NPR reported in 2016, Chinese consumers actively seek out U.S.-made New Balance sneakers because they believe they're better made than those manufactured in Asia. This perception apparently applies to a broad range of American-made goods.

have been working alongside automation for more than two centuries. A sewing machine automates hand-stitching. A loom automates hand-weaving. In general complex, low-cost assemblies like apparel-making don't lend themselves to full automation because they involve so many individual operations that can be done very well by humans for little money. In fact, Marty Bailey likes to say that people are the most amazing machines in the world.

But yes, a resilient future depends on good policymaking to ensure that the workforce is well positioned for technological change and won't slip through the cracks every time the demand for skills shifts. It was unduly cruel for policymakers to go whole hog for the knowledge/service economy without containing the cost of higher education. We can do better. MIT's 2020 report "The Work of the Future: Building Better Jobs in an Age of Intelligent Machines" argues that government and innovation can, and should, work hand in hand to "innovate to rebalance the desire of employers for low-cost, minimal commitment, and maximal flexibility, with the necessity that workers receive fair treatment, reasonable compensation, and a measure of economic security. The U.S. must craft and enforce fair labor standards, ensure effective collective bargaining, set a well-calibrated federal minimum wage, extend the scope and flexibility of its unemployment insurance system, and modernize its dysfunctional system of employer-based health insurance."

Shifting policy focus from economic growth to lifelong skills training for Americans would herald a new, worker-centered era. Could coal miners be retrained for jobs in green energy, for example? The Biden administration recently dedicated $450 million to convert coal mines to wind and solar farms. Notably, to take advantage of government credits, developers must pay prevailing wages and use apprentices. The Biden administration has also developed tens of billions in bonuses and tax credits to develop the next generation of energy workers to phase out petroleum and coal industries without creating undo harm to those communities.

These changes can't come soon enough. The health of our planet, and all of humanity, depend on everyone making more sustainable choices.

One final thought about the New Americans who power domestic manufacturing: Most people don't abandon their family and country for opportunity. They uproot their lives to survive. Those of us who are the children, grandchildren, or great-grandchildren of immigrants are likely descendants of people who were fleeing, rather than going toward, somewhere. Our ancestors may have left for the same reasons Makenga and her family did. Because their countries fell apart. Dictators rise. Climates change. They had to choose: stay and die, or give up everything and run.

My great-grandfather Joseph Rabinowitz fled Poland in 1888 at the age of sixteen. At the time, the tsar was avenging an assassination attempt by unleashing his people and the police on the Jews, who had lived alongside Russia's various ethnic groups for five hundred years. The new Russian rhetoric set Eastern Europe's ever-present anti-Semitic kindling ablaze, a fire that would rage westward, igniting the Nazis. But first, there were pogroms. Angry mobs from neighboring towns swept into Jewish villages to kill and destroy and loot while policemen stood by, or sometimes joined in. The antagonists seized Jews' belongings, expelled them from universities, and periodically massacred them in their homes.

Joseph Rabinowitz arrived penniless in a small community called Woodbine in the Pine Barrens of southern New Jersey. The town had been founded by Baron Maurice de Hirsch, a wealthy German banker determined to save Eastern Europe's Jews; he imagined that Woodbine would grow into a Jewish farming collective. But the soil proved too sandy to support agriculture. When immigrants struggled to make a living off the land, the Baron de Hirsch Fund built a clothing factory that eventually supported the majority of the Jewish immigrants who landed there.

Joseph was resourceful and well liked. He was elected mayor of

Woodbine and helped finance the construction of the synagogue, which still stands. At the factory, he was promoted up the management ladder until he was running the place. When he landed a government contract to make uniforms during World War I, the Fund voted to sell him the business for $1. Joseph then encouraged the workers to take over the factory, but they chose not to. Maybe they didn't want to take on the risk. Joseph was successful enough to send my grandmother and her five siblings to the University of Pennsylvania in the 1920s. Just before the Great Depression he built a ten-story apartment building on the corner of 23rd and Walnut Streets in Philadelphia, which also still stands.

It takes a lot to convince people to abandon everything they know and move to a country where they have no roots and cannot speak the language. Joseph's brother Chaim made a different choice. He stayed in Poland. He and my great-grandfather lived parallel lives, raising children and grandchildren, until the Nazis invaded Poland. Chaim's entire family perished in concentration camps.

My paternal great-grandparents escaped oppression in Ukraine and arrived in the U.S. with nothing and managed to set up a women's clothing business in Philadelphia. Their son, Abe Levitt, my grandfather, took over the family business. Most of Abe's employees were Italian immigrants—and they were unionized. Abe spent much of his adult life driving from New York to Chicago, selling his line to the sophisticated buyers of high-end department stores. But he forbade my father from entering the factory. "This will not be your life," he told him, and my father obliged. Through Abe's business connections, my grandmother had an enviable wardrobe. Before she died, she gave me a stunning thick wool jacket in deep burgundy, made in the 1950s. The label reads: "Sam G, Division of Sam Gruenbaum, Inc." Seventy-some years later, the garment looks brand new. Sewed into a seam in the lining is a faded ILGWU tag.

The history of manufacturing is Americans' shared heritage. It is the story of immigration, hard work, and luck. Ben and Whitney built a company that made Makenga's and Anaam's and Khalid's lives in

America possible, just as countless people have before them. Certainly, factory work is demanding. But the rebirth of manufacturing—supported by labor and environmental protections—offers immigrants, New Americans, high school grads, skilled workers, tech savants, and fiercely independent-minded entrepreneurs an opportunity to forge a new, more resilient American dream.

ACKNOWLEDGMENTS

Most people who write books begin as avid readers, and I'm no exception. When I was a kid, I'd lie on my parents' scratchy wool rug in the hallway, propped up on elbows, deciphering the Sunday comics section in the now-defunct *Philadelphia Bulletin.* Later, I graduated to *New Yorker* cartoons. It was just a matter of time before I became a book fiend. A heartfelt thank-you to every editor, writer, and illustrator who gave kids like me a reason to pick up a newspaper or magazine. And an additional thank-you to the papermakers, ink makers, typesetters, designers, press operators, and truck drivers who helped produce and deliver the newspapers, magazines, and books I've read over my lifetime, including *Making It in America.*

Ultimately, this book is about family, and my interest in where things were made began with my own. My parents, Jerry and Julie Levitt, have always stressed the importance of supporting American workers by buying domestically made goods. When my dad came home one day in a new beige Volkswagen Rabbit in the early 1980s, for example, he made a point of telling me that this German car was made in the USA. The Rabbit was the first European automobile built by Americans, in Westmoreland County, Pennsylvania, 280 miles from my childhood home.

I've tried to follow my parents' lead, but it's not always easy finding American-made things. Searching online, you encounter plenty of bait and switch, so I appreciate the websites set up to guide consumers to authentic domestic products. These aggregators aren't perfect, especially since companies switch up manufacturing decisions frequently. If you really care, you've got to read the small print. Fortunately, some of my kitchen supplies were made in the USA, including my Anchor Hocking glass containers. My Danner hiking boots, which will last a lifetime, were made in the USA. My husband carries around an American-made Duluth Trading Company duffel bag.

Admittedly, my interest in where things were made has led to awkward moments. When I was very young, my grandmother gave me a doll she'd bought on a trip to Israel. After a quick examination of it, I asked her why something from Israel was made in Japan. Some forty years later this question remains as relevant as ever. Grandma Nettie lived to age 106 and died while I was wrestling with the final draft of this manuscript. I miss her deep faith in human progress. She'd witnessed nearly the entire twentieth century and at the end of her days often said that she'd like to return in fifty years, just to see all the new technological marvels.

My maternal grandmother, Zelda Meranze, never forgot the faces of the neighborhood children she went to school with who worked at her father's clothing factory in a small town in southern New Jersey. It was Grandma Zel who first told me about the Triangle Shirtwaist Fire. Although she was just a little girl in 1911, she must have felt a strong connection to the tragedy. Perhaps in part to atone, she married Joe Meranze, a redheaded labor lawyer who represented, among others, the press workers at the *Philadelphia Inquirer.* Grampa Joe's stationery sported a tiny union-made stamp in the upper-left corner. That man believed in buying in bulk. Three decades after he passed away, I still have boxes of those envelopes with his Philadelphia address.

My brother Dan Levitt lives 13,000 miles away, which means he's always awake when I need him most (at dawn) for pep talks, wisdom nuggets, perspective, and a good laugh. A quick talk with him is a great way to start a productive writing day.

This book would not exist without Brian Kevin, the former editor of *Down East* magazine. Quirky, funny, endlessly inquisitive, Brian is a true believer in the power of a good story. Brian introduced me to American Roots during the pandemic and agreed to run my longer story about Ben and Whitney, "American Roots Runs Deep" (a headline that must have driven the copy editor insane), in the November 2020 issue. He didn't expect the piece I submitted. For the record, here's an excerpt of an email he sent to me after his initial read:

> I think if you'd have described to me a draft that had 400 words about Ben's labor affinity and zero words about the company's COVID outbreak, I'd have said, nix all but a short graf of union stuff and use that space to tell us how they avoided becoming an ironic disaster story when COVID struck. But of course, damned if that labor stuff isn't really interesting and essential. So what I'm inclined to do, if you're game, is to say let's tack another $500 onto the fee, and could you please dive into this draft where I've left space for it and some notes about it and give us, you know, 500 words or so about this whole second part of their COVID saga that we've left out. What do you say to that, and can it be accomplished by Monday morning?

And that was the birth of *Making It in America.*

Ben and Whitney Waxman trusted me, opened up their business and lives to me, and worked their insane schedules around my hurry-up-and-wait pace. In short, there would be no book without them. There is no way to properly articulate the depth of my gratitude to them. For the sake of brevity, I'll just leave it at thank you and hope they know how deeply I mean that. *Game on.*

David Patterson, VP at Stuart Krichevsky Literary Agency, is a total rock star and has the vintage guitars to prove it. David is also the premier arbiter of good book ideas. I discovered multiple times that he's exceptionally skilled at saying no in the nicest possible way. But he said yes to *Making It in America.*

Denise Oswald, editrix extraordinaire. Holy moly, this woman is good at what she does, and the book world is much better for having her in it. Denise is the best kind of editor: a reader's advocate, a true collaborator, a booklover. If this work is at all readable, that's due to her succinct, straightforward queries which graced nearly every page of several drafts. Denise once referred to publishing my first book as a "knife fight." I hope she found this one was a little easier.

I'm insanely lucky to live in a book-rich region. Through the Minuteman Library Network, a consortium of dozens of public and academic libraries in Greater Boston, I've been able to access almost every publication I need. If Minuteman doesn't have it, Boston Public Library usually does. If not, I might find it at the Boston Athenaeum, a member-supported library that hasn't unloaded any of its collection since its founding in 1807.

It's important to acknowledge our pandemic support group whenever we can, and throughout 2020 and 2021, I walked at least a thousand miles around Boston with the impressively well-read Rachel Salzman. We wore out several pairs of sneakers* while discussing everything under the sun, including *Making It in America.*

And a big thank-you to Hillary Rayport and Anupreeta Das, two brilliant women who inspire me every day with their intelligence and resilience, and gave me much to think about as I worked on this book.

Finally, as ever, grateful to you, Mr. Slade, my erudite madman.

* Made in Vietnam.

BIBLIOGRAPHY

"Academy Award Winning Documentary Harlan County USA (1976)." Clapboard Tales Collections. YouTube, February 5, 2018.

Adamson, Glenn. *Craft: An American History.* New York: Bloomsbury, 2022.

Amengual, Matthew, and Sarosh Kuruvilla. "Introduction to a Special Issue on Improving Private Regulation of Labor in Global Supply Chains: Theory and Evidence." *ILR Review* 73, no. 4 (2020): 809–16.

American Fashion Podcast—Fashion Business Conversations. https://american fashionpodcast.com/townhall/.

Andersen, Kurt. *Evil Geniuses: The Unmaking of America: A Recent History.* New York: Random House, 2021.

"Annual Report of the Secretary of the Treasury on the State of the Finances, Report on Manufactures, December 1791; On the Establishment of a Mint, January 1791." FRASER—St. Louis Fed, https://fraser.stlouisfed.org/title /annual-report-secretary-treasury-state-finances-194/report-manufactures -december-1791-establishment-a-mint-january-1791-5630.

"The Biden Plan to Ensure the Future Is 'Made in All of America' by All of America's Workers." https://joebiden.com/made-in-america/.

Bidwell, Percy W. "The Agricultural Revolution in New England." *American Historical Review* 26, no. 4 (1921): 683–702.

Blom, Philipp. *Nature's Mutiny: How the Little Ice Age Transformed the West and Shaped the Present.* New York: Liveright, 2019.

Bradford, Amy. "History of Linen." *TOAST,* April 16, 2018, https://us.toa.st /blogs/magazine/history-of-linen.

Broadberry, Stephen, and Bishupriya Gupta. "Lancashire, India, and Shifting Competitive Advantage in Cotton Textiles, 1700–1850: The Neglected Role of Factor Prices." *Economic History Review* 62, no. 2 (2009): 279–305.

Brooks, Richard R. *As Steel Goes.* New Haven: Yale University Press, 1940.

Brown, Sherrod. *Myths of Free Trade: Why American Trade Policy Has Failed,* revised and updated. New York: The New Press, 2006.

Cassidy, John. "The Biggest Challenge Facing Joe Biden's New Economic Team." *New Yorker,* December 1, 2020, https://www.newyorker.com/news/our -columnists/the-biggest-challenge-facing-joe-bidens-new-economic-team.

"Child Labour in the Fashion Supply Chain." *The Guardian,* https://labs.the guardian.com/unicef-child-labour/.

Chomsky, Noam. *Profit over People: Neoliberalism and Global Order.* New York: Seven Stories Press, 1999.

Chua, Jasmin Malik. "Why California Could Be the Sustainable Fashion Capital of the US." *Sourcing Journal,* July 27, 2020, https://sourcingjournal.com /denim/denim-innovations/california-eco-friendly-fashion-capital-boyish -jeans-sustainable-fashion-alliance-222041/.

Clean Clothes Campaign. *Un(der) Paid in the Pandemic: An Estimate of What the Garment Industry Owes Its Workers.* 2020, www.cleanclothes.org.

Cline, Elizabeth L. *Overdressed: The Shockingly High Cost of Cheap Fashion.* New York: Penguin, 2013.

"Complete Process of Textile Manufacturing Fiber to Complete Garment." YouTube, https://www.youtube.com/watch?v=5nUjGNDImIk&ab_channel =TextileVlog.

The Cotton Museum at the Memphis Cotton Exchange, Memphis, Tennessee. https://memphiscottonmuseum.org.

Cowie, Jefferson, and Jefferson R. Cowie. *Stayin' Alive: The 1970s and the Last Days of the Working Class.* New York: The New Press, 2010.

Crawford, Lucy. *History of the White Mountains: The History of the White Mountains from the First Settlement of the Upper Coos and Pequaket (1846).* Edited by John T. B. Mudge. Etna, NH: Durand Press, 1999.

Dalrymple, William. *The Anarchy: The East India Company, Corporate Violence, and the Pillage of an Empire.* New York: Bloomsbury, 2019.

Dean, Ninette. "The Up and Down History of the Zipper." *Smithsonian Libraries and Archives/Unbound,* May 3, 2010, https://blog.library.si.edu /blog/2010/05/03/the-up-an-down-history-of-the-zipper/.

Dini, Ridwan Karim. "How the West's Obsession with Fast Fashion Compounds an Environmental Nightmare in Ghana." Public Radio International, October 18, 2021.

Donaldson, Tara. "US, China Affirm Plans to Implement Phase One Trade Deal." *Sourcing Journal,* May 8, 2020.

Douglas, Audrey W. "Cotton Textiles in England: The East India Company's Attempt to Exploit Developments in Fashion, 1660–1721." *Journal of British Studies* 8, no. 2 (1969): 28–43, Cambridge.org.

Eban, Katherine. *Bottle of Lies: The Inside Story of the Generic Drug Boom.* New York: Ecco, 2019.

"Economic Indicators—International Trade." U.S. Census Bureau, https://www
.census.gov/economic-indicators/#intl_trade. Accessed December 11, 2022.

Eisenhower, Dwight. "Remarks at Dedication of AFL-CIO," June 4, 1956. The
American Presidency Project.

"Elias Howe: Inventor of the Sewing Machine." *ThoughtCo,* December 19, 2018.

"Experience Hogs & Heifers NYC in Virtual Reality." (Press Alt plus A for Accessibility Version.) *YouVisit.*

Fagan, Brian. *The Little Ice Age: How Climate Made History, 1300–1850.* New
York: Basic Books, 2000.

Friedman, Arthur. "Under USMCA, Labor 'Magnifying Glass' Coming to Mexican Factories." *Sourcing Journal,* May 28, 2020.

Friedman, Arthur, and Jessica Binns. "Support at House Hearing to Punish China
over Uyghur Forced Labor." *Sourcing Journal,* September 17, 2020.

Gilpin, Toni. *The Long Deep Grudge: A Story of Big Capital, Radical Labor, and
Class War in the American Heartland.* Chicago: Haymarket Books, 2020.

Graeber, David. *Bullshit Jobs: A Theory.* New York: Simon & Schuster, 2018.

Green, Mark. "Trade Talk: Should Labor Standards Be Included in Free Trade
Agreements with the United States? Implications for Asia." Wilson Center.

Greenhouse, Steven. *Beaten Down, Worked Up: The Past, Present, and Future of
American Labor.* New York: Knopf, 2019.

Gross, Andrew. *Button Man: A Novel.* New York: St. Martin's, 2019.

Ha, Thi Minh. "Vietnam Factory Workers Laid Off as West Cuts Imports."
Agence France-Presse/Yahoo News, December 14, 2022, https://news.yahoo
.com/vietnam-factory-workers-laid-off-022438549.html. Accessed December 15, 2022.

Hachfield, David. "What Makes Up the Price of a Zara Hoody." *Public Eye,*
November 20, 2019.

"Historic Backlog of Cargo Ships at the Port of Long Beach." *Long Beach Local
News,* October 12, 2021.

"How Dutch-Based Vlisco Became One of Africa's Most Popular Fashion Companies." *How We Made It in Africa,* September 26, 2014.

"Impact Report 2020/2021." *Labour Behind the Label.* https://labourbehindthe
label.org/resources/reports/.

Irwin, Douglas A. *The Aftermath of Hamilton's "Report on Manufactures."* National
Bureau of Economic Research, September 2003.

Jacobs, William, and Nellie Spiller. "The Westbrook Historical Society." The
Westbrook Historical Society.

Judis, John B. *The Nationalist Revival: Trade, Immigration, and the Revolt Against
Globalization.* New York: Columbia Global Reports, 2018.

Katz, Daniel. *All Together Different: Yiddish Socialists, Garment Workers, and the
Labor Roots of Multiculturalism.* New York: NYU Press, 2013.

Keir, Malcolm. "Some Influences of the Sea Upon the Industries of New England."
Geographical Review 5, no. 5 (1918): 399–404.

Khalid, Asma, and Barbara Sprunt. "'Build Back Better': Joe Biden Outlines Economic Recovery Plan." NPR, July 9, 2020.

Klein, Christopher. "How America's Industrial Revolution Was Launched by Spies." History.com, January 10, 2019.

Klein, Matthew C., et al. *Trade Wars Are Class Wars: How Rising Inequality Distorts the Global Economy and Threatens International Peace.* New Haven: Yale University Press, 2020.

Klein, Naomi. *The Shock Doctrine: The Rise of Disaster Capitalism.* New York: Picador, 2008.

Kobayashi, Kazuo. "Indian Cotton Textiles in the Eighteenth-Century Atlantic Economy." Excerpt from "The British Atlantic Slave Trade and Indian Cotton Textiles: The Case of Thomas Lumley & Co." *Socio-Economic History* 77, no. 3 (2011).

Labor 411. "Making It Easy to Support Good Jobs." http://labor411.org/.

Ladenburg, Thomas. "The Causes of the American Revolution." *Digital History,* 2007.

Lazazzera, Milena. "Inside Italy's Shadow Economy." *New York Times,* September 20, 2018.

Longfellow, Rickie. "The Evolution of Mississippi Highways—Back in Time—General Highway History—Highway History—Federal Highway Administration." Federal Highway Administration, May 14, 2019, https://www.fhwa.dot .gov/infrastructure/back0503.cfm. Accessed December 11, 2022.

Loomis, Erik. *Out of Sight: The Long and Disturbing Story of Corporations Outsourcing Catastrophe.* New York: The New Press, 2015.

MacArthur, John R. *The Selling of Free Trade: NAFTA, Washington, and the Subversion of American Democracy.* Berkeley: University of California Press, 2001.

"MacEdward Leach and the Songs of Atlantic Canada—'Tha Mo Bhreachdan Dubh fo'n Dìle (My Black Plaid is Soaked).'" Memorial University of Newfoundland.

Macy, Beth. *Factory Man: How One Furniture Maker Battled Offshoring, Stayed Local—and Helped Save an American Town.* New York: Little, Brown and Company, 2015.

"Maine History Online—Mills and Changing Cities." *Maine Memory Network,* www.mainememory.net.

Manyika, James. "Current State of Manufacturing." National Institute of Standards and Technology, April 22, 2021.

Mercogliano, Salvatore R. "Why Military Sealift Command Needs Merchant Mariners at the Helm." Center for International Maritime Security, www .cimsec.org.

Mestricht, Keith, and Mark A. Pinsky. *Organized Money: How Progressives Can Leverage the Financial System to Work for Them, Not Against Them.* New York: The New Press, 2019.

Montgomery, David R. *Dirt: The Erosion of Civilizations.* Berkeley: University of California Press, 2012.

Moran, William. *The Belles of New England: The Women of the Textile Mills and the Families Whose Wealth They Wove.* New York: St. Martin's Press, 2002.

Ndegwa, Dorcas. "Vlisco to Africa: Your Money Is No Good Here." Most Influential People of African Descent (MIPAD), www.mipad.org.

Penny, Louise. "U.S. Exports of Used Clothing Creating Waste Nightmare." CBS News, September 16, 2021.

Perley, Sidney. *Historic Storms of New England.* Beverly, MA: Commonwealth Editions, 2001.

Phillips, Matt. "The Long Story of U.S. Debt, from 1790 to 2011, in 1 Little Chart." *The Atlantic,* November 13, 2012.

Piketty, Thomas. *Capital in the Twenty-First Century.* Translated by Arthur Goldhammer. Cambridge: Harvard University Press, 2017.

"Planet Money Makes a T-Shirt." *NPR Visuals,* December 2, 2013, https://apps.npr.org/tshirt/#/cotton.

"Pullovers, Cardigans etc. of Cotton, Knit." The Observatory of Economic Complexity, https://oec.world.

Rabushka, Alvin. "The Colonial Roots of American Taxation, 1607–1700." Hoover Institution, August 1, 2002.

Reich, Robert B. *Saving Capitalism: For the Many, Not the Few.* New York: Knopf, 2016.

Riley, Tonya. "What It Means to Be a Working-Class Clothing Brand in America Today." *Esquire,* July 14, 2017.

Rivard, Paul E. *A New Order of Things: How the Textile Industry Transformed New England.* Hanover, NH: University Press of New England, 2002.

Robertson, Michael. *The Last Utopians: Four Late Nineteenth-Century Visionaries and Their Legacy.* Princeton: Princeton University Press, 2018.

Rosen, Ellen Israel. *Making Sweatshops: The Globalization of the U.S. Apparel Industry.* Berkeley: University of California Press, 2002.

"Route 66: 1926–1945 (U.S.)." National Park Service, November 17, 2021, https://www.nps.gov/articles/route-66-1926-1945.htm.

Shell, Ellen Ruppel. *The Job: Work and Its Future in a Time of Radical Change.* New York: Crown, 2018.

Smil, Vaclav. *Made in the USA: The Rise and Retreat of American Manufacturing.* Cambridge: MIT Press, 2015.

Smith, S. D. "The Market for Manufactures in the Thirteen Continental Colonies, 1698–1776." *Economic History Review* 51, no. 4 (1998): 676–708.

Sprovieri, John. Editorial. *Assembly Magazine.*

"The States Leading the U.S. Manufacturing Resurgence." Area Development, https://www.areadevelopment.com/RegionalReports/Q1-2013/states-leading-US-manufacturing-resurgence-2665542.shtml. Accessed December 11, 2022.

Stein, Judith. *Pivotal Decade: How the United States Traded Factories for Finance in the Seventies.* New Haven: Yale University Press, 2010.

Stephenson, M. J. "Wool Yields in the Medieval Economy." *Economic History Review* 41, no. 3 (1988): 368–91.

Stiglitz, Joseph E. *People, Power, and Profits: Progressive Capitalism for an Age of Discontent.* New York: W. W. Norton, 2020.

Stoll, Steven. *Ramp Hollow: The Ordeal of Appalachia.* New York: Farrar, Straus & Giroux, 2017.

"Support Good Jobs." *Union Label,* https://unionlabel.org/do-buy/support-good -jobs/.

Susskind, Daniel. *A World Without Work: Technology, Automation, and How We Should Respond.* New York: Henry Holt and Company, 2020.

Suzman, James. *Work: A Deep History, from the Stone Age to the Age of Robots.* New York: Penguin, 2022.

Taft, Philip, and Philip Ross. "American Labor Violence: Its Causes, Character, and Outcome." *DiText,* http://www.ditext.com/taft/violence.html.

Terkel, Studs. *Working.* New York: Pantheon, 1974.

Thomas, Dana. *Fashionopolis: The Price of Fast Fashion—and the Future of Clothes.* New York: Penguin, 2019.

"Trade in Goods with China, Available Years: 1992–2022." U.S. Census Bureau, https://www.census.gov/foreign-trade/balance/c5700.html.

"2022 Sourcing Report." *Sourcing Journal,* https://sourcingjournal.com/report/.

Tyler, Gus. *Look for the Union Label: A History of the International Ladies' Garment Workers' Union.* Armonk, NY: M. E. Sharpe, 1995.

"Unease in the Golden Age: Clearly Vicious as a Matter of Policy: The Fight Against Federal-Aid—Federal Aid Legislation—Highway History—Federal Highway Administration." Federal Highway Administration, https://www .fhwa.dot.gov/infrastructure/hwyhist04a.cfm.

"Unionwear's Featured TedX Talk: Made Right Here—Fashion—News & Press." *Unionwear,* June 29, 2015, https://unionwear.com/news-and-press/unionwears -featured-tedx-talk-made-right-here/.

U.S. Department of Labor, Bureau of Labor Statistics. *History of Wages in the United States from Colonial Times to 1928.* Washington, D.C.: U.S. Government Printing Office, 1934.

"Utexrwa, Rhoda to Boost Silk Production." *New Times,* May 21, 2010, https:// www.newtimes.co.rw/section/read/20015.

Walling, Philip. "Britain's Sheep Are Vanishing and So Is Our History." *Daily Mail,* May 2, 2014, https://www.dailymail.co.uk/news/article-2618349/Britains -sheep-vanishing-history-disappearing-them.html.

Watson, Traci. "See the World's Oldest Dress." *National Geographic,* February 18, 2016, https://www.nationalgeographic.com/history/article/160218-oldest-dress -egypt-tarkhan-archaeology.

Weed, Peter, et al. "A Daunting Maze of Barriers." *Maine Monitor,* May 4, 2019, https://www.themainemonitor.org/a-daunting-maze-of-barriers/.

Weeks, Linton. "Tragedy Gives the Hoodie a Whole New Meaning." March 24, 2012. NPR.

"When I Buy a Garment, What Portion of the Cost Goes to the Workers?" Clean Clothes Campaign, November 20, 2019, www.cleanclothes.org.

"Why We No Longer Manufacture in Scotland." The Tartan Blanket Co., August 7, 2020.

Wilde, Robert. "Did Cotton Drive the Industrial Revolution?" *ThoughtCo,* October 10, 2019.

Williams, James. "How the Pandemic Is Reshaping American Manufacturing." Merrow Manufacturing, July 16, 2020.

Willis, Sofia. "How Sustainable Dyeing Is Changing the Textile Industry." Plug and Play Tech Center, March 22, 2021.

Witwer, David, and Catherine Rios. *Murder in the Garment District: The Grip of Organized Crime and the Decline of Labor in the United States.* New York: The New Press, 2020.

Wong, Ruth Grace. "Making Zippers in the USA!" *Medium,* May 14, 2018.

INDEX

Higgins, Mike, 180
Hine, Lewis, 134, 195
Hoffa, Jimmy, 185
Hogs & Heifers, New York City, 87–89
hoodie/sweatshirt
  as an American icon, 140
  brief history of, 132–40
  case of Trayvon Martin and, 138–39
  Champion adds the hood, 136
  Champion brand, 135–36
  evolving significance of, 137
  Fetterman and, 139
  first sweatshirt born, 135
  Lemon and, 140
  Macron and, 139–40, 140n
  manufacturing of, offshored, 140
  "Million Hoodies March," 139
  "no hoodie" policies, 138
  Rocky movies and, 136–37, 137n
  Russell brand, 135, 136
  as symbol of subversion, 137–38
  as workwear, 136
  worn by union men and women, 138
  Zelensky and, 139–40
  Zuckerberg and, 138
"Horo Once More I Would Shout for Joy,"
  (Scottish Gaelic song), 43–44
Horowitz, Fran, 257
Howard, Ron, 100
Howe, Elias, 144
  sewing machine and, 144–45
  zipper patent, 145

IDEA (International Institute for
  Democracy and Electoral
  Assistance), 23
ILGWU (International Ladies Garment
  Workers Union), 105, 181–82, 184,
  303
  "Look for the union label," 197
IMF (International Monetary Fund), 71,
  246
imports, xi, xiii
  amount processed through California
    ports, xii, 238
  apparel and footwear, 19, 231
  costs vs. costs of made in America, 21
  Covid pandemic and, 24–25

damage to the U.S. economy and
  workers, 69, 295
demand for, xii, 26n
in early America, 7
environmental impact of textile
  manufacturing and, 21–22
factory safety and, 22
flooding the U.S., 74
free trade paradigm and, 24
hunger among foreign workers, 25
impact of pursuit of cheaper labor, 24
income inequality and, 23
international trade and, 12
major brands and, 74
NAFTA and, 15–16
Nike and, 25
pharmaceuticals, 299, 299n
political problems and, 23–24
poverty and, 21
quality and, 22
questions about workers, 20
regulation and, 12
shuttering of U.S. factories and, 74
tariffs and, 7, 8, 11, 13, 16, 198, 286n
tariffs recommended by the ITIPF, 68
U.S. annual trade deficit to China, 68
U.S. dependency on, 295
U.S. port backups, xi–xiii, 275
Zara hoodie example, 20–21, *21*
See also China; NAFTA; *specific
  countries*
India
  Amazon and, 270
  American cotton and, 156
  British East India Company and,
    12–13
  exports from, 27n, 156, 263, 299
  Monsanto and cotton crop, 154–55
Indonesia, 12, 25, 123
Industrial Revolution, 6–7, 9
International Alliance of Theatrical Stage
  Employees Local 114, 216
International Brotherhood of Teamsters,
  184, 185
International Union of Painters and Allied
  Trades, 158–60
International Workers of the World, 76
Iraq War, 121

Merrow family, 40, 244

Mestrich, Keith, 287–88

Mexico

American oil exported to, 295

American textile and clothing
production in, 18, 27, 139, 263, 264

free trade and, 14, 15

NAFTA and, 18, 25–26, 139

USMCA and, 19, 286n

Whirlpool production in, 78–79

workers immigrate to the U.S., 121

Miners for Democracy, 65

Monsanto, 154, 155

Moody, Lemuel, 37

Moonrise Kingdom (film), 119

Moran, James, 213

Morello, Tom, 95

Morris, Jeff, 207–8, 210

NAFTA (North American Free Trade
Agreement), 15–16

American companies closed, jobs
lost, 18

American workers' income decline
after, 19

closing of New England's textile mills
and, 45–46

impact on Mexico, 25–26

killing of garment industry, 118

offshoring and, 260, 261, 263

passage of, 192

replaced by USMCA, 19, 286, 286n

National Association of Manufacturers, 4

National Child Labor Committee, 134

National Consumers League, 182, 183

Nearing, Helen and Scott, 33–34

Neel, Alice, 59n

Negro Motorist Green Book, The, 207

New Balance, 26, 300n

New York Times

despair in global garment industry, 25

on Fetterman's hoodie, 139

NFL (National Football League), 288,
288n

NFLPA (NFL Players Association),
288–89

Nguesso, Sassou, 246–47

Niekerk, David, 269

Nike, 24, 25, 26–27, 262, 291

9/11 terrorist attacks, 49, 74, 87, 88

Nixon, Richard, 72–73, 147, 184

NLRB (National Labor Relations Board),
54, 57, 58, 108, 112n, 286

Amazon union votes and, 241–42

Noxubee, Mississippi, 152–53

Obama, Barack, 74, 76, 78, 94

Olsen, Glenn, 163–64

Opower, Inc., 188–89

OPRRE (Office of Public Roads and Rural
Engineering), 203

Organized Money (Mestrich), 288

OSHA (Occupational Safety and Health
Administration), 108, 112n, 158, 184

Outside Business Journal, 130

OXO, 270

Painters District Council 35, 217

Pakistan, 156, 263

Parkdale, North Carolina, 170

Patagonia company, 110, 130

Paton, Elizabeth, 25

Pendleton Woolen Mills, 26–27

Pennsylvania

J&L Steel and, 54–55, 58–59

labor movement in, 54–59

loss of manufacturing, 20

opioid epidemic in, 61

presidential race (2004), 61

Waxman organizing in, 52–53, 61–62

Perkins, Frances, 183

Peterson, Gary, 162–64, 165, 171

Philadelphia, Pennsylvania, 20, 55, 137n,
142, 195, 207, 274, 303

Pilchman, Ned, 166–71

American Fabrics and, 166–70,
235–36

China cornering the cotton market
and, 231–32, 234

partner, Gary, 231–35, 237

pessimism about America
manufacturing, 170–71

Pinchot, Gifford, 58

Pinochet, Augusto, 72–73

Polartec, 105

Pollock, Jackson, 59n

A NOTE ABOUT THE AUTHOR

Rachel Slade is the acclaimed author of *Into the Raging Sea,* a national best seller, *New York Times* Notable Book, and a winner of the Maine Literary Award for nonfiction and the Mountbatten Award for Best Book. A former staff editor and writer at *Boston* magazine and *The Boston Globe,* Slade has won national awards in civic journalism, reporting, and criticism. She lives with her husband in Brookline, Massachusetts, and Rockport, Maine.

A NOTE ABOUT THE TYPE

This book was set in Adobe Garamond. Designed for the Adobe Corporation by Robert Slimbach, the fonts are based on types first cut by Claude Garamond (ca. 1480–1561).

Composed by North Market Street Graphics
Lancaster, Pennsylvania

Printed and bound by Lakeside Book Company
Harrisonburg, Virginia

Designed by Michael Collica

HOW TO MAKE AN ALL-AMERICAN HOODIE

OUR STORY BEGINS IN MISSISSIPPI, WHERE THE COTTON IS GROWN, HARVESTED, AND GINNED . . .

THEN SPUN INTO YARN IN SOUTH CAROLINA.

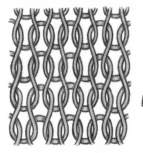

YARN IS CUSTOM-KNIT INTO FLEECE AND DYED IN NORTH CAROLINA . . .

. . . THEN ROLLED ONTO BOLTS AND SHIPPED TO FALL RIVER, MASSACHUSETTS.

AN EIGHT-PERSON TEAM SEWS TOGETHER THE BACK AND TWO FRONTS AT THE SHOULDER, SETS THE SLEEVES AND HOOD, AND TOPSTITCHES THE SEAMS.

ONE STITCHER CLOSES THE SIDES, A SECOND ATTACHES THE CUFFS, A THIRD ATTACHES THE WAISTBAND.

THE NEXT STITCHER PREPARES THE FRONT EDGES WITH SEAM TAPE.

ZIPPERS ARE MADE IN CALIFORNIA.

ONE WORKER SETS THE RIGHT SIDE OF THE ZIPPER; ANOTHER SETS THE LEFT. THE LAST PERSON ON THE LINE TOPSTITCHES THE ZIPPERS.

AN INSPECTOR LOOKS FOR FLAWS AND SNIPS STRAY THREADS.